WARSHIPS
of the
BRITISH & COMMONWEALTH
NAVIES
SECOND EDITION

H. T. Lenton

LONDON

IAN ALLAN

Contents

© Ian Allan Ltd. 1966
This edition 1969

SBN 7110 0065 4

Published by Ian Allan Ltd., Terminal House, Shepperton, Surrey and printed by Crampton & Sons Ltd., Sawston, Cambridge.

Introduction

The gratifying response to the first edition of *British & Commonwealth Navies* has resulted in this second edition being published earlier than planned, and despite the limited passage of time the opportunity has been taken to thoroughly revise the work and bring it up-to-date.

A feature of the first edition—the grouping of the vessels into seven main functional divisions—has been retained as the innovation was very favourably received; but another feature—the general arrangement drawings—had to be dropped as it was not possible to incorporate the increased number available together with the extra information that has been included. However, arrangements have been made for these drawings to be secured separately as noted on the jacket back flap.

During 1967/8 the following additions were made to the Royal Navy's combatant strength: three missile-armed and nuclear-powered submarines (each 7,000 tons); the nuclear-powered submarine WARSPITE (4,500 tons) and the conventionally-powered ONYX (2,410 tons); four " Leander " class frigates (each 2,350 tons); and the assault ship INTREPID (10,550 tons) and three LCM(9) (each 176 tons). Further support afloat was provided by the MCM vessel ABDIEL (1,460 tons), the helicopter ship ENGADINE (8,000 tons), two ammunition ships (each 19,000 tons) and two store ships (each 15,500 tons); while auxiliary vessels included four LS(L)s for the Ministry of Transport (each 5,560 tons), four surveying vessels (each 990 tons), two water boats and three coastal tankers (each 285 tons gross), and four medium berthing tugs (each 152 tons gross).

Commonwealth construction comprised the missile-armed destroyer BRISBANE (3,370 tons), two "Oberon" class submarines (each 2,410 tons), and 16 patrol boats (each 100 tons) for the Royal Australian Navy; two "Oberon" class submarines (each 2,410 tons) for the Royal Canadian Navy; four gun/torpedo boats (each 95 tons) and eleven patrol boats (each 109 tons) for the Royal Malaysian Navy; and the fast gunboat PAHLAWAN for Brunei. The newly formed Jamaican Coast Guard passed three small patrol boats (each 60 tons) into service, all of which were built in the United States.

A questionable acquisition to Commonwealth naval strength are those vessels transferred, or scheduled for transfer, to India and Ghana from the U.S.S.R. For India these include four " F " class submarines, five " Kronstadt " class frigates, six " P4 " type torpedo boats, and two " Poluchat 1 " class LSM(R); while Ghana has received four 90-ton patrol boats. The frigate/despatch vessel ordered by the latter country in the U.K. was completed in 1968 and was immediately put up for sale.

The civil strife in Nigeria resulted in the brief emergence of the Biafran Navy during 1967 and again in 1968. The seaward defence boat IBADAN (ex-*Montford*) was seized and renamed VIGILANCE by Biafra but was sunk by Nigerian forces on 26/7/67 and was subsequently recaptured on 10/9/67 at Port Harcourt. In 1968, Biafran efforts to secure the

3

old MTB GAY FORESTER, now renamed FREEDOM and re-engined with Maybach diesel engines, suffered a setback when the craft was arrested and held at Gibraltar while en-route. Following Singapore's secession from Malaysia the latter transferred the patrol boat PANGLIMA to them to form the nucleus of a small naval force, and this was followed by Singapore placing an order with Vosper Thornycroft for six of their standard 110 ft. patrol boats.

Early in 1968 the British Government announced yet a further painful re-appraisal of defence policy. All forces are to be withdrawn from the Far East—except Hong Kong and Persian Gulf—by 1971, after which what remains of the carrier fleet will be phased-out. On a more immediate basis the carrier VICTORIOUS was paid-off for disposal instead of re-commissioning, and the construction of nuclear-powered submarines is to be slowed down as an economic measure. Land-based air power—earlier proclaimed as the substitute for carrier aviation—has been abandoned, and while its ability to provide air cover for the fleet east of Suez was always questionable, any surface forces deployed in this area subsequent to 1971 are now assured that they will lack this vital element.

The power vacuum thus left in the Indian Ocean will undoubtedly be fully exploited by the U.S.S.R. and gives a deeper significance to the naval aid they have proffered to India. Whether the United States will attempt to fill this void remains problematical, but it is unlikely that they will be able to do anything while they remain involved in Viet-Nam. The planned British withdrawal has made its impact on Australia where the Royal Australian Navy was not slow to press for the acquisition of a strike carrier, and an American vessel was uppermost in their mind.

While organisational changes have not been spectacular they nevertheless could have far wider consequences than is evident at this stage when the planned withdrawal from the Far East is completed. The traditional Home and Mediterranean fleets were merged into a single Western Fleet and the mixed escort squadrons are to be disbanded; British submarines stationed in Australia and Canada were withdrawn as these Commonwealth Navies placed their own units in commission; and Canada merged her armed services into a single unit known as the Canadian Armed Forces whose Maritime Command embraces the former Royal Canadian Navy (still referred to as such in this volume). It appeared pointless to continue to include the South African Navy among those of the Commonwealth as the existing arms ban can only result in the complete severance of ties, and they have therefore been excluded. Ironically, with the closing of the Suez Canal and the consequent re-routing of much British trade round the Cape, at no stage has the desirability of having a friendly South Africa lying directly athwart this route been more vital.

As usual, I am particularly indebted to the Director of Public Relations (Royal Navy) for generous assistance with information and photographs, and to the information services of the Commonwealth navies who have been no less forthcoming; to the publishers of *Shipbuilding & Shipping Record* and *Naval Record* for the loan of certain blocks; and to my colleagues in the Warships Records Club and the World Ship Society.

London, 1969.

H.T.L.

FLEET VESSELS

[Block courtesy *International Marine Design & Equipment*

Victorious

Pt. No.	Name	Builder	Laid down	Launched	Completed	Disposition
R.38	VICTORIOUS	Vickers-Armstrongs (Tyne)	4. 5.37	14. 9.39	15. 5.41	Portsmouth for disposal

Machinery contract: Engined Wallsend Slipway. Re-boilered Foster Wheeler during modernisation.

"*Illustrious*" *class:* **VICTORIOUS**

Sole survivor of a class of six, this vessel—which originally displaced 22,600/29,100 tons, had dimensions of 751(oa) ×95¾×29⅓ feet, and was armed with sixteen 4·5-inch D.P. (8×2) and forty-eight 2-pounder A.A. (6×8) guns—introduced the armoured flight deck and hangar to carriers.

Modernised at H.M. Dockyard, Portsmouth, between 1950–58 she was lengthened by some 30 feet; had an 8¾-deg. angled flight deck, steam catapults, and mirror landing aid fitted; was equipped with modern GW and air direction and control radar, tactical display system, and operations room; was re-boilered, had remote machinery control room installed, and generating capacity increased to 4,200kW.; and was re-armed with twelve 3-inch D.P. (6×2) and six 40mm. A.A. (1×6) guns, each mounting with its own HA.DCT.

These modifications increased displacement by nearly 8,000 tons and draught by 1¾ feet, while aircraft capacity is variable depending on types borne. Refitted 1962–63 when gun armament was reduced, and flight deck strengthened— to operate the heaviest naval aircraft—and extended outboard of island to provide access between fore and aft ends. Black top to funnel and rigged with lattice mainmast.

Sister ships ILLUSTRIOUS, FORMIDABLE and INDOMITABLE, and near sister ships IMPLACABLE and INDEFATIGABLE, were scrapped 1953–56.

Displacement: 30,530/35,500 tons.

Dimensions: 673(pp) 781(oa)×103¼ (146¾ across FD)×28½/31 feet.

Machinery: Six Foster Wheeler boilers (440 lb/in² at 750°F); three shafts; Parsons geared turbines, S.H.P. 110,000= 31 knots; O.F. 4,850 tons.

Protection: Main belt 4½ inches, hangar side 4½ inches, flight deck 3½ inches, hangar deck 2½ inches.

Armament: Eight 3-inch A.A. (4×2), four 3-pounder saluting (4×1) guns; twenty-eight aircraft and eight helicopters. Two steam catapults, two lifts, and four arrester wires.

Complement: 2,400.

[Block courtesy *Shipbuilding & Shipping Record*

Above and **left:**
Eagle

Right: Bridge of *Eagle.*

Below: Stern and bow view of *Eagle.*

"Audacious" class: **EAGLE**

This class was much improved over the IMPLACABLE with enlarged dimensions to operate heavier aircraft, double armoured hangars with 17½ feet headroom to accommodate United States naval aircraft on which the Royal Navy was then dependant, thicker flight deck armour and enhanced damage control arrangements, and the provision of permanent deck parks to accommodate additional aircraft.

Fitted with an interim angled deck and mirror landing aid in 1956–57, the EAGLE was completely modernised at H.M. Dockyard, Devonport, between 1959–64 and was provided with an 8½-deg. angled deck, steam catapults, and a comprehensive display radar system. The four twin 4·5-inch D.P. gun turrets at the fore end of the flight deck and the light A.A. armament were removed and replaced by six quadruple Seacat launchers, each with its own HA.DCT, disposed three to starboard, two to port, and one aft. She was also re-rigged with two lattic masts stepped forward and aft of the funnel.

At present the most modern carrier in the Royal Navy, the EAGLE now forms a distinct sub-group from her former sister ship ARK ROYAL (see following page).

Displacement: 43,000/50,000 tons.

Dimensions: 720(pp) 811¾(oa) × 112¾ (171 across FD) × 31/35 feet.

Machinery: Eight Admiralty 3-drum boilers; four shafts; Parsons geared turbines, S.H.P. 152,000 = 31½ knots; O.F. 5,500 tons.

Protection: Details not available.

Armament: Twenty-four Seacat (6×4) G.W.S.; eight 4·5-inch D.P. (4×2), four 3-pounder saluting (4×1) guns; thirty-four aircraft and ten helicopters. Two steam catapults and two lifts.

Complement: 2,637.

Pt. No.	Name	Builder	Laid down	Launched	Completed	Disposition
R.05	EAGLE (ex-*Audacious*) ...	Harland & Wolff ...	24.10.42	19. 3.46	1.10.51	Home/Far East

Machinery contract: Engined by builder.

"Audacious" class: **ARK ROYAL**

Completed after the EAGLE, the ARK ROYAL originally incorporated a 5½-deg. angled deck, steam catapults, and a deck edge lift port side amidships in addition to the two centre line units: the last two items being first fittings in the Royal Navy.

The deck edge lift only served the upper hangar but encroached on hangar space and was removed in 1959. The overhang of the angled deck led to the suppression of the two port forward gun turrets, the two starboard forward turrets were removed in 1959, and the forward turret on each side aft in 1964. Thirty-six 40mm. A.A. (5×6 and 6×1) guns were taken out at various times and replaced by two quadruple and one twin mounting.

Refitted in 1961 with improved steam catapults and mirror landing aid, the ARK ROYAL had a stump lattice mast added before the lattic foremast, and retained the short tripod mainmast stepped abaft the funnel. There was little likelihood of her being modernised on the same scale as the EAGLE—as the time involved would take up some half of her active remaining life while the cost involved would go halfway towards a new carrier—but the total abandonment of the carrier replacement programme resulted in the ARK ROYAL starting an extensive refit in 1967.

Displacement: 43,060/50,390 tons.
Dimensions: 720(pp) 810¼(oa) × 112¾ (164½ across FD) × 31/35 feet.
Machinery: Eight Admiralty 3-drum boilers (400 lb/in² at 600°F); four shafts; Parsons geared turbines, S.H.P. 152,000=31½ knots; O.F. 5,500 tons.
Protection: Details not available.
Armament: Four 4·5-inch D.P. (2×2), fourteen 40mm. A.A. (2×4 and 3×2), two 2-pounder saluting (2×1) guns; forty aircraft and eight helicopters. Two steam catapults and two lifts.
Complement: 2,345.

Pt. No.	Name	Builder	Laid down	Launched	Completed	Disposition
R.09	ARK ROYAL (ex-*Irresistible*)	Cammell Laird ...	3. 5.43	3. 5.50	25. 2.55	Devonport refitting

Machinery contract: Engined by builder.

"*Hermes*" *class:* **CENTAUR**

This class was an improvement over the war-built light fleet carriers of the "Colossus" and "Majestic" classes with double the power for an additional 5 knots of speed, accompanied by increased dimensions which resulted in more hangar space and a lightly armoured flight deck.

Construction was arrested by the termination of hostilities and four units (the ARROGANT, MONMOUTH, POLYPHEMUS, and the original HERMES) were cancelled. Three of the remaining units—ALBION, BULWARK, and CENTAUR—were completed to a modified design, which considerably increased their original displacement of 18,300 tons and resulted in a 2-knot loss of speed, and included a 5¾-deg. angled deck; while the final unit—the second HERMES (ex-*Elephant*)—had further extensive modification worked in placing her in a sub-class of her own.

The ALBION and BULWARK were later converted to commando carriers during 1959–62, leaving only the CENTAUR able to operate fixed wing aircraft, and she had steam catapults installed in 1957. Owing to her relatively small size and limited hangar space the CENTAUR does not now meet modern requirements but is, nevertheless, still capable of active employment although laid-up in reserve.

Displacement:	22,000/27,000 tons.
Dimensions:	650(pp) 737¾(oa) × 90 (123 across FD) × 23/27 feet.
Machinery:	Four Admiralty 3-drum boilers; two shafts; Parsons geared turbines, S.H.P. 80,000 = 27½ knots; O.F. 3,500 tons.
Protection:	Flight deck 1 inch.
Armament:	Twenty 40mm. A.A. (1 × 6, 5 × 2, 4 × 1), four 3-pounder slauting (4 × 1) guns; seventeen aircraft and eight helicopters. Two steam catapults, two lifts, and five arrester wires.
Complement:	1,390.

Pt. No.	Name	Builder	Laid down	Launched	Completed	Disposition
R.06	CENTAUR...	Harland & Wolff ...	30. 5.44	22. 4.47	1. 9.53	Plymouth reserve

Machinery contract: Engined by builder.

Above and below: *Hermes.*

"*Hermes*" class (*modernised*): **HERMES**

Like her sister ships, construction of the HERMES was suspended after the war, and she was advanced to the launching stage only to clear the slip for more urgent mercantile tonnage, after which work on her was again suspended.

Construction was resumed in 1957 to include all technical advances which included a 6½-deg. angled deck, steam catapults, deck edge lift, mirror landing aid, and comprehensive display system radar. Also, her electrical supply was changed from d.c. to a.c. and the generator power stepped up to 5,440kW. For ABC defence measures there was a wash-down system, boxed-in boilers, and control room from which the main and auxiliary machinery could be remotely operated. The deck edge lift was the first in the Royal Navy not to encroach on hangar space. When refitted 1965-66 the ten 40mm. A.A. (5×2) guns were replaced by four quadruple Seacat launchers.

The HERMES was the most up-to-date carrier in the Royal Navy on completion but, like the CENTAUR, she suffers from limited hangar capacity although she can operate the most modern aircraft but in too few numbers. Unlike her near sister ships the HERMES stepped her solitary lattice mast abaft the funnel.

Displacement: 23,000/27,800 tons.

Dimensions: 650(pp) 744¼(oa) ×90 (144½ across FD) ×24/28 feet.

Machinery: Four Admiralty 3-drum boilers; two shafts; Parsons geared turbines, S.H.P. 80,000=27½ knots; O.F. 3,500 tons.

Protection: Flight deck 1 inch.

Armament: Sixteen Seacat (4×4) G.W.S.; twenty aircraft and eight helicopters. Two steam catapults, two lifts, and four arrester wires.

Complement: 2,100.

Pt. No.	Name	Builder	Laid down	Launched	Completed	Disposition
R.12	HERMES (ex-*Elephant*) ...	Vickers-Armstrongs (Barrow)	21. 6.44	16. 2.53	18.11.59	Home/Far East

Machinery contract: Engined by builder.

FLEET VESSELS

Dreadnought at sea on the surface.

Note bull-nosed bow and partially submerged stern.

Prototype: **DREADNOUGHT**

While both the "Porpoise" and "Oberon" classes possessed good anti-submarine qualities, they were limited in speed and radius by conventional propulsion, and the most effective answer to the nuclear-powered submarine—whether missile or torpedo armed—was a similar vessel specifically equipped for the role. Unfortunately, the cost of such a vessel was so high that only a portion of the anti-submarine effort can be expended in this direction, and the major contribution must still be conducted from relatively cheaper surface forces.

The adoption of nuclear propulsion enabled the **DREADNOUGHT** to adopt the full form most suitable for continuous submerged operation, and consequently she was made short and full with a bull-nosed bow. It was originally intended to install a British nuclear reactor, but in 1958 an agreement was reached with the United States for the supply of an American-built reactor and, in consequence, the construction of the **DREADNOUGHT** was advanced. For optimum performance a single shaft was found preferable to a multi-shaft installation, and with no draught limitation a large diameter propeller could be shipped. For maximum reliability all control and essential auxiliary machinery was duplicated. Range is practically unlimited and is more dictated by the physical state of the crew and the need to replenish consumable stores and armament.

The **DREADNOUGHT** has the speed to tactically combine with a carrier group where she would powerfully reinforce the anti-submarine screen; or provide anti-submarine cover for an amphibious force faced with an ocean passage; or be deployed as a hunter/killer vessel, either singly or as a unit of an anti-submarine group.

Displacement: 3,000/4,000 tons.
Dimensions: 265¾(pp) ....(oa) × 32¼ × 26 feet.
Machinery: One pressurised water-cooled reactor; one shaft; Westinghouse geared turbines, S.H.P. 15,000 = 15/30 knots.
Armament: Six 21-inch T.T. (all forward).
Complement: 88.

Pt. No.	Name	Builder	Laid down	Launched	Completed	Disposition
S.101	DREADNOUGHT ...	Vickers-Armstrongs (Barrow)	12. 6.59	21.10.60	17. 4.63	3rd Submarine Squadron

Machinery contracts: Rolls-Royce and Westinghouse.

The *Valiant* exercising on the surface with a naval helicopter. As this type of submarine is designed for continuous submerged operation it has a poor surface performance as shown by the wake.

" *Valiant* " *class:* **CHURCHILL, CONQUEROR, SUPERB, VALIANT, WARSPITE.**
Improved " *Valiant* " *class:* **TWO** unnamed.

This class is generally similar to the **DREADNOUGHT** but with slightly enlarged dimensions and a British-built nuclear propulsion plant.

Capable of undertaking submerged patrols of long endurance at continuous high speed, staying submerged for over two months if necessary. In view of this particular attention has been paid to the habitability, while an improved underwater distilling plant will provide unlimited fresh water.

The armament of homing torpodes will be controlled by the latest weapon control equipment, and together with long range sonar, inertial navigation system and ability to measure ice clearance when operating under the polar caps, means that the only physical limitations imposed on their sphere of operations is where there is insufficient depth of water.

Orders were placed with Vickers (Barrow) in 1967/8 for enlarged and improved " *Valiant* " class submarines.

Displacement: 3,500/4,500 tons.
Dimensions: 285(pp) ....(oa)$\times 33\frac{1}{4} \times 30$ feet.
Machinery: One pressurised water-cooled reactor; one shaft; English Electric geared turbines, S.H.P. 20,000$=$20/35 knots.
Armament: Six 21-inch T.T. (all forward).
Complement: 103.

Pt. No.	Name	Builder	Laid down	Launched	Completed	Disposition
S.46	CHURCHILL	Vickers-Armstrongs (Barrow)	30.6.67	20.12.68	....	Building, 3rd Submarine Squadron
S.105	CONQUEROR	Cammel Laird	5.12.67	28. 8.69	....	Building
S.106	SUPERB	Vickers (Barrow)	68	....	....	Building
S.102	VALIANT ... ... (ex-*Inflexible*)	Vickers-Armstrongs (Barrow)	22. 1.62	3.12.63	18. 7.66	3rd Submarine Squadron
S.103	WARSPITE...	Vickers-Armstrongs (Barrow)	10.12.63	25. 9.65	18. 4.67	3rd Submarine Squadron
S.107	A	Vickers (Barrow)	....	....	....	Ordered
S.108	B	Vickers (Barrow)	....	....	....	Ordered

Machinery contracts: Pressurised water-cooled reactor by Rolls-Royce & Associates (a consortium of Foster Wheeler, Rolls-Royce, and Vickers-Armstrongs), geared turbines by English Electric, and electric motors by L.S.E.

Resolution running on the surface.

[Block courtesy *Shipbuilding & Shipping Record*

"*Resolution*" *class:* **RENOWN, REPULSE, RESOLUTION, REVENGE**

The Royal Navy's entire seaborne nuclear deterrent force is represented by this class of four vessels. They are longer than their anti-submarine counterparts because of the addition of the missile compartment amidships—between the sail and machinery spaces—where the Polaris missiles are vertically stowed and can be fired from below the surface. They are also provided with torpedo tubes so that they can also undertake an anti-submarine role should the occasion arise.

All nuclear submarines have auxiliary electric propulsion with power supplied by either diesel generators (when on the surface or using the snort) or a bank of batteries (when fully submerged).

A fifth unit of this class was projected but was cancelled early in 1965, which enabled the order for the CHURCHILL (see previous page) to be advanced by some six months.

Displacement: .,.../7,000 tons.

Dimensions: 360(pp) 425(oa) × 33 × 30 feet.

Machinery: One pressurised water-cooled nuclear reactor; one shaft; English Electric geared turbines, S.H.P. 20,000 = 20/35 knots.

Armament: Sixteen Polaris (16 × 1) G.W.S.; six 21-inch T.T. (all forward).

Complement: 141.

Pt. No.	Name	Builder	Laid down	Launched	Completed	Disposition
S.26	RENOWN	Cammell Laird ...	25. 6.64	25. 2.67	15.11.68	10th Submarine Squadron
S.23	REPULSE	Vickers-Armstrongs (Barrow)	2. 9.65	4.11.67	28. 9.68	10th Submarine Squadron
S.22	RESOLUTION	Vickers-Armstrongs (Barrow)	26. 2.64	15. 9.66	2.10.67	10th Submarine Squadron
S.27	REVENGE	Cammell Laird ...	19. 5.65	15. 3.68	....	Building, 10th Submarine Squadron

Machinery contracts: Pressurised water-cooled reactor by Rolls-Royce & Associates and geared turbines by English Electric.

FLEET VESSELS

"Battle" class (second group): **AGINCOURT, AISNE, BARROSA, CORUNNA**

Former destroyers converted to radar picket duties during 1961–62. Modifications effected included the removal of both banks of T.T. and the entire light A.A. armament; the after shelter deck extended well forward to just short of the funnel; a heavier lattice foremast stepped to carry the large AW scanner; a tripod mast stepped aft; a quadruple Seacat launcher mounted on the after superstructure; and the provision of a comprehensive operations room. Some 40 tons of permanent ballast had to be added to compensate for the additional topweight.

At present they serve with the mixed frigate squadrons composed of mutually supporting specialised vessels, but have the speed to tactically combine with carrier task groups if so required.

Displacement: 2,780/3,430 tons.
Dimensions: 355(pp) 379(oa) $\times$ 40$\frac{1}{4}$ $\times$ 12$\frac{3}{4}$/14$\frac{1}{4}$ feet.
Machinery: Two Admiralty 3-drum boilers (400 lb/in^2 at 650°F); two shafts; Parsons geared turbines, S.H.P. 50,000 = 35$\frac{3}{4}$/31$\frac{1}{4}$ knots; O.F. 680 tons.
Armament: Four Seacat (1 $\times$ 4) G.W.S.; four 4·5-inch D.P. (2 $\times$ 2), two 20mm. A.A.(2 $\times$ 1) guns; one A/S mortar (Squid).
Complement: 232.

Pt. No.	Name			Builder		Laid down	Launched	Completed	Disposition
D.86	AGINCOURT	...	...	Hawthorn Leslie	...	12.12.43	29. 1.45	25. 6.47	Portsmouth reserve
D.22	AISNE	...	...	Vickers-Armstrongs (Tyne)		26. 8.43	12. 5.45	20. 3.47	1st Division, Western Fleet; for disposal.
D.68	BARROSA	...	...	Clydebank	.	28.12.43	17. 1.45	14. 2.47	Far East
D.97	CORUNNA	...	...	Swan Hunter	...	12. 4.44	29. 5.45	6. 6.47	Portsmouth reserve

Machinery contracts: Aisne engined by Parsons, *Corunna* by Wallsend Slipway, all others by builders.

"*Weapon*" *class:* **BROADSWORD, CROSSBOW, SCORPION**

This class were a new conception in destroyer design when completed, and were fitted as fleet escorts with emphasis on good anti-aircraft and anti-submarine qualities but still retaining a torpedo armament for attacking major surface units.

The close of the Second World War resulted in sixteen being cancelled, and the remaining four were completed as two distinct groups. Originally intended to ship three twin 4-inch A.A. mountings, one was replaced by A/S mortars sited forward in two units (BATTLEAXE and BROADSWORD) and aft in the other two (CROSSBOW and SCORPION), while two additional twin 40mm. A.A. mountings to be placed between the torpedo tubes were suppressed The unit machinery arrangement had boiler and engine rooms alternated which lessened the risk of total loss of power due to battle damage.

Converted to radar pickets in 1958–59 they were less elaborately equipped than the "Battle" class conversions, and had both banks of T.T. removed; the after superstructure extended forward with a lattice mast stepped at its fore end to carry the AW scanner. The BATTLEAXE and BROADSWORD had the positions of the A/S mortars and the after twin 4-inch mounting transposed—making them uniform with the other pair—and the former was scrapped in 1964.

Displacement: 2,280/2,935 tons.

Dimensions: 341½(pp) 365(oa) × 38 × 12½/13¾ feet.

Machinery: Two Foster Wheeler boilers (430 lb/in² at 750°F); two shafts; Parsons geared turbines, S.H.P. 40,000 = 36¾/31½ knots; O.F. 600 tons.

Armament: Four 4-inch A.A. (2×2), six 40mm. A.A. (2×2 and 2×1) guns; two except *Scorpion* one A/S mortar (Squid except *Scorpion* Limbo).

Complement: 234.

Pt. No.	Name	Builder	Laid down	Launched	Completed	Disposition
D.31	BROADSWORD	Yarrow	20. 7.44	5. 2.46	4.10.48	Rosyth for disposal
D.96	CROSSBOW	Thornycroft	26. 8.44	20.12.45	4. 3.48	Portsmouth reserve
D.64	SCORPION (ex-*Tomahawk*, (ex-*Centaur*)	White	16.12.44	15. 8.46	17. 9.47	Rosyth for disposal

Machinery contracts: All engined by builders.

FLEET VESSELS

Above: *Agincourt.*

Below: *Battleaxe* (now scrapped).

Former " Battle " class destroyer *Agincourt* modified as aircraft direction vessel.

FLEET VESSELS

Assiniboine after conversion to a helicopter carrying destroyer.

Pt. No.	Name	Builder	Laid down	Launched	Completed	Disposition
DDH.234	ASSINIBOINE	Marine Industries ...	19. 5.52	12. 2.54	16. 8.56	Royal Canadian Navy, 7th Escort Squadron
DDH.233	FRASER	Burrard	11.12.51	19. 2.53	28. 6.57	Completed Canadian Yarrow, Royal Canadian Navy, 5th Escort Squadron
DDH.230	MARGAREE	Halifax Shyd.	12. 9.51	29. 3.56	5.10.57	Royal Canadian Navy, 7th Escort Squadron
DDH.229	OTTAWA	Canadian Vickers ...	8. 6.51	29. 4.53	10.11.56	Royal Canadian Navy, 7th Escort Squadron
DDH.206	SAGUENAY	Halifax Shyd.	4. 4.51	30. 7.53	15.12.56	Royal Canadian Navy, 1st Escort Squadron
DDH.205	ST. LAURENT	Canadian Vickers ...	22.11.50	30.11.51	29.10.55	Royal Canadian Navy, 5th Escort Squadron
DDH.203	SKEENA	Burrard	1. 6.51	19. 8.52	30. 3.57	Royal Canadian Navy, 3rd Escort Squadron

Machinery contracts: St. Laurent engined by Yarrow, others by builders.

"St. Laurent" class: **ASSINIBOINE, FRASER, MARGAREE, OTTAWA, SAGUENAY, ST LAURENT, SKEENA**

The first Commonwealth warships of post-Second World War design, these vessels were also the first major naval units to be wholly designed in Canada. As completed they were flush-decked vessels with a radiused sheer strake and a modified turtle back f'oc'sle, well able to maintain speed in adverse weather condtitions, and sufficiently fast to engage the new generation of fast submarines.

Originally armed with two twin 3-inch D.P. and two single 40mm. A.A. guns and two A/S mortars, they were modified in 1963–65 when the after 3-inch mounting was replaced by a landing pad for an A/S helicopter; a hangar was worked-in abaft the funnel whose uptakes were divided—and set abreast—to provide increased hangar space, and addition which also necessitated the removal of both the amidships 40mm. A.A. guns; one A/S mortar was removed owing to the limited space now available abaft the landing pad; and the freeboard right aft was reduced to facilitate the working of variable depth sonar over the stern. The open twin 3-inch mounting on the fo'c'sle has now been enclosed by a gun shield, and the A/S armament augmented by the addition of torpedoes.

Displacement: 2,265/2,800 tons.

Dimensions: 361(wl) 366(oa) × 42 × 13¼/000 feet.

Machinery: Two Babcock & Wilcox boilers; two shafts; English Electric geared turbines, S.H.P. 30,000=28½ knots; O.F. 000 tons.

Armament: Two 3-inch D.P. (1 × 2) guns; one A/S mortar (Limbo); one A/S helicopter.

Complement: 250.

FLEET VESSELS

Talwar, note single 40 mm. A.A. guns abaft funnel not in Royal Navy vessels.

Pt. No.	Name	Builder	Laid down	Launched	Completed	Disposition
F.77	BLACKPOOL	Harland & Wolff ...	20.12.54	14. 2.57	14. 8.58	Royal New Zealand Navy (1966)
F.73	EASTBOURNE	Vickers-Armstrongs (Tyne)	13. 1.54	29.12.55	9. 1.58	Completed Vickers-Armstrongs (Barrow), 17th Frigate Squadron
F.63	SCARBOROUGH... ...	Vickers-Armstrongs (Tyne)	11. 9.53	4. 4.55	10. 5.57	17th Frigate Squadron
F.65	TENBY	Cammell Laird ...	23. 6.53	4.10.55	18.12.57	17th Frigate Squadron
F.43	TORQUAY	Harland & Wolff ...	11. 3.53	1. 7.54	10. 5.56	17th Frigate Squadron
F.36	WHITBY	Cammell Laird ...	30. 9.52	2. 7.54	10. 7.56	20th Frigate Squadron
F.140	TALWAR	Cammell Laird ...	7. 6.57	18. 7.58	26. 4.59	Indian Navy
F.143	TRISHUL	Harland & Wolff ...	19. 2.57	18. 6.58	13. 1.60	Indian Navy

Machinery contracts: Eastbourne and Scarborough engined by Vickers-Armstrongs (Barrow), and others by builders.

28

"Whitby" class: **BLACKPOOL, EASTBOURNE, SCARBOROUGH, TALWAR, TENBY, TORQUAY, TRISHUL, WHITBY**

The Royal Navy's first post-war frigate programme embraced three specialised types—the anti-submarine (type 12), anti-aircraft (type 41), and aircraft direction (type 61) vessels—as it was not considered possible to combine their individual qualities within a single hull of moderate dimensions. They were thus mutually supporting vessels and needed to be deployed in groups to secure all-round effectiveness against attack.

The A/S frigates proved generally similar to the Royal Canadian Navy vessels which had only shortly preceded them, and while the hull line differed it had the same object in view of maintaining speed in adverse conditions to counter fast submarines which could otherwise exploit surface weather conditions to their advantage. The "Whitby" class hull was of all-welded prefabricated sections with a prominent half-raised fo'c'sle to secure lift forward and the break in deck level occurring well aft to preserve longitudinal strength. It has proved a most sea-kindly hull form and has been largely adhered to since. Although moderately powered, an adequate speed was attained by a combination of fine hull form with double reduction gearing for low propeller revolutions.

The armament comprised a twin 4·5-inch D.P. turret foward, controlled by a radar-fitted HA/LA.DCT on the bridge; a twin 40mm. A.A. mounting abaft the funnel; and two A/S mortars in wells farther aft. The original provision to ship twelve tubes for A/S torpedoes (one twin training and four fixed on each side) was only of short duration, and was only fitted to the earlier vessels and has since been removed. The BLACKPOOL was loaned to the Royal New Zealand Navy in 1966 as a temporary measure.

Displacement: 2,150/2,560 tons.

Dimensions: 360(pp) 370(oa) × 41 × 11¼/14 feet.

Machinery: Two Babcock & Wilcox boilers; two shafts; English Electric geared turbines, S.H.P. 30,000=30 knots; O.F. 370 tons except *Indian Navy vessels* 400 tons.

Armament: Two 4·5-inch D.P. (1×2), two except *Indian Navy vessels* four 40mm. A.A. (1×2:1×2 and 2×1) guns; two A/S mortars (Limbo).

Complement: 152 (189 in leaders) except *Indian Navy vessels* 231.

FLEET VESSELS

Puma, like *Lynx*, has combined mast and funnel aft.

Pt. No.	Name	Builder	Laid down	Launched	Completed	Disposition
F.37	JAGUAR	Denny...	2.11.53	20. 7.57	12.12.59	Home/Far East
F.14	LEOPARD	H.M. Dockyard (Portsmouth)	25. 3.53	23. 5.55	30. 9.58	Home/Far East
F.27	LYNX	Clydebank	13. 8.53	12. 1.55	14. 3.57	Home/Far East
F.34	PUMA	Scotts	16.11.53	30. 6.54	27. 4.57	Home/Far East
F.137	BEAS	Vickers-Armstrongs (Tyne)	29.11.56	9.10.58	24. 5.60	Indian Navy
F.139	BETWA	Vickers-Armstrongs (Tyne)	29. 5.57	15. 9.59	8.12.60	Indian Navy
F.31	BRAHMAPUTRA (ex-*Panther*)	Clydebank	20.10.55	15. 3.57	31. 3.58	Indian Navy

Machinery contracts: Jaguar engined by Crossley; *Beas, Betwa,* and *Leopard* by Vickers-Armstrongs (Barrow); *Lynx* by Crossley and British Polar; *Brahmaputra* by British Polar; and *Puma* by H.M. Dockyard (Chatham).

"Leopard" class: **BEAS, BETWA, BRAHMAPUTRA, JAGUAR, LEOPARD, LYNX, PUMA**

Together with the type 61 aircraft direction frigates (see following pages) these vessels (type 41 anti-aircraft frigates) were built to form mutually self-supporting groups with the type 12 anti-submarine frigate (see preceding pages).

Both types adopted a shorter but generally similar hull form to the type 12, and were originally to be propelled by geared turbines of about half the power installed in the type 12. As no suitable steam plant of this power was readily available they were fitted with the initial mark of the Admiralty standard range diesel engine then under development: four units being coupled to each shaft via gearing. The exhaust uptakes were led up inside the lattice fore- and mainmasts, and the JAGUAR was provided with controllable pitch propellers—the first Royal Navy vessel to be so fitted.

The twin 4·5-inch turrets fore and aft were fully automatic and controlled by the combined HA/LA.DCT on the bridge and by an HA.DCT aft, and were supplemented for close range work by a twin 40mm. A.A. mounting aft. It is intended to replace the twin 40mm. by a quadruple Seacat launcher in the near future. Only a single A/S mortar was installed on the quarterdeck.

The original PANTHER of this class was completed for the Indian Navy and renamed, while a second ship of the same name was to have become the type 61 GLOUCESTER. A combined mast and funnel has replaced the lattice mainmast in LYNX and PUMA.

Displacement: 2,300/2,520 tons except *Indian Navy vessels* 2,250/2,515 tons.

Dimensions: 330(pp) 340(oa) × 40 × 11¼ except *Indian Navy vessels* 11/12¾ feet.

Machinery: Two shafts; 16-cyl. ASR.1 diesel engines (four/shaft), B.H.P. 12,400 = 25 knots; O.F. 230 tons.

Armament: Four 4·5-inch D.P. (2 × 2), two 40mm. A.A. (1 × 2) guns; one A/S mortar (Squid).

Complement: 205 except *Indian Navy vessels* 210.

Lincoln, together with *Llandaff*, still retain lattice masts.

Pt. No.	Name			Builder			Laid down	Launched	Completed	Disposition
F.59	CHICHESTER	...	...	Fairfield	...	...	26. 6.53	21. 4.55	16. 5.58	Home/Far East
F.99	LINCOLN ...	...	...	Fairfield	...	...	1. 6.55	6. 4.59	7. 7.60	Home/Far East
F.61	LLANDAFF	...	...	Hawthorn Leslie	...	...	27. 8.53	30.11.55	11. 4.58	Home/Far East
F.32	SALISBURY	...	...	H.M. Dockyard De onport)		...	23. 1.52	25. 6.53	27. 2.57	Devonport refitting

Machinery contracts: Salisbury engined by Vickers-Arn strongs (Barrow), all others by British Polar.

"Salisbury" class: CHICHESTER, LINCOLN, LLANDAFF, SALISBURY

Generally similar to the preceding "Leopard" class except that the after 4·5-inch turret was suppressed and replaced by additional radar while an enlarged operations room was provided between decks and the twin 40mm. A.A. mounting was moved further aft.

The final unit of this class—the LINCOLN—was fitted with controllable pitch propellers, and had a higher after superstructure to take a quadruple Seacat launcher but temporarily shipped a single 40mm. A.A. gun in lieu.

The merit of this class is not readily apparent unless the present day necessity to detect targets at long range, and then assimilate and relay this information through extensive communications facilities, is fully appreciated. The equipment required for these purposes is bulky and complex, so that the design problem is more one of volume than weight and consequently not easily resolved, although satisfactory development has been made in this direction.

Three further units of this class were projected: the EXETER and GLOUCESTER (ex-type 41 *Panther*) were cancelled, while the COVENTRY was finally completed as a "Leander" class. A combined mast and funnel has replaced both lattice masts in the CHICHESTER, and the lattice mainmast in SALISBURY.

Engine room layout.

[Block courtesy *Shipbuilding & Shipping Record.*

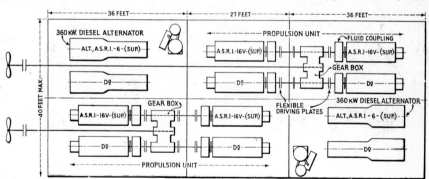

Displacement: 2,170/2,350 tons.
Dimensions: 330(pp) 340(oa) × 40 × 10¾/12½ feet.
Machinery: Two shafts; 16-cyl. ASR.1 diesel engines (four/shaft), B.H.P. 12,400 = 25 knots; O.F. 230 tons.
Armament: Two 4·5-inch D.P. (1 × 2), two except *Lincoln* one 40mm. A.A. (1 × 1/2) guns; one A/S mortar (Squid).
Complement: 207.

Restigouche

"*Restigouche*" *class:* CHAUDIERE, COLUMBIA, GATINEAU, KOOTENAY, RESTIGOUCHE, ST. CROIX, TERRA NOVA

Generally similar to the "St. Laurent" class as completed, and incorporated small modifications as a result of experience with the earlier vessels.

The bridge projected conspicuously forward of the superstructure, and the forward twin 3-inch A.A. mounting was raised above the level of the fo'c'sle deck.

All are to be taken in hand, starting in 1966, for alteration similar to the " St. Laurent " class, but with Asroc rocket assisted A/S torpedoes supplementing the Limbo A/S mortar (one to be removed), the addition of variable depth and Jezebel passive sonar, and the removal of the after win 3-inch A.A. mounting to provide a landing pad and hangar for the A/S helciopter, which will result in a 5 ft. increase of overall length.

Displacement: 2,365/2,900 tons.
Dimensions: 361(wl) 366(oa) × 42 × $13\frac{1}{2}$/... feet.
Machinery: Two Babcock & Wilcox boilers; two shafts; English Electric geared turbines, S.H.P. 30,000 = 28 knots; O.F. ... tons.
Armament: Four 3-inch A.A. (2 × 2) guns; two A/S mortars (Limbo).
Complement: 246.

Pt. No.	Name	Builder	Laid down	Launched	Completed	Disposition
DDE.235	CHAUDIERE	Halifax	30. 7.53	13.11.57	14.11.59	Royal Canadian Navy, 2nd Escort Squadron
DDE.260	COLUMBIA	Burrard	11. 6.53	1.11.56	7.11.59	Royal Canadian Navy, 2nd Escort Squadron
DDE.236	GATINEAU	Davie Sbdg.	30. 4.53	3. 6.57	17. 2.59	Royal Canadian Navy, 5th Escort Squadron
DDE.258	KOOTENAY	Burrard	21. 8.52	15. 6.54	7. 3.59	Royal Canadian Navy, 1st Escort Squadron
DDE.257	RESTIGOUCHE ...	Canadian Vickers ...	15. 7.53	22.11.54	7. 6.58	Royal Canadian Navy, 3rd Escort Squadron
DDE.256	ST. CROIX	Marine Industries ...	15.10.54	15.11.56	4.10.58	Royal Canadian Navy, 2nd Escort Squadron
DDE.259	TERRA NOVA	Victoria	14.11.52	21. 6.55	6. 6.59	Royal Canadian Navy, 3rd Escort Squadron

Machinery contracts: All engined by builders.

35

Yarra—note quadruple Seacat launcher installed aft and two HA/LA.DCTs

The *Rothesay* recently completed a refit at H.M. Dockyard, Rosyth, when a hangar (off-centred to port) and a landing deck were added aft for a helicopter which resulted in the forward 3-barrelled A/S mortar being removed. A quadruple launcher or Seacat missiles, together with its director, was mounted on the hangar roof in place of the former 40mm gun; single 20mm guns have been added in the after corner of the superstructure on each side and, a little forward, 6-barrelled 3-inch rocket launchers (not shown in photograph) have been added with the 2-inch rocket flare projector mounted on top. The masts have been plated-in.

FLEET VESSELS

Pt. No.	Name	Builder	Laid down	Launched	Completed	Disposition
F.115	BERWICK	Harland & Wolff ...	16. 6.58	15.12.59	1. 6.61	Chatham refitting
F.106	BRIGHTON	Yarrow	23. 7.57	30.10.59	28. 9.61	Chatham refitting
F.113	FALMOUTH	Swan Hunter	23.11.57	15.12.59	25. 7.61	Rosyth refitting
F.108	LONDONDERRY... ...	White	15.11.56	20. 5.58	18.10.61	1st Destroyer Squadron, Rosyth refitting
F.103	LOWESTOFT	Stephen	9. 6.58	23. 6.60	26. 9.61	Chatham refitting
F.126	PLYMOUTH	H.M. Dockyard (Devonport)	1. 7.58	20. 7.59	11. 5.61	Chatham refitting
F.129	RHYL	H.M. Dockyard (Portsmouth)	29. 1.58	23. 4.59	31.10.60	West Indies
F.107	ROTHESAY	Yarrow	6.11.56	9.12.57	23. 4.60	Home/Far East
F.101	YARMOUTH	Clydebank	29.11.57	23. 3.59	26. 3.60	Portsmouth refitting
F.05	PARRAMATTA	Cockatoo	3. 1.57	31. 1.59	4. 7.61	Royal Australian Navy, 3rd Destroyer Squadron
F.07	YARRA	H.M.A. Dockyard (Williamstown)	9. 4.57	30. 9.58	7.61	Royal Australian Navy, 3rd Destroyer Squadron
F.111	OTAGO (ex-*Hastings*) ...	Thornycroft	5. 9.57	11.12.58	22. 6.60	Royal New Zealand Navy
F.148	TARANAKI	White	27. 6.58	19. 8.59	28. 3.61	Royal New Zealand Navy
F.22	DERWENT	H.M.A. Dockyard (Williamstown)	16. 6.59	17. 6.61	4.64	Royal Australian Navy, 3rd Destroyer Squadron
F.21	STUART	Cockatoo	20. 3.59	8. 4.61	27. 6.63	Royal Australian Navy, 3rd Destroyer Squadron
F.64	SWAN	H.M.A. Dockyard (Williamstown)	16. 8.65	16.12.67	....	Royal Australian Navy, 3rd Destroyer Squadron
F.74	TORRENS	Cockatoo	12. 8.65	28. 9.68	....	Royal Australian Navy, 3rd Destroyer Squadron

Machinery contracts: Falmouth engined by Wallsend Slipway, Plymouth and Yarmouth by English Electric, and others by builders.

"Rothesay" class: **BERWICK, BRIGHTON, DERWENT, FALMOUTH, LONDONDERRY, LOWESTOFT, OTAGO, PARRAMATTA, PLYMOUTH, RHYL, ROTHESAY, STUART, SWAN, TARANAKI, TORRENS, YARMOUTH, YARRA**

These vessels differ internally from the "Whitby" class, and their layout has been modified as a result of experience with the latter.

The superstructure abaft the funnel was built-up to a ship a quadruple Seacat launcher, together with its DCT and missile handling and control arrangements, but this is not fitted at present in the Royal Navy vessels except in ROTHESAY and YARMOUTH and a single 40mm. A.A. gun was mounted in lieu. The funnel was made a little thicker, slightly raked, and fitted with a domed top. The ROTHESAY and YARMOUTH had their 40mm. A.A. gun replaced by a quadruple Seacat launcher and a helicopter added when refitted 1965-67, and the remaining Royal Navy units are to be similarly modified.

The Royal Australian Navy vessels had a tubular foremast and a more conspicious mainmast than other units of the class. The DERWENT, STUART, SWAN and TORRENS were made flush-decked and had a modified A/S armament and variable depth sonar.

The original HASTINGS was completed for the Royal New Zealand Navy, while a second ship of the same name—together with the FOWEY and WEYMOUTH—were finally completed as units of the "Leander" class (see p. 49). Three further vessels of this class—PRESIDENT KRUGER (F.150), PRESIDENT PRETORIUS (F.145), and PRESIDENT STEYN (F.147)—were built for the South African Navy but had no provision for Seacat and shipped two 40mm. A.A. guns aft.

Displacement: 2,150/2,560 tons.

Dimensions: 360(pp) 370(oa) × 41 × 12¾/14 feet.

Machinery: Two Babcock & Wilcox boilers; two shafts; English Electric geared turbines, S.H.P. 30,000=30 knots; O.F. 370 tons.

Armament: Four Seacat (1×4) G.W.S. in *Rothesay, Yarmouth, R.A.N.* and *R.N.Z.N. vessels* only; two 4·5-inch D.P. (1×2), one except *Rothesay, Yarmouth, R.A.N.* and *R.N.Z.N. vessels* nil 40mm. A.A. guns; two A/S mortars (Limbo) except *Derwent, Stuart, Swan* and *Torrens* one A/S G.W.S. (Ikara); one A/S helicopter in *Rothesay* and *Yarmouth.*

Complement: 200 except *R.N.Z.N. vessels* 219 and *R.A.N. vessels* 250.

Quarter view of *Fife* showing helicopter landing deck and missile ramps aft

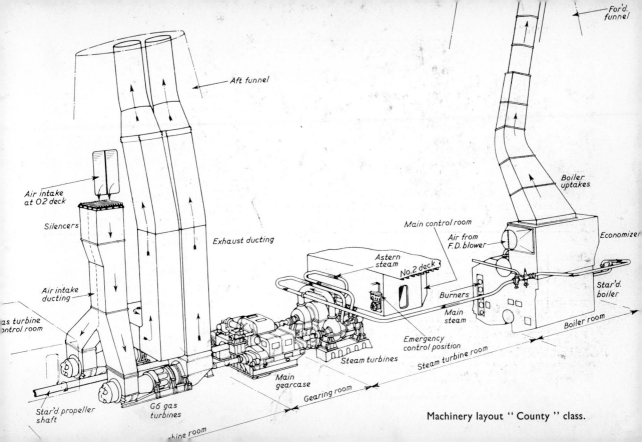

Machinery layout "County" class.

For'd funnel

Aft funnel

Air intake at O2 deck

Silencers

Exhaust ducting

Air intake ducting

Gas turbine control room

Star'd propeller shaft

G6 gas turbines

...hine room

Main gearcase

Gearing room

Steam turbines

Steam turbine room

Emergency control position

Astern steam

No.2 deck

Main control room

Air from F.D. blower

Burners

Main steam

Boiler uptakes

Economizer

Star'd boiler

Boiler room

FLEET VESSELS

Kent and earlier units have mainmast further aft than later units

Pt. No.	Name	Builder	Laid down	Launched	Completed	Disposition
D.18	ANTRIM	Fairfield	20. 1.66	19.10.67	....	Building
D.02	DEVONSHIRE	Cammell Laird ...	9. 3.59	10. 6.60	15.11.62	Home/Far East
D.20	FIFE	Fairfield	31. 5.62	9. 7.64	21. 6.66	Home/Far East
D.19	GLAMORGAN	Vickers-Armstrongs (Tyne)	13. 9.62	9. 7.64	13.10.66	Home/Far East
D.06	HAMPSHIRE	Clydebank	26. 3.59	16. 3.61	15. 3.63	Home/Far East
D.12	KENT	Harland & Wolff ...	1. 3.60	27. 9.61	15. 8.63	Home/Far East
D.16	LONDON	Swan Hunter	26. 2.60	7.12.61	14.11.63	Western Fleet flagship
D.21	NORFOLK	Swan Hunter	15. 3.66	16.11.67	....	Building

Machinery contracts: *Antrim* engined by Harland & Wolff (steam) and A.E.I. and Yarrow (two gas each); *Devonshire* by A.E.I. except for one set of steam by builders; *Fife* by Harland & Wolff (steam and gas); *Glamorgan* by Parsons (steam) and Yarrow (gas); *Hampshire* by builders (steam) and White and Yarrow (two gas each); *Kent* by builders except for one set of steam by A.E.I.; *London* by Wallsend Slipway (steam), A.E.I. (two gas), Thornycroft and Yarrow (one gas each); and *Norfolk* by Harland & Wolff (steam) and A.E.I. and Yarrow (two gas each).

"*County*" *class*: **ANTRIM, DEVONSHIRE, FIFE, GLAMORGAN, HAMPSHIRE, KENT, LONDON, NORFOLK**

Although officially classed as guided missile (armed) destroyers these vessels were not a continuation of the obsolescent destroyer category, but were so rated so that destroyer scantlings were kept firmly in mind all through the design stage—especially as regards to equipment—in order to keep size to an acceptable minimum. Designed to provide long and close range anti-aircraft cover for fast carrier groups, they are fleet escorts approaching the size of the conventional cruiser which, in turn, has been largely supplanted by the modern frigate.

Innovations in their design were the long- and close-range sea-to-air missile systems, and combined steam and gas turbine machinery for main propulsion which was first tried out in the "Tribal" class (see p. 95). As they will spend the greater majority of their time under way using the long life steam plant, for the relatively short periods for which full speed is required their power is boosted by the short-life gas turbines which are more economic in weight and space. In addition, the latter enabled them to get under way immediately from the dead condition while the steam plant is being flashed-up—an important consideration in this nuclear age.

Control arrangements for the armament comprise a DCT for the beam riding Seaslug missiles at the after end of the superstructure; DCT's close abaft the after funnel on each side for the Seacat missiles; and a combined HA/LA.DCT on the bridge for the gun armament, which is principally carried to provide gunfire support for troops ashore and for bombardment purposes. No anti-submarine weapons are carried, but a target detected by the ship-borne sonar would be engaged by either the helicopter, which is armed with A/S homing torpedoes, or by other anti-submarine vessels of the screen. The last four units (ANTRIM, FIFE, GLAMORGAN, and NORFOLK) are fitted with Seaslug Mk. II of greater range and a limited capability against surface vessels.

Displacement:	5,600/6,200 tons.
Dimensions:	505(pp) 521½(oa) × 54 × 16/20 feet.
Machinery:	Two Babcock & Wilcox boilers (700 lb/in² at 900°F); two shafts; A.E.I. steam and gas (two/shaft) geared turbines, S.H.P. 30,000 (steam) + 30,000 (gas) = 32½ knots; O.F. 600 tons.
Armament:	Two Seaslug (1 × 2), eight Seacat (2 × 4) G.W.S.; four 4·5-inch D.P. (2 × 2); four 2-pounder saluting (4 × 1), two 20mm. A.A. (2 × 1) guns; one A/S helicopter.
Complement:	440.

Annapolis

"MacKenzie" class: **ANNAPOLIS, MACKENZIE, NIPIGON, QU'APPELLE, SASKATCHEWAN, YUKON**

Generally similar to the "Restigouche" class but with improved habitability, while the last two units—ANNAPOLIS and NIPIGON—were completed to a modified design.

With the last two the boiler uptakes were divided and led-up as twin funnels, set abreast, to provide increased space for the helicopter hangar positioned between and abaft them; a helicopter landing deck replaced the after twin 3-inch A.A. mounting, and enabled only a single A/S mortar to be shipped, but the A/S armament was augmented by the addition of a helicopter fitted to carry A/S torpedoes; and the hull was cut down right aft to work the variable depth sonar over the stern.

Similar modifications were extended to the entire "St. Laurent" class, and the remaining units of the "Restigouche" and "Mackenzie" classes will be similarly altered in due course, and will result in twenty homogeneous anti-submarine vessels of high quality.

Displacement: 2,335/2,900 tons.
Dimensions: 361(wl) 366(oa) × 42 × 13½/... feet.
Machinery: Two Babcock & Wilcox boilers; two shafts; English Electric geared turbines, S.H.P. 30,000 = 28 knots; O.F. ... tons.
Armament: Four except *Annapolis* and *Nipigon* two 3-inch A.A. (1/2 × 2) guns; two except *Annapolis* and *Nipigon* one A/S mortar (Limbo); one A/S helicopter in *Annapolis* and *Nipigon* only.
Complement: 246.

Pt. No.	Name	Builder	Laid down	Launched	Completed	Disposition
DDH.265	ANNAPOLIS	Halifax Shyd.	... 7.60	27. 4.63	19.12.64	Royal Canadian Navy, 3rd Escort Squadron
DDE.261	MACKENZIE	Canadian Vickers ...	15.12.58	25. 5.61	6.10.62	Royal Canadian Navy, 2nd Escort Squadron
DDH.266	NIPIGON	Marine Industries ...	... 4.60	10.12.61	30. 5.64	Royal Canadian Navy, 1st Escort Squadron
DDE.264	QU'APPELLE	Davie Sbdg.	... 1.60	2. 5.60	14. 9.63	Royal Canadian Navy, 2nd Escort Squadron
DDE.262	SASKATCHEWAN ...	Victoria	29.10.59	31. 1.61	16. 2.63	Completed Canadian Yarrow, Royal Canadian Navy, 2nd Escort Squadron
DDE.263	YUKON	Burrard	23. 3.60	27. 7.61	25. 5.63	Royal Canadian Navy, 2nd Escort Squadron

Machinery contracts: All engined by builders.

Bow and stern view of
Naiad.

[Blocks courtesy of
*Shipbuilding & Shipping
Record*

Quarter view of *Danae* showing Seacat and HA.DCT on hangar roof, single mortar well offset to port, and ramp cut in stern for working VDS.

FLEET VESSELS

Pt. No.	Name	Builder	Laid down	Launched	Completed	Disposition
F.12	ACHILLES	Yarrow	27.10.67	21.11.68	....	Building
F.114	AJAX (ex-*Fowey*)	Cammell Laird ...	19.10.59	16. 8.62	11.12.63	Home/Far East
F.57	ANDROMEDA	H.M. Dockyard (Portsmouth)	25. 5.66	24. 5.67	4. 7.68	
F.38	ARETHUSA	White	17. 9.62	5.11.63	29. 9.65	Home
F.56	ARGONAUT	Hawthorn Leslie ...	27.11.64	8. 2.66	5. 9.67	NATO Standing Squadron
F.10	AURORA	Clydebank ...	1. 6.61	28.11.62	9. 4.64	Home
F.69	BACCHANTE	Vickers (Tyne) ...	25.10.66	29. 2.68	....	Building
F.75	CHARYBDIS	Harland & Wolff ...	27. 1.67	28. 2.68	6. 6.69	
F.28	CLEOPATRA	H.M. Dockyard (Devonport)	19. 6.63	25. 3.64	1. 3.66	Home/Middle East
F.47	DANAE	H.M. Dockyard (Devonport)	16. 1.65	21.10.65	10.10.67	Home
F.104	DIDO (ex-*Hastings*) ...	Yarrow	2.12.59	22.12.61	18. 9.63	Home/Far East
F.16	DIOMEDE	Yarrow	30. 1.68	15. 4.69	....	Building
F.15	EURYALUS	Scotts	2.11.61	6. 6.63	16. 9.64	Home/Far East
F.18	GALATEA	Swan Hunter ...	29.12.61	23. 5.63	25. 4.64	Home
F.58	HERMIONE	Stephen	10.12.65	26. 4.67	11. 7.69	Completed by Yarrow
F.52	JUNO	Thornycroft ...	16. 7.64	24.11.65	18. 7.67	1st Division, Western Fleet
F.60	JUPITER	Yarrow	3.10.66	4. 9.67	....	Building
F.109	LEANDER (ex-*Weymouth*)	Harland & Wolff ...	10. 4.59	28. 6.61	27. 3.63	Home/Far East
F.45	MINERVA	Vickers-Armstrongs (Tyne)	27. 7.63	19.12.64	13. 5.66	Home/Middle East
F.39	NAIAD	Yarrow	30.10.62	4.11.63	15. 3.65	Home/Far East
F.127	PENELOPE... (ex-*Coventry*)	Vickers-Armstrongs (Tyne)	14. 3.61	17. 8.62	1.11.63	2nd Training Squadron
F.42	PHOEBE	Stephen	3. 6.63	8. 7.64	15. 4.66	Home/Far East
F.71	SCYLLA	H.M. Dockyard (Devonport)	17. 5.67	8. 8.68	....	Building
F.40	SIRIUS	H.M. Dockyard (Portsmouth)	9. 8.63	22. 9.64	15. 6.66	Home
F.	A	Yarrow	....	....	....	Building
F.	B	Yarrow	....	....	....	Building.
F.	CANTERBURY	Yarrow	13. 4.69	....	....	Building for Royal New Zealand Navy
F.55	WAIKATO...	Harland & Wolff ...	10. 1.64	18. 2.65	16. 9.66	Royal New Zealand Navy
F.	NILGIRI	Mazagon Dock ...	15.10.66	23.10.68	....	Building for Indian Navy
F.	C	Mazagon Dock ...	....	....	....	Projected for Indian Navy
F.	D	Mazagon Dock ...	....	....	....	Projected for Indian Navy

" *Leander* " *class:* **ACHILLES, AJAX, ANDROMEDA, ARETHUSA, ARGONAUT, AURORA, BACCHANTE, CANTERBURY, CHARYBDIS, CLEOPATRA, DANAE, DIDO, DIOMEDE, EURYALUS, GALATEA, HERMIONE, JUNO, JUPITER, LEANDER, MINERVA, NAIAD, NILGIRI, PENELOPE, PHOEBE, SCYLLA, SIRIUS, WAIKATO,** and **FOUR** unnamed vessels (two only projected)

The policy adopted by the earlier specialised frigates (types 12, 41, and 61) was reversed with these vessels to give them a general purpose capability.

The hull was made flush-decked with a ramp cut into the stern for working the variable depth sonar; tubular masts replaced the former lattice ones; the detached superstructures forward and aft were joined and a hangar placed at its after end; the deck aft of the hangar was left clear as a helicopter landing area, and only sufficient space remained aft to ship a single A/S mortar. The GW radar is carried on the mainmast, and the anti-aircraft qualities enhanced by the addition of Seacat (not yet fitted in earlier units which still temporarily mount 40mm. A.A. guns) and anti-submarine qualities by the addition of variable depth sonar and a helicopter armed with A/S torpedoes. To compensate for the additional topweight they have had to ship permanent ballast, and the last eleven units (ACHILLES, ANDROMEDA, BACCHANTE, CANTERBURY, CHARYBDIS, DIOMEDE, HERMIONE, JUPITER, SCYLLA, and two unnamed) have had their beam increased by 2 feet, and Sea Dart may replace Seacat in them. It is now proposed to re-arm some—if not all—with the Ikara A/S G.W.S.

They have nevertheless proved a most successful class, and their design has been adopted by the Royal Netherlands Navy for six very similar vessels, while the Indian Navy has the construction of three units in local yards.

Displacement: 2,350/2,760 tons.

Dimensions: 360(pp) 372(oa) × 41 except *Achilles, Andromeda, Bacchante, Charybdis, Diomede, Hermione, Jupiter* and *Scylla* 43 × 13½/14½ feet.

Machinery: Two Babcock & Wilcox boilers (550 lb/in² at 860°F); two shafts; English Electric geared turbines, S.H.P. 30,000 = 30 knots; O.F. .... tons.

Armament: Four Seacat (1×4—not in *Ajax, Aurora, Dido, Euryalus, Galatea, Leander* and *Penelope*) G.W.S.; two 4·5-inch D.P. (1×2), two 40mm. A.A. (2×1—in *Ajax, Aurora, Dido, Eurylus, Galatea, Leander* and *Penelope*) guns; one A/S mortar (Limbo); one A/S helicopter.

Complement: 251/263.

Machinery contracts: A, B, *Achilles, Andromeda, Argonaut, Canterbury, Charybdis, Danae, Diomede, Hermione, Nilgiri, Scylla,* and *Sirius* engined by White: *Cleopatra* by Cammell Laird, *Galatea* by Wallsend Slipway, and others by builders.

FLEET VESSELS

Machinery layout of earlier "Leander" class.

Machinery layout of later "Leander" class.

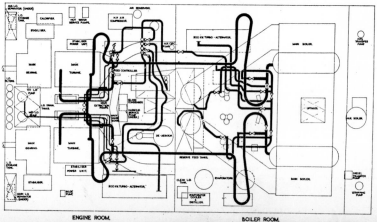

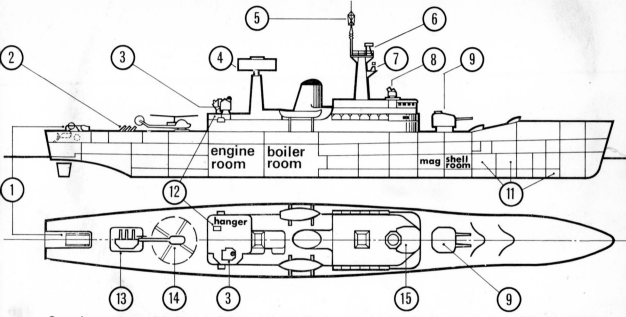

General arrangement of the "Leander" class: 1 Variable depth sonar; 2 3-barrelled 12-inch A/S mortar; 3 Seacat director; 4 General warning radar; 5 HF/DF aerial; 6 Surveillance radar; 7 Navigational radar; 8 Gun director; 9 Twin 4·5-inch turret; 10 Magazine and shell room; 11 Sonar compartment; 12 Seacat missile launcher; 13 A/S mortar well; 14 Wasp helicopter; 15 Enclosed bridge

[Block courtesy *Naval Record*

Canadian "Tribal" class.

Canadian " Tribal " class : **ALGONQUIN, ATHABASKAN, HURON, IROQUOIS.**

Considerably larger than the destroyer escorts of the "St. Laurent" and subsequent classes, these vessels approximate the size of the eight missile-armed general purpose frigates cancelled in 1963.

The hull has a long raised fo'c'sle deck terminating at the after end of the hangar, and drops a further deck level at the stern, over which the variable depth sonar is worked. The helicopter landing deck is sited abaft the hangar at fo'c'sle deck level, and provided with a double haul down Beartrap.

The profile is clean with two detached superstructures—the bridge block and helicopter hangar—joined by a narrow casing on which the lattice mast and a slim funnel is stepped. The single 5-inch gun is mounted forward of the bridge, and the A/S mortar in a well abaft the helicopter landing deck. Design features include flume stabilising tanks, a pre-wetting system and NBCD citadel, bridge control of main engines, and provision is made for later shipping a close range A.A. missile system.

While the original provision was to install steam burbine propulsion, developing S.H.P. 30,000 for a speed of 27 knots, it is now intended to provide gas turbines of greater power which will raise speed by 3 knots and enlarge the radius of action. This will inevitably result in some modification to the superstructure to provide the necessary air intakes, etc.

Displacement : .,.../4,100 tons.
Dimensions : 398(pp) 425¾(oa) × 50 × 14/... feet.
Machinery : Two shafts (c.p. propellers); Pratt & Whitney geared gas turbines, S.H.P. 44,000 + 6,200 = 30 (max)/.... (cruising) knots; O.F. ... tons.
Armament : One 5-inch D.P. gun; four 21-inch A/S (2 × 2) T.T.; one A/S mortar (Limbo); two helicopters.
Complement : 200 (+50 for training).

Pt. No.	Name	Builder	Laid down	Launched	Completed	Disposition
DDH.283	ALGONQUIN	Davie Shipbuilding ...	....	....	....	Building for Royal Canadian Navy
DDH.281	ATHABASKAN	Davie Shipbuilding ...	....	....	....	Building for Royal Canadian Navy
DDH.282	HURON	Marine Industries ...	....	....	....	Building for Royal Canadian Navy
DDH.280	IROQUOIS	Marine Industries ...	....	....	....	Building for Royal Canadian Navy

Machinery contracts : United Aircraft of Canada.

Bow and quarter views of the *Perth*.

"Charles F. Adams" class: **BRISBANE, HOBART, PERTH**

These were the first major Commonwealth warships to be constructed in a foreign yard, but they met Royal Australian Navy requirements for a missile-armed destroyer of smaller size than the Royal Navy "County" class.

The bow-mounted sonar is housed in a bulbous forefoot, and for engaging submarines at long range they are fitted with Ikara torpedo-carrying missile mounted forward of the deckhouse between the funnels (which distinguishes them from their United States Navy counterparts), and for shorter range work there are triple banks of tubes for A/S torpedoes abreast the fore end of the bridge, to port and starboard. For aerial defence a single-arm launcher for Tartar sea-to-air missiles is provided aft, together with two 5-inch D.P. guns in fully automatic turrets fore and aft.

Steam conditions are in advance of the Royal Navy and automatic combustion control is provided for the boilers. The hull is typically American: flush-decked with clipper stem and marked sheer forward so that the forward and after turrets are at the same level although the latter is mounted on the superstructure. This class has earned a high reputation in the United States Navy for their overall ability as anti-aircraft and anti-submarine units, and they are undoubtedly versatile vessels, able to steam fast and hit hard, and are well equipped for a variety of roles.

Displacement: 3,370/4,500 tons.
Dimensions: 420(pp) 437(oa) $\times$ 47 $\times$ 15/22 feet.
Machinery: Four Foster Wheeler boilers (1,200 lb/in^2); two shafts; General Electric geared turbines, S.H.P. 70,000 = 35 knots; O.F. 900 tons.
Armament: One Tartar G.W.S.; two 5-inch D.P. (2 $\times$ 1) guns; six 12-inch A/S (2 $\times$ 3) T.T.; two A/S G.W.S. (2 $\times$ 1-Ikara).
Complement: 333.

Pt. No.	Name	Builder	Laid down	Launched	Completed	Disposition
D.41	BRISBANE	Defoe Sbdg.	16. 2.65	5. 5.66	16.12.67	Royal Australian Navy, 1st Destroyer Squadron
D.39	HOBART	Defoe Sbdg.	26.10.62	9. 1.64	18.12.65	Royal Australian Navy, 1st Destroyer Squadron
D.38	PERTH	Defoe Sbdg.	21. 9.62	26. 9.63	22. 5.65	Royal Australian Navy, 1st Destroyer Squadron.

Machinery contracts: Engined by builders.

55

FLEET VESSELS

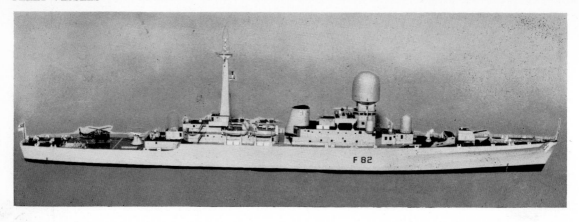

Although classed as a destroyer the type 82 is more representative of an upward expansion of the frigate design, and a conspicuous feature is the Anglo-Dutch CDS radar carried over the bridge and enclosed in a plastic dome. The Vickers Mk. 8 4·5-inch gun and the Ikara launcher are positioned forward; and the Sea Dart launcher A/S mortar (in a well to starboard), and A/S helicopter aft.

Pt. No.	Name	Builder	Laid down	Launched	Completed	Disposition
D.	BRISTOL	Swan Hunter	15.11.67	30. 6.69	....	Building

Machinery contracts: Engined by A.E.I. (steam turbines) and Rolls-Royce (gas turbines).

Type 82: **BRISTOL**

The specialised frigates (types 12, 41 and 61) resulted from the Admiralty policy that all the desirable escort qualities could not be included within a single hull of moderate dimensions: a policy later reversed by the "Leander" class where by a combination of technical development and some reduction in specialist qualities a wholly satisfactory general purpose frigate was evolved with only marginal increases in dimensions.

With this vessel (type 82) the general purpose capability has been much improved by highly sophisticated weapon systems together with complex methods of detection and its associated automatic plotting arrangements. As a result size has been more than doubled with an even greater increase in cost as compared with the "Leander" class. Despite the design excellence of the type 82 it is obvious that only a few vessels of this quality can be constructed, they will further accentuate the numerical shortage already experienced by the Royal Navy in this category, and with the carrier replacement programme now abandoned even their usefulness is questionable. Although four units were originally projected, three were subsequently cancelled following the placing of the initial order on 4/10/66.

For aerial defence they will ship the Sea Dart guided missile system aft, which is superior to the Seaslug missile at very high and low levels, has an accelerated re-action time, an improved target handling capacity, and is a more compact weapon system. For anti-submarine warfare the Australian Ikara system has been adopted, enabling submarines to be attacked at long range, and is positioned forward of the bridge. Finally, a single 4·5-inch D.P. is carried in a turret on the fo'c'sle and two 40mm. guns aft.

The superstructure is formed of the flush-sided square blocks that is now current practice, with the GW radar over the fore bridge, the missile guidance radar aft, and additional scanner units abreast and forward of the bridge: all enclosed by conspicuous dome-topped plastic weather screens. A single tubular mast is stepped against the after bridge, with the W/T aerials led forward to spreaders on the bridge and on and abaft the funnel, together with the usual array of whip aerials. Arrangements are also provided for working variable depth sonar over the stern. Main propulsion is by steam and gas turbines—the latter for boost power—remotely operated from a central control room, with controllable pitch propellers.

Displacement: 5,650/6,750 tons.

Dimensions: 490(pp) 507(oa) × 55 × 17/22½ feet.

Machinery: Two .... boilers; two shafts; A.E.I. steam and Rolls-Royce gas geared turbines, S.H.P. 30,000 (steam)+44,000 (gas) =35/32 knots; O.F. ... tons.

Armament: Two Sea Dart (1 × 2) G.W.S.; one 4·5-inch D.P., two 40mm. A.A. (2 × 1) guns; one A/S G.W.S. (Ikara), one A/S mortar (Limbo); one A/S helicopter.

Complement: 433.

Model showing approximate appearance of type 42 destroyer with the target illuminator radar enclosed by plastic domes fore and aft, and the surveillance radar on the bridge.

Type 42: **ONE** unnamed vessel.

This vessel is a scaled-down version of the type 82, and while it lacks the long range A/S weapons of the latter greater reliance is placed on the helicopter—which is provided with a hangar—for launching A/S torpedoes or ATS missiles. The remainder of the armament is grouped forward and comprises a single 4·5-inch D.P. gun in a turret and a twin launch ramp for Sea Dart STA missiles.

Main propulsion is by a COGOG arrangement of gas turbines which resulted in considerable savings in weight and space as compared with the COSAG arrangement of steam and gas turbines in the type 82.

Displacement: 3,250/.,... tons.
Dimensions: ....(pp) ....(oa) × ... × .../... feet.
Machinery: Two shafts (c.p. propellers); Rolls-Royce geared gas turbines S.H.P. 44,000/7,200 =32/.. knots; O.F. ... tons.
Armament: Two Sea Dart (1×2) G.W.S.; one 4.5-inch D.P., two 20mm. A.A. (2×1) guns; one helicopter.
Complement: 300.

Pt. No.	Name	Builder	Laid down	Launched	Completed	Disposition
D.	Unnamed	Vickers (Barrow) ...	....	....	....	Building

Machinery contracts: Engined by Rolls-Royce.

Type 21: **ONE** unnamed vessel.

A simplified frigate whose design was prepared jointly by Vosper Thornycroft and Yarrow for a vessel of less complexity and cost than the type 12. Like the type 42 COGOG propulsion was adopted together with a helicopter for long range A/S operations, but with less sophisticated surveillance radar and data automation. The 4·5-inch D.P. gun is mounted in a turret on the foredeck, the quadruple Seacat launcher on the hanagr roof aft, and the tubes for A/S torpedoes amidships.

Displacement: 2,500/.,... tons.
Dimensions: ....(pp) 384(oa) × ... × .../... feet.
Machinery: Two shafts (c.p. propellers); Rolls-Royce geared gas turbines S.H.P. 44,000/7,200 =35/.. knots; O.F. ... tons.
Armament: Four Seacat (1×4) G.W.S.; one 4·5-inch D.P. gun; six 12-inch A/S (2×3) T.T.; one helicopter.
Complement: 170.

Pt. No.	Name	Builder	Laid down	Launched	Completed	Disposition
F.	Unnamed	Vosper Thornycroft (Woolston)	....	....	....	Building

Machinery contracts: Engined by Rolls-Royce.

Thermopylae (left) and *Trump* (right) showing different conning towers of second and third groups.

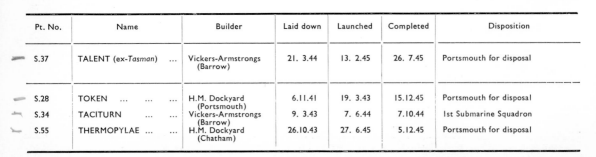

Pt. No.	Name	Builder	Laid down	Launched	Completed	Disposition
S.37	TALENT (ex-*Tasman*) ...	Vickers-Armstrongs (Barrow)	21. 3.44	13. 2.45	26. 7.45	Portsmouth for disposal
S.28	TOKEN	H.M. Dockyard (Portsmouth)	6.11.41	19. 3.43	15.12.45	Portsmouth for disposal
S.34	TACITURN	Vickers-Armstrongs (Barrow)	9. 3.43	7. 6.44	7.10.44	1st Submarine Squadron
S.55	THERMOPYLAE	H.M. Dockyard (Chatham)	26.10.43	27. 6.45	5.12.45	Portsmouth for disposal

" *T* " *class: First group*—**TALENT.** *Second group*—**TACITURN, THERMOPYLAE, TOKEN.** *Third group*—**TABARD, TIPTOE, TRUMP.**

This class dated from 1935 and during the Second World War performed the bulk of the overseas patrol work. They were developed from the "L", "O", "P" and "R" classes and were a single hull design, with saddle tanks, of riveted (earlier boats) or welded (later boats) construction.

The *first group* (riveted construction) were streamlined and fitted with the snort air mast 1955–60 to improve underwater performance, which resulted in the removal of all external T.T. and deck guns. The former conning tower was enclosed by a large sail which provided a streamlined housing for the snort, radar, and W/T masts, while a small enclosed bridge was positioned at the foot of the sail at its fore end.

The *second* and *third groups* (welded construction) were lengthened in 1951–56 by an additional section inserted between the diesel and electric motor rooms—which accommodated a further pair of electric motors and extra battery stowage—and increased submerged speed and endurance. The *third group* had a more conspicuous sail and were without the small enclosed bridge at its foot. Now primarily intended for anti-submarine work they are silent running.

This class originally comprised fifty-nine units, of which five were cancelled; fifteen were war losses; five—Royal Netherlands Navy TIGERHAAI (ex-*Tarn*) and ZWAARDVISCH (ex-*Talent*—since scrapped), and Israeli DAKAR (ex-*Totem*—since lost), DOLPHIN (ex-*Truncheon*) and LEVIATHAN (ex-*Turpin*)—were sold; and twenty-seven scrapped.

Displacement: 1,090/1,575 tons *first group*, 1,280/1,700 tons *second group*, 1,310/1,740 tons *third group*.
Dimensions: 265(pp) 273½(oa) *first group*, 277(pp) 285½(oa) *Thermopylae*, 279(pp) 287½(oa) *Taciturn*, 285(pp) 293½(oa) *third group* × 26½ × 14¾ feet.
Machinery: Two shafts, diesel/electric motors, B.H.P./S.H.P. 2,500/2,900 except *first group* 1,450=15/15 except *first group* 10½ knots; O.F. 250 tons except *first group* 132 tons.
Armament: Six 21-inch T.T. (all forward—twenty short torpedoes).
Complement: 65 except *first group* 59.

Pt. No.	Name	Builder	Laid down	Launched	Completed	Disposition
S.42	TABARD	Scotts	6. 9.44	21.11.45	25. 6.46	4th Submarine Squadron, for disposal
S.32	TIPTOE	Vickers-Armstrongs (Barrow)	10.11.42	25. 2.44	13. 6.44	1st Submarine Squadron
S.33	TRUMP	Vickers-Armstrongs (Barrow)	31.12.42	25. 3.44	9. 7.44	4th Submarine Squadron, for disposal

Machinery contracts: Diesel engines for *Tally Ho, Tiptoe,* and *Trump* by Clydebank; others by builders.

FLEET VESSELS

Artful.

Pt. No.	Name	Builder	Laid down	Launched	Completed	Disposition
S.61	ACHERON	H.M. Dockyard (Chatham)	26. 8.44	25. 3.47	17. 4.48	Rosyth refitting
S.72	AENEAS	Cammell Laird ...	10.10.44	25.10.45	31. 7.46	1st Submarine Squadron
S.41	ALARIC	Cammell Laird ...	31. 5.44	18. 2.46	11.12.46	1st Submarine Squadron
S.65	ALCIDE	Vickers-Armstrongs (Barrow)	1. 2.45	12. 4.45	18.10.46	1st Submarine Squadron
S.66	ALDERNEY	Vickers-Armstrongs (Barrow)	6. 2.45	25. 6.45	10.12.46	Portsmouth for disposal
S.67	ALLIANCE...	Vickers-Armstrongs (Barrow)	13. 3.45	26. 7.45	14. 5.47	1st Submarine Squadron
S.68	AMBUSH	Vickers-Armstrongs (Barrow)	17. 5.45	24. 9.45	22. 7.47	1st Submarine Squadron

"A" class: **ACHERON, AENEAS, ALARIC, ALCIDE, ALDERNEY, ALLIANCE, AMBUSH, AMPHION, ANCHORITE, ANDREW, ARTEMIS, ARTFUL, ASTUTE, AURIGA**

This class was designed in the Second World War for Pacific operations, and were basically enlarged "T" class with slightly higher speed and greater endurance when surfaced.

They were of pre-fabricated and welded construction, and when the arrangements for their production were sufficiently advanced they were put in hand and, at the same time, no further "T" class were ordered. A similar arrangement was worked for the war built frigates when switching from the riveted "River" class to the pre-fabricated and welded "Loch/Bay" class. The end of hostilities resulted in thirty units of the "A" class being cancelled, while a further unit—the AFFRAY—was accidently lost on 16/4/51, and one unit—the AUROCHS—was scrapped.

All have been streamlined (resulting in the removal of external T.T. and deck guns), have been equipped with the snort air mast, and fitted with a conspicuous sail over the former conning tower. During the Indonesian confrontation a 4-inch gun was added to those units then serving in Far East.

Displacement: 1,120/1,620 tons.
Dimensions: 269¼(pp) 283(oa) × 22¼ × 17/00 feet.
Machinery: Two shafts; diesel/electric motors, B.H.P./S.H.P. 4,300/1,250 = 18/9 knots; O.F. 159 tons.
Armament: Six 21-inch T.T. (four forward and two aft—sixteen torpedoes).
Complement: 60.

Pt. No.	Name	Builder	Laid down	Launched	Completed	Disposition
S.43	AMPHION ... ... (ex-*Anchorite*)	Vickers-Armstrongs (Barrow)	14.11.43	31. 8.44	27. 3.45	7th Submarine Squadron, for disposal
S.64	ANCHORITE (ex-*Amphion*)	Vickers-Armstrongs (Barrow)	19. 7.45	22. 1.46	18.11.47	Portsmouth for disposal
S.63	ANDREW	Vickers-Armstrongs (Barrow)	13. 8.45	6. 4.46	16. 3.48	7th Submarine Squadron
S.49	ARTEMIS	Scotts	28. 2.44	26. 8.46	15. 8.47	1st Submarine Squadron
S.96	ARTFUL	Scotts	8. 6.44	22. 5.47	2. 2.48	1st Submarine Squadron, for disposal
S.47	ASTUTE	Vickers-Armstrongs (Barrow)	4. 4.44	30. 1.45	30. 6.45	1st Submarine Squadron
S.69	AURIGA	Vickers-Armstrongs (Barrow)	7. 6.44	29. 3.45	12. 1.46	1st Submarine Squadron

Machinery contracts: Artful engined by Brotherhood, others by builders.

Porpoise.

Pt. No.	Name			Builder			Laid down	Launched	Completed	Disposition
S.06	CACHALOT	...	...	Scotts ...	...	...	1. 8.55	11.12.57	1. 9.59	7th Submarine Squadron
S.05	FINWHALE	...	...	Cammell Laird	...		18. 9.56	21. 7.59	19. 8.60	Portsmouth refitting
S.04	GRAMPUS...	...	...	Cammell Laird	...		16. 4.55	30. 5.57	19.12.58	1st Submarine Squadron
S.03	NARWHAL	...	...	Vickers-Armstrongs (Barrow)			15. 3.56	25.10.57	4. 5.59	1st Submarine Squadron

"*Porpoise*" *class:* CACHALOT, FINWHALE, GRAMPUS, NARWHAL, PORPOISE, RORQUAL, SEALION, WALRUS

The first post-war operational submarines, this class incorporated experience accrued from the German type XXI and the modifications extended to the "T" and "A" class submarines, together with much improved habitability in order to undertake prolonged submerged patrols.

In order to reduce engine noise transmission diesel-electric propulsion was adopted while snorting. When fully submerged power is drawn from large capacity batteries and by connecting the two battery groups in series—to give 880V on load—a limited burst of high speed can be secured. The large sail encloses the periscope standards (one fitted with a sextant), the snort, radar, and W/T masts, and enables speed to be maintained when snorting.

They come as close to true submarines as conventional propulsion allows and would spend the greater proportion of their patrols at snort depth, only going deep to attack or escape detection. Except for leaving, and entering, harbour they would not operate on the surface at all, and have a radius of action suitable for world-wide employment. A 20mm. A.A. gun is temporarily carried by RORQUAL.

Displacement: 1,605/2,405 tons.
Dimensions: 241(pp) 295¼(oa) × 26½ × 18 feet.
Machinery: Two shafts; 16-cyl. ASR.1 diesel engines/electric motors, B.H.P./S.H.P. 3,500/4,500 = 15/19 knots; O.F. .... tons.
Armament: Eight 21-inch T.T. (six forward and two aft—sixteen long and ten short torpedoes).
Complement: 70.

Pt. No.	Name	Builder	Laid down	Launched	Completed	Disposition
S.01	PORPOISE	Vickers-Armstrongs (Barrow)	15. 6.54	25. 4.56	16. 4.58	3rd Submarine Squadron
S.02	RORQUAL	Vickers-Armstrongs (Barrow)	15. 1.55	5.12.56	24.10.58	7th Submarine Squadron
S.07	SEALION	Cammell Laird ...	5. 6.58	31.12.59	25. 7.61	3rd Submarine Squadron
S.08	WALRUS	Scotts	12. 2.58	22. 9.59	8. 2.61	3rd Submarine Squadron

Machinery contracts: Diesel engines for *Cachalot* and *Walrus* by H.M. Dockyard (Chatham), others by builders. Electric motors for all by English Electric.

FLEET VESSELS

Opossum

Pt. No.	Name	Builder	Laid down	Launched	Completed	Disposition
S.09	OBERON	H.M. Dockyard (Chatham)	28.11.57	18. 7.59	24. 2.61	Portsmouth refitting
S.17	OCELOT	H.M. Dockyard (Chatham)	17.11.60	5. 5.62	31. 1.64	1st Submarine Squadron
S.10	ODIN	Cammell Laird ...	27. 4.59	4.11.60	3. 5.62	3rd Submarine Squadron
S.12	OLYMPUS	Vickers-Armstrongs (Barrow)	4. 3.60	14. 6.61	7. 7.62	1st Submarine Squadron
S.14	ONSLAUGHT	H.M. Dockyard (Chatham)	8. 4.59	24. 9.60	14. 8.62	7th Submarine Squadron
S.21	ONYX	Cammell Laird ...	16.11.64	18. 8.66	25.11.67	3rd Submarine Squadron
S.19	OPOSSUM	Cammell Laird ...	21.12.61	23. 5.63	5. 6.64	Devonport refitting
S.20	OPPORTUNE	Scotts	26.10.62	14. 2.64	28.12.64	Devonport refitting
S.16	ORACLE	Cammell Laird ...	26. 4.60	26. 9.61	14. 2.63	3rd Submarine Squadron
S.11	ORPHEUS	Vickers-Armstrongs (Barrow)	16. 4.59	17.11.59	25.11.60	Chatham refitting
S.13	OSIRIS	Vickers-Armstrongs (Barrow)	26. 1.62	29.11.62	11. 1.64	Devonport refitting
S.15	OTTER	Scotts	14. 1.60	15. 5.61	20. 8.62	3rd Submarine Squadron
S.18	OTUS	Scotts	31. 5.61	17.10.72	5.10.63	1st Submarine Squadron

"*Oberon*" *class:* **OBERON, OCELOT, ODIN, OJIBWA, OKANAGAN, OLYMPUS, ONONDAGA, ONSLAUGHT, ONSLOW, ONYX, OPOSSUM, OPPORTUNE, ORACLE, ORPHEUS, OSIRIS, OTTER, OTUS, OTWAY, OVENS, OXLEY**

Generally similar to the "Porpoise" class but with improved anti-submarine equipment. An aluminium casing was experimentally fitted in the ORPHEUS, but this was altered to glass reinforced plastic laminate in the later boats, which has been generally adopted and extended to include the sail in the most recent construction.

Internal modifications in the Royal Canadian Navy vessels include more extensive air-conditioning to meet the more severe operating conditions they will generally experience, and conversion machinery to supply 400 c/s 3-phase electrical power to suit Canadian equipment.

While the "Oberon" class have been described—not without justification—as the best conventional submarines built, it is unlikely that any further units of this type will be built except, perhaps, for Commonwealth navies still lacking submarine experience.

Displacement: 1,610/2,410 tons.
Dimensions: 241(pp) 295¼(oa) × 26½ × 18 feet.
Machinery: Two shafts; 16-cyl. ASR.1 diesel-electric motors, B.H.P./S.H.P. 3,500/4,500 = 15/19 knots; O.F. . . . tons.
Armament: Eight 21-inch T.T. (six forward and two aft—sixteen long and ten short torpedoes).
Complement: 68.

Pt. No.	Name	Builder	Laid down	Launched	Completed	Disposition
SS.72	OJIBWA (ex-*Onyx*) ...	H.M. Dockyard (Chatham)	27. 9.62	29. 2.64	23. 9.65	Royal Canadian Navy
SS.74	OKANAGAN	H.M. Dockyard (Chatham)	25. 3.65	17. 9.66	4. 9.67	Royal Canadian Navy
SS.73	ONONDAGA	H.M. Dockyard (Chatham)	18. 6.64	25. 9.65	22. 6.67	Royal Canadian Navy
S.60	ONSLOW	Scotts	29. 5.67	3.12.68	....	Building for Royal Australian Navy
S.59	OTWAY	Scotts	29. 6.65	29 11 66	....	Building for Royal Australian Navy
S.70	OVENS	Scotts	17. 6.66	4.12.67	15. 4.69	Royal Australian Navy
S.57	OXLEY	Scotts	2. 7.64	24. 9.65	18. 4.67	Royal Australian Navy

Machinery contracts: Diesel engines for *Opossum*, *Opportune*, *Oracle*, and *Osiris* by British Polar; for all *R.A.N. vessels* by Cammell Laird; and others by builders. Electric motors by English Electric except *R.C.N. vessels* by A.E.I.

French " Daphne " class: **HANGOR** and **TWO** unnamed vessels

As the British Government had considered that the Indian and Pakistani navies were better suited to maintaining surface forces only, there was little co-operation to meet the demands from both navies for submarines and the training of their crews. Consequently, both navies looked to foreign sources of supply: India to the U.S.S.R. and Pakistan to France. Similarly, the British embargo on arms to South Africa resulted in this navy also turning to France for submarines when an order for three " Daphne " class was placed with Chantiers Dubigeon-Normandie, Nantes.

Displacement: 869/1,043 tons.
Dimensions: . . . .(pp) 189½(oa) × 19¼ × 14¾ feet.
Machinery: Two shafts; 12-cylinder SEMT-Pielstick diesel engines/electric motors B.H.P./S.H.P. 1,300/1,600 = 13/15½ knots; O.F. . . . tons.
Armament: Twelve 21-inch T.T. (eight fwd and four aft).
Complement · 50.

Pt. No.	Name	Builder	Laid down	Launched	Completed	Fate
S.	A	Ch. Nav. Le Ciotat .. (Le Trait)	1.12.67	...12.68	... 6.69	Building for Pakistani Navy
S.	B	Ch. Nav. Le Ciotat .. (Le Trait)	8. 7.68	...12.69	... 6.70	Building for Pakistani Navy
S.	HANGOR	Brest Dockyard ..	28. 6.69	....	....	Building for Pakistani Navy

Machinery contracts: Diesel engines by Chantiers de l'Atlantique, and electric motors by Jeumont-Schneider.

Russian " F " class: **KALVARI, KANDHERI,** and **TWO** unnamed

No reliable details are available on these conventionally powered submarines which were scheduled for transfer to the Indian Navy during 1968.

ESCORT VESSELS

"*Majestic*" *class:* BONAVENTURE, MELBOURNE, VIKRANT

Four units of this class had their construction suspended at the end of the Second World War and, of these, MELBOURNE was completed between 1949–55, BONAVENTURE 1952–57, and VIKRANT 1957–61: all to modernised designs on sale to Commonwealth navies. Modifications included a 7½-deg. (5½-deg. in MELBOURNE) angled deck, steam catapult, and mirror landing aid. The fourth unit, the LEVIATHAN, was never completed and was not finally scrapped until 1968. Her boilers were removed and were used to re-boiler the Royal Netherlands Navy carrier KAREL DOORMAN (ex-*Venerable*) in 1966/7, which was sold to the Brazilian Navy and renamed 25th DE MAYO in 1968.

Both BONAVENTURE and MELBOURNE are now used as anti-submarine aircraft carriers and only VIKRANT continues to operate strike aircraft, although all retain this capability to a limited extent.

Of the two remaining units of this class MAGNIFICENT was scrapped in 1956, and SYDNEY (ex-*Terrible*) was converted into a troop transport by the Royal Australian Navy in 1962–63.

Displacement: 16,000/20,000 tons except *Vikrant* 19,500 tons.
Dimensions: 630(pp) 700 *Vikrant*/701½ *Melbourne*/704 *Bonaventure* (oa) ×80¼ (123 except *Melbourne* 126 across FD) × 21/25 feet.
Machinery: Four Admiralty 3-drum boilers (400 lb/in² at 700°F); two shafts; Parsons geared turbines, S.H.P. 40,000= 24½ knots; O.F. 3,200 tons.
Armament: Four 3-inch D.P. (2×2—*Bonaventure* only), three 6-pounder saluting (3×1—*Bonaventure* only), fifteen *Vikrant*/twenty-five *Melbourne* 40mm. A.A. (4×2 and 7×1/7×2 and 11×1) guns; eight aircraft and thirteen helicopters *Bonaventure*/ten aircraft and ten helicopters *Melbourne*/sixteen aircraft *Vikrant*. One steam catapult and two lifts.
Complement: 1,250 *Melbourne*/1,343 *Vikrant*/1,370 *Bonaventure* (1,450 war).

Pt. No.	Name	Builder	Laid down	Launched	Completed	Disposition
CVL.22	BONAVENTURE (ex-*Powerful*)	Harland & Wolff ...	27.11.43	27. 2.45	17. 1.57	Royal Canadian Navy (1957), Atlantic
R.21	MELBOURNE (ex-*Majestic*)	Vickers-Armstrongs (Barrow)	13. 4.43	28. 2.45	27.10.55	Royal Australian Navy (1955)
R.11	VIKRANT (ex-*Hercules*) ...	Vickers-Armstrongs (Tyne)	14.10.43	22. 9.45	4. 3.61	Completed Harland & Wolff, Indian Navy (1961)

Machinery contracts: Vikrant engined by Parsons, other two by builders.

ESCORT VESSELS

A landing deck and hangar for four A/S helicopters has replaced the after gun turret and its HA/LA.DCT in *Blake*, and below the landing deck are the accommodation and workshops for the air complement.

Pt. No.	Name	Builder	Laid down	Launched	Completed	Disposition
C.99	BLAKE (ex-*Tiger*, ex-*Blake*)	Fairfield	17. 8.42	20.12.45	8. 3.61	Western Fleet
C.34	LION (ex-*Defence*) ...	Scotts	24. 6.42	2. 9.44	22. 2.60	Completed Swan Hunter; Devonport in reserve
C.20	TIGER (ex-*Bellerophon*) ...	Clydebank	1.10.41	25.10.45	18. 3.59	Devenport refitting

Machinery contracts: Lion engined by Wallsend Slipway, others by builders.

"*Minotaur*" *class:* BLAKE, LION, TIGER

This class was originally generally similar to the later units of the "Fiji" class except that the hangar structure abaft the bridge was omitted, an extra twin 4-inch A.A. mounting was shipped in lieu of "X" turret, and radar-fitted control arrangements were provided for a numerically reduced—but more effective—light A.A. armament.

The first group comprised two vessels (one transferred to the Royal Canadian Navy on completion), both since scrapped, while of the second group of ten vessels—which had a foot more beam and more modern HA.DCT's—five were cancelled (four only projected and not further advanced), one scrapped, and three had their construction suspended between 1949–55 while a revised design was prepared. As completed, these last three had a fully automatic and radar-controlled main and secondary gun armament, all carried in turrets with an individual HA/LA.DCT for each turret, so that they could simultaneously engage five air, or surface, targets. The high rate of fire of automatic guns meant increased magazine stowage, which together with the weighty turret installations, both contributed to numerically limiting the gun armament. The revised design also incorporated more extensive superstructure forward and aft, lattice masts, caps to the funnels, and ABC defence measures.

In BLAKE and TIGER the after 6-inch gun turret has been removed and replaced by a large hangar abaft the main-mast to accommodate four A/S helicopters, with a landing deck extending to the stern. To make the hull a stable plat-form five pairs of fin stabilisers have been installed, and quadruple Seacat launchers have replaced the 3-inch turrets amidships. Their primary role is as command ships but, if required, a company of Royal Marines can be accommodated and put ashore by helicopters, while the forward 6-inch turret was retained to provide ground fire support. The ships thus have a versatile role in anti-submarine and/or amphibious operations.

At present the LION has not been put in hand for conversion and is in reserve with her full cruiser armament of four 6-inch (2×2) and six 3-inch (3×2) D.P. guns.

Displacement: 9,550/12,080 tons.

Dimensions: 538(pp) $555\frac{1}{2}$(oa) $\times 64 \times 18/21$ feet.

Machinery: Four Admiralty 3-drum boilers; four shafts; Parsons geared turbines, S.H.P. 80,000=$31\frac{1}{2}$ knots; O.F. 1,850 tons.

Protection: Main belt $3\frac{1}{4}$–$3\frac{1}{2}$ (abreast magazines) inches closed by bulkheads 2 inches, complete deck 2 inches. Turrets $1\frac{1}{2}$ (crown)–2 (rear)–3 (face) inches, barbettes $\frac{3}{4}$–1 inch. DCT's $\frac{1}{2}$ inch.

Armament: Eight Seacat (2×4) G.W.S.; two 6-inch D.P. (1×2), two 3-inch D.P. (1×2) guns; four A/S helicopters.

Complement: 900.

ESCORT VESSELS

Besides changes in armament the *Athabaskan* was re-rigged with a lattice foremast and stump mainmast, an HA/LA.DCT replaced the former HA.DCT on the bridge, prominent funnel caps and whip aerials were added, and the after shelter deck extended to enclose handling arrangements for the A/S mortar projectiles. The four single 40mm. A.A. guns were mounted abreast the after funnel and at the fore end of the after shelter deck.

Pt. No.	Name	Builder	Laid down	Launched	Completed	Disposition
DDE.219	ATHABASKAN	Halifax	15. 5.44	4. 5.46	20. 2.48	Royal Canadian Navy, Altantic reserve

Machinery contracts: Engined by builders.

Old " Tribal " class: **ATHABASKAN**

These former destroyers were designed in 1935 in answer to large foreign contemporaries which individually outclassed the standard British units. Compared with the latter the "Tribal" class carried double the number of guns and only half the torpedo armament, but had an enhanced light A.A. battery.

A total of sixteen were built for the Royal Navy, and both the Royal Australian and Canadian Navies each planned a further flotilla of seven units. The R.A.N. later cancelled the last four units of their programme, while the R.C.N. not only completed their programme but built an additional vessel to replace one which had become a war loss.

An early modification with the R.N. vessels was the substitution of "X" mounting by a twin 4-inch A.A., and the R.A.N. and R.C.N. vessels were so completed except that the final R.C.N. pair had twin 4-inch A.A. in all four positions. In addition, the last four R.C.N. vessels all had a foot more beam to partly compensate for topweight added.

Only four R.N. vessels survived the war and were scrapped soon after, but the R.A.N. and R.C.N. units were further modified for escort work. The R.A.N. vessels had "Y" mounting removed, the after shelter deck extended aft, and an A/S mortar mounted on the quarterdeck. The R.C.N. vessels underwent several conversions, and ultimately followed the layout of the R.A.N. vessels but with a more modern and effective armament. Both "A" and "B" mountings were exchanged for twin 4-inch A.A. and "X" mounting for a twin 3-inch A.A., "Y" mounting was removed and the after shelter deck extended aft, and two A/S mortars were mounted on the quarterdeck.

All R.A.N. and five R.C.N. bessels have since been scrapped, another R.C.N. vessel converted into a naval museum at Toronto, and the ATHABASKAN is unlikely to be retained long. Considered large and expensive vessels for their day, they strike an interesting comparison with present day 1st rate escorts which would find their dimensions minimal.

Displacement: 2,200/2,800 tons.

Dimensions: 355½(pp) 377½(oa) × 37½ × 10/13½ feet.

Machinery: Three Admiralty 3-drum boilers; two shafts; Parsons geared turbines, S.H.P. 44,000=36/32 knots; O.F. 520 tons.

Armament: Four 4-inch A.A. (2×2), two 3-inch A.A. (1×2), four 40mm. A.A. (4×1) guns; four 21-inch (1×4) T.T.; two A/S mortars (Squid).

Complement: 240.

ESCORT VESSELS

" O " and " P " classes: **TIPPU SULTAN, TUGHRIL**

These vessels were the first war-programmed destroyers in which the design was standardised to speed production. While generally adopting the dimensions, longitudinal framing, and two boiler arrangement of the "J" class, they reverted to single guns and quadruple T.T. but with provision for an enhanced light A.A. battery. In fact, none of them shipped their designed armament as completed owing to war production difficulties.

Of the sixteen vessels comprising the two flotillas, five were war losses; one was transferred to the Turkish Navy in 1946—the GAYRET (ex-*Oribi*, ex-*Observer*)—as replacement for a war acquisition subsequently lost, and three to the Pakistani Navy in 1949–51 (TARIQ (ex-*Offa*) since scrapped); and seven were scrapped.

One of the immediate post-war requirements was to counter the actual (and potential) increased submerged speed of submarines, and only destroyers possessed the required margin of speed necessary. As a stop-gap measure, until a

Pt. No.	Name	Builder	Laid down	Launched	Completed	Disposition
260	TIPPU SULTAN (ex-*Onslow*, ex-*Pakenham*)	Clydebank	1. 7.40	31. 3.41	8.10.41	Pakistani Navy (1949)
261	TUGHRIL (ex-*Onslaught*, ex-*Pathfinder*)	Fairfield	14. 1.41	9.10.41	19. 6.42	Pakistani Navy (1951)
F.02	QUEENBOROUGH ...	Swan Hunter	6.11.40	16. 1.42	10.12.42	Royal Australian Navy (1945), for disposal
F.03	QUIBERON	White	14.10.40	31. 1.42	22. 7.42	Royal Australian Navy (1945), for disposal
F.04	QUICKMATCH	White	6. 2.41	11. 4.42	30. 9.42	Royal Australian Navy (1945), for disposal
F.138	RAPID	Cammell Laird ...	16. 6.41	16. 7.42	20. 2.43	Rosyth for training
F.185	RELENTLESS	Clydebank	20. 6.41	15. 7.42	30.11.42	Portsmouth reserve, for disposal.

Machinery contracts: Queenborough engined by Wallsend Slipway, others by builders.
Conversion contracts: Tippu Sultan Grayson, Rollo & Clover 1957–59, *Tughril* C. & H. Crighton 1957–59, *R.A.N. vessels* Cockatoo (two) and H.M.A. Dockyard (Williamstown—two) 1951-57; *Rapid* Stephen 1952-53; and *Relentless* H.M. Dockyard (Portsmouth) 1952-53.

new generation of anti-submarine vessels were designed and put into production, two kinds of destroyer conversions to fast A/S vessels were put in hand: the type 15 full conversion and the type 16 limited conversion.

The latter was adopted for these vessels which involved little more than re-arming. "A" gun was removed, "B" gun was replaced by a twin 4-inch A.A. mounting, single 40mm. A.A. replaced the light A.A. in each bridge wing, the multiple 2-pounder A.A. mounting abaft the funnel was taken out, the forward bank of T.T. was removed and the after bank retained for A/S torpedoes, a twin 40mm. A.A. replaced the light A.A. mounted between the tubes, "X" gun was replaced by two A/S mortars, and "Y" gun was replaced by a single 40mm. A.A. This, together with modern radar, sonar, and communications equipment well fitted them for the A/S role, and only in recent years have they started to pass out of service as replaced by new construction.

Displacement: 1,800/2,300 tons.

Dimensions: $328\frac{3}{4}$(pp) 345(oa) $\times 35 \times 10/13\frac{1}{2}$ feet.

Machinery: Two Admiralty 3-drum boilers; two shafts; Parsons geared turbines, S.H.P. 40,000 $= 36\frac{3}{4}/31\frac{1}{2}$ knots; O.F. 500 tons.

Armament: Two 4-inch A.A. (1 $\times$ 2), five 40mm. A.A. (1 $\times$ 2 and 3 $\times$ 1) guns; four 21-inch (1 $\times$ 4) T.T.; two A/S mortars (Squid).

Complement: 170.

Left: *Tippu Sultan* type 16 (limited conversion). **Right:** *Quadrant* modified type 15 (full conversion).

ESCORT VESSELS

"Q" and "R" classes: **QUEENBOROUGH, QUIBERON, QUICKMATCH, RAPID, RELENTLESS**

These vessels formed the second group of war standard destroyers and, except they were dimensionally slightly larger, differed little from the first group.

Of the sixteen vessels comprising the two flotillas, two were war losses; one—Royal Netherlands Navy BANCKERT (ex-*Quillam*—since scrapped)—was sold; five were transferred to the Royal Australian Navy (QUADRANT and QUALITY since scrapped) in 1945 and three to the Indian Navy in 1949; and three were scrapped. The Indian Navy vessels have remained largely unaltered and are listed in the amphibious warfare section (p. 123).

The remaining vessels underwent full conversion to fast anti-submarine vessels, and in this respect the "R" class units were the prototype type 15 conversions. With them the upper deck was razed, and the fo'c'sle deck extended well aft and a side-to-side superstructure erected forward of the funnel with a half-raised enclosed bridge at its fore end. The A/S mortars were arranged *en echelon* at the after end of the fo'c'sle deck with a twin 4-inch A.A. mounting—and its HA.DCT—forward of them. Two twin sets of tubes for A/S torpedoes were also provided, to port and starboard, but were later removed. Finally, a twin 40mm. A.A. mounting was placed on the superstructure forward super-firing over the enclosed bridge. Re-rigged with two lattice masts and fitted with modern radar, sonar, plotting, and communications equipment they possessed both the weaponry and the speed to counter fast submarines able to operate continuously submerged.

The Royal Australian Navy vessels were also converted on generally similiar lines, except that the twin 40mm. A.A. mounting was placed at the fore end of the superstructure in place of the half-raised wheelhouse, which was sited further aft on this deck and made full height.

Displacement: 2,200 ("*Q*" class) or 2,300 ("*R*" class)/2,700 tons.

Dimensions: $339\frac{1}{2}$(pp) $358\frac{1}{4}$(oa) $\times 35\frac{3}{4} \times 11\frac{1}{2}/14\frac{1}{2}$ feet.

Machinery: Two Admiralty 3-drum boilers; two shafts; Parsons geared turbines, S.H.P. $40,000 = 36\frac{3}{4}/31\frac{1}{2}$ knots; O.F. 590 tons.

Armament: Two 4-inch A.A. (1×2), two 40mm. A.A. (1×2) guns; two A/S mortars (Limbo except *Quadrant*, *Rapid* and *Roebuck* Squid).

Complement: 174.

Troubridge, modified type 15 conversion with twin 40mm. mounting forward of frigate bridge.

Grenville, original type 15 conversion with twin 40mm. mounting abaft bridge.

The third group of war standard destroyers embraced ten flotillas—the "S" to "W". "Z" and "C" (four groups) classes —and incorporated more refinement than was possible with the earlier groups as war production was better able to meet requirements.

None of the "S" class remain in service, one was a war loss; two were transferred to the Royal Norwegian Navy on completion—the SVENNER (ex-*Shark*) and STORD (ex-*Success*)—of which the former became a war loss and the latter has since been scrapped; three—Royal Netherlands Navy KORTENAER (ex-*Scorpion*, ex-*Sentinel*), EVERTSEN (ex-*Scourge*) and PIET HIEN (ex-*Serapis*)—were sold (all since scrapped); and two were scrapped.

All the "T" class were given type 16 limited conversions except the TROUBRIDGE which received a type 15 full conversion and is listed on the following page. The limited conversion were generally similar to the "O" and "P" classes except that two additional 40mm. A.A. guns were mounted abaft the funnel. Only TROUBRIDGE of this class now remain in service, the remaining seven being scrapped during 1965-66.

ESCORT VESSELS

Pt. No.	Name	Builder	Laid down	Launched	Completed	Disposition
F.09	TROUBRIDGE	Clydebank	10.11.41	23. 9.42	8. 3.43	Home
F.197	GRENVILLE	Swan Hunter	1.11.41	12.10.42	27. 5.43	Home
F.83	ULSTER	Swan Hunter	12.11.41	9.11.42	30. 6.43	2nd Training Squadron
F.17	ULYSSES	Cammell Laird ...	14. 3.42	22. 4.43	23.12.43	Devonport for disposal
F.53	UNDAUNTED	Cammell Laird ...	8. 9.42	19. 7.43	3. 3.43	2nd Training Squadron
F.08	URANIA	Vickers-Armstrongs (Barrow)	18. 6.42	19. 5.43	18. 1.44	Devonport for disposal
DDE.224	ALGONQUIN (ex-*Valentine*, ex-*Kempenfelt*)	Clydebank	8.10.42	2. 9.43	28. 2.44	Royal Canadian Navy (1944), Pacific reserve.
F.50	VENUS	Fairfield	12. 1.42	23. 2.43	28. 8.43	Devonport for disposal
F.29	VERULAM	Fairfield	26. 1.42	22. 4.43	10.12.43	2nd Training Squadron
F.41	VOLAGE	White	31.12.42	15.12.43	26. 5.44	Portsmouth for disposal
F.159	WAKEFUL	Fairfield	3. 6.42	30. 6.43	17. 2.44	Portsmouth for training
F.187	WHIRLWIND	Hawthorn Leslie ...	31. 7.42	30. 8.43	20. 7.44	Portsmouth for disposal
F.102	ZEST	Thornycroft	21. 7.42	14.10.43	20. 7.44	Home/Far East, for disposal
DDE.226	CRESCENT	Clydebank	16. 9.43	20. 7.44	21. 9.45	Royal Canadian Navy (1945), Pacific reserve

Machinery contracts: Grenville and Ulster engined by Wallsend Slipway, others by builders.

"T", "U", "V", "W" and "Z" classes: ALGONQUIN, CRESCENT, GRENVILLE, TROUBRIDGE, ULSTER, ULYSSES, UNDAUNTED, URANIA, VENUS, VERULAM, VOLAGE, WAKEFUL, WHIRLWIND, ZEST

All war standard destroyers which were given type 15 full conversions to fast anti-submarine vessels. Of the thirty-two vessels forming the "U" to "W" and "Z" classes one was a war loss; two were transferred to the Royal Canadian Navy on completion—ALGONQUIN (ex-*Valentine*, ex-*Kempenfelt*) and SIOUX (ex-*Vixen*)—of which the latter has since been scrapped; nine—Yugoslavian KOTOR (ex-*Kempenfelt*, ex-*Valentine*) and PULA (ex-*Wager*), South African JAN VAN RIEBEECK (D.278 ex-*Wessex*, ex-*Zenith*), SIMON VAN DER STEL (D.237 ex-*Whelp*), and VRYSTAAT (F.157 ex-*Wrangler*), Egyptian EL QUAHER (ex-*Myngs*) and EL FATEH (ex-*Zenith,* ex-*Wessex*), and Israeli ELATH (ex-*Zealous*) and YAFFA (ex-*Zodiac*)—were sold; and nine were scrapped.

An open bridge has replaced the twin 40mm. A.A. mounting in VENUS and WAKEFUL while they are serving as training vessels, and VERULAM and WAKEFUL had the twin 4-inch A.A. mounting removed in addition and replaced by a deckhouse. In TROUBRIDGE, ULSTER and ZEST the half-raised bridge has been replaced by a frigate bridge mounted over, and farther aft, on the superstructure, with the twin 40mm. A.A. mounting moved forward and partially overhanging the fore end of the superstructure, and only ULSTER is fitted with fixed tubes for A/S torpedoes. Helicopter landing pads were added aft in GRENVILLE (since removed) and UNDAUNTED. Both the Royal Canadian Navy vessels have enlarged bridges and conspicuous funnel caps. In ALGONQUIN the twin 3-inch A.A. mounting is before the bridge and the twin 4-inch A.A. aft, but these positions are transposed in the CESRCENT, while both have launching racks for A/S torpedoes. Damaged stern section in ULSTER was replaced by corresponding section from URCHIN (since scrapped) in 1966.

Displacement: 2,240/2,850 tons except *R.C.N. vessels* 2,100/2,700 tons.
Dimensions: 339½(pp) 362¾(oa)×35¾×11½/14½ except *R.C.N. vessels* 13½ feet.
Machinery: Two Admiralty 3-drum boilers; two shafts; Parsons geared turbines, S.H.P. 40,000=36¾/31¼ knots; O.F. 580 tons.
Armament: Two 4-inch A.A. (1×2), two 3-inch A.A. (1×2 in *R.C.N. vessels* only), two 40mm. A.A. (1×2 except *R.C.N. vessels* 2×1) guns; eight 21-inch (8×1 fixed) in *Ulster* only; two except *Crescent* one A/S mortars (Squid in "V" and "W" classes, Limbo in *Troubridge*, "U" class, *Zest* and *Crescent*).
Complement: 195 except *Algonquin* 230 and *Crescent* 250.

Conversion contracts: Troubridge H.M. Dockyard (Portsmouth) & White 1955–57; *Grenville* 1953–54; *Ulster* 1952–53 and *Zest* 1954–56 H.M. Dockyard (Chatham); *Ulysses* 1952–53 H.M. Dockyard (Devonport); *Undaunted* 1952–54 and *Volage* 1952 White; *Urania* Harland & Wolff (Liverpool) 1953–54; *Whirlwind* 1952–53 Palmer; *Venus* 1952; *Verulam* H.M. Dockyard (Portsmouth) 1952; *Algonquin* 1954 and *Crescent* 1956 H.M.C. Dockyard (Esquimalt); *Wakeful* Scott's 1952–53.

ESCORT VESSELS

Caprice with frigate bridge and quadruple Seacat launcher aft.

Carysfort with open bridge and 40mm gun aft.

" C " class (CA group): **CAMBRIAN, CAPRICE, CARYSFORT, CAVALIER**

The final group (CA, CH, CO and CR groups) of war standard destroyers generally followed the earlier groups except that the light A.A. armament was more variable as completed.

The CA group were more extensively modified to improve their anti-submarine qualities than their sister groups when the after bank of torpedo tubes and "X" gun were removed, the after shelter deck extended forward, and two A/S mortars mounted on it. The light A.A. guns abaft the funnel were replaced by a deckhouse, and the twin 40mm. A.A. originally mounted between the torpedo tubes was moved aft on to the extended after shelter deck. The bridgework was altered in all, and while the first four to be refitted (CARRON, CARYSFORT, CAVALIER and CAVENDISH) retained the old type of open bridge, with additions, the last four (CAESAR, CAMBRIAN, CAPRICE and CASSANDRA) were provided with a lower, enclosed frigate type bridge. A Mk. VI HA.DCT was shipped on the bridge of all.

The superstructure at the fore end of the after shelter deck was heightened to incorporate a quadruple Seacat launcher (finally only shipped in CAPRICE and CAVALIER), the torpedo tubes have been removed from the four surviving units, and the other four scrapped.

Displacement: 2,020/2,600 tons.
Dimensions: 339½(pp) 362¾(oa) × 35¾ × 10½/13¾ feet.
Machinery: Two Admiralty 3-drum boilers (300 lb/in² at 640°F); two shafts; Parsons geared turbines, S.H.P. 40,000= 36¾/31¼ knots; O.F. 580 tons.
Armament: Four Seacat (1×4) G.W.S. in *Caprice* and *Cavalier;* three 4.5-inch D.P. (3×1), two except *Cambrian* and *Carysfort* three 40mm. A.A. (2/3×1) guns; two A/S mortars (Squid).
Complement: 186.

Pt. No.	Name	Builder			Laid down	Launched	Completed	Disposition
D.85	CAMBRIAN (ex-*Spitfire*) ...	Scotts ...	...	...	14. 8.42	10.12.43	17. 7.44	Completed by Clydebank; Home/Far East, for disposal
D.01	CAPRICE (ex-*Swallow*) ...	Yarrow	...	...	28. 9.42	16. 9.43	5. 4.44	Home/Far East
D.25	CARYSFORT (ex-*Pique*) ...	White ...	...	...	12. 5.43	25. 7.44	20. 2.45	Home/Far East, for disposal
D.73	CAVALIER (ex-*Pellew*) ...	White ...	...	...	28. 2.43	7. 4.44	22.11.44	Home/Far East

Machinery contracts: All engined by builders.

ESCORT VESSELS

"C" class (*CH, CO and CR groups*): **ALAMGIR, CHEVRON, JAHANGIR, SHAH JEHAN**

Except that they were provided with RPC mountings for their 4·5-inch D.P. guns, additional weight which entailed suppressing the forward bank of torpedo tubes, there three groups were otherwise similar to the CA group, and some had hulls of all-welded construction.

Of the twenty-four vessels originally comprising the three flotillas, thirteen (including the entire CO group) were scrapped; two—Royal Canadian Navy CRESCENT and CRUSADER (since scrapped)—were transferred on completion; and eight—Pakistani Navy ALAMGIR (ex-*Creole*), JAHANGIR (ex-*Crispin*), SHAH JEHAN (ex-*Charity*) and TAIMUR (ex-*Chivalrous*—since scrapped); and Royal Norwegian Navy BERGEN (ex-*Cromwell*), OSLO (ex-*Crown*), STAVANGER (ex-*Crystal*) and TRONDHEIM (ex-*Croziers*—since scrapped)—were sold.

They were similarly modified to the CA group to improve their anti-submarine capability but with less structual alteration. Two A/S mortars replaced "X" gun but no alterations were made to the bridge or the after shelter deck.

Displacement: 1,900/2,545 tons except *CR group* 1,920/2,560 tons.
Dimensions: 339½(pp) 362¾(oa) × 35¾ × 10¼/13¾ feet.
Machinery: Two Admiralty 3-drum boilers (300 lb/in² at 640°F); two shafts; Parsons geared turbines, S.H.P. 40,000 = 36¾/31¼ knots; O.F. 580 tons.
Armament: Three 4·5-inch D.P. (3 × 1), six 40mm. A.A. (1 × 2 and 4 × 1) guns; four 21-inch (1 × 4) T.T.; two A/S mortars (Squid).
Complement: 175 except *Pakistani Navy vessels* 200.

Pt. No.	Name	Builder	Laid down	Launched	Completed	Disposition
D.51	CHEVRON	Stephen	18. 3.43	23. 2.44	23. 8.45	Rosyth for disposal
164	SHAH JEHAN (ex-*Charity*)	Thornycroft	9. 7.43	30.11.44	19.11.45	Pakistani Navy (1959)
160	ALAMGIR (ex-*Creole*) ...	White	3. 8.44	22.11.45	14.10.46	Pakistani Navy (1958)
162	JAHANGIR (ex-*Crispin*, ex-*Craccher*)	White	1. 2.44	23. 6.45	10. 7.46	Pakistani Navy (1958)

Machinery contracts: All engined by builders.

Modified " Black Swan " class: **CAUVERY, KISTNA**

The ultimate development of the escort sloop, these vessels rendered excellent service during the Second World War, and enjoyed a large measure of success against German submarines when deployed as support groups in the North Atlantic.

Although very well armed for their size, the provision of only a single HA.DCT did circumscribe their effectiveness as anti-aircraft vessels, and in spite of their heavy A.A. battery it was as anti-submarine vessels they they excelled. Two directors were also provided, abreast the funnel to port and starboard, for the light A.A. armament. Principally because of insufficient speed they were phased-out of service post-war. The Indian Navy vessels had "X" mounting and the light A.A guns on the quarterdeck removed to provide additional accommodation.

Of the thirty-six units originally comprising this class (including four for the Royal Indian Navy), five were cancelled; five were war losses (the LARK was later salved by the Russian Navy and placed in service as the NEPTUN but has since been scrapped); four—Egyptian Navy TARIK (ex-*El Malek Farouq*, ex-*Whimbrel*), and West German HIPPER (ex-*Actaeon*), SCHARNHORST (ex-*Mermaid*) and SCHEER (ex-*Hart*)—were sold; and twenty (including two Pakistani Navy units) were scrapped.

Displacement: 1,470/1,925.
Dimensions: 282(pp) 299½(oa) × 38½ × 9¼/11¼ feet.
Machinery: Two Admiralty 3-drum boilers; two shafts; Parsons geared turbines, S.H.P. 4,300 = 19¾/18 knots; O.F. 370 tons.
Armament: Four 4-inch A.A. (2 × 2), four 40mm. A.A. (4 × 1) guns.
Complement: 219.

Pt. No.	Name	Builder	Laid down	Launched	Completed	Disposition
F.110	CAUVERY	Yarrow	28.10.42	15. 6.43	21.10.43	Indian Navy, 12th Frigate Squadron
F.46	KISTNA	Yarrow	14. 7.42	22. 4.43	26. 8.43	Indian Navy, 12th Frigate Squadron

Machinery contracts: All engined by builders.

ESCORT VESSELS

"River" class: **ANTIGONISH, BEACON HILL, JONQUIERE, LAUZON, STE. THERESE, STETTLER**

These vessels re-introduced the frigate category to the Commonwealth navies, and were successors to the smaller corvettes which—designed for coastal escort duties—were not, unnaturally, found wanting in size for ocean work.

The main object behind the design was increased size and better ability to maintain speed under ocean conditions, as compared with the corvette, together with a greater radius of action. The gun armament was light—but nevertheless sufficient to deal with a surfaced submarine—and deck space was primarily devoted to A/S weapons. These frigates were built in U.K., Canadian, and Australian yards, and were very similar vessels but with some modification in armament in some Canadian- and Australian-built units. Reciprocating machinery was installed more as a matter of necessity than choice as turbine production facilities were non-existent in Canada.

The Canadian-built vessels of this class originally consisted of eighty-eight vessels and, of these, nineteen were cancelled; three were war losses; ten were built for the United States Navy, but only two were turned over and the balance transferred to the Royal Navy until the end of hostilities when they were returned; twelve—the Dominican MELLA (ex-*Presidente Trujillo*, ex-*Carlplace*); Chilean BAQUEDANO (ex-*Esmeralda*, ex-*Glace Bay*, ex-*Lauzon*), CAVADONGA (ex-*Sea Cliff*, ex-*Megantic*), and IQUIQUE (ex-*Joliette*); Israeli MISGAV (ex-*Strathadam*), MISNAK (ex-*Hallowell*) and MIVTAKH (ex-mercantile *Violetta*, ex-*Orkney*) of which the last two later became the Singhalese Navy GAJABAHU and MAHASENA (since scrapped) respectively; Peruvian FERRE (ex-*Poundmaker*) and PALACIOS (ex-*St. Pierre*), and Royal Norwegian Navy DRAUG (ex-*Penetang*, ex-*Rouyn*), GARM (ex-*Giffard*) and TROLL (ex-*Prestonian*, ex-*Beauharnois*)—were sold, together with a further five sold-out commercially; three—ST. CATHERINES, ST. STEPHEN and STONETOWN (last two sold-out commercially)—were transferred to the Canadian Coast Guard

Pt. No.	Name	Builder	Laid down	Launched	Completed	Disposition
DE.301	ANTIGONISH	Canadian Yarrow ...	2.10.43	10. 2.44	4. 7.44	Royal Canadian Navy, Esquimalt for disposal
DE.303	BEACON HILL	Canadian Yarrow ...	16. 7.43	6.11.43	16. 5.44	Royal Canadian Navy, 7th Frigate Squadron
DE.318	JONQUIERE	G. T. Davie	16. 2.43	28.10.43	10. 5.44	Royal Canadian Navy, Esquimalt for disposal
DE.322	LAUZON (ex-*Glace Bay*)...	G. T. Davie	1. 7.43	10. 6.44	30. 8.44	Royal Canadian Navy, for disposal
DE.309	STE. THERESE ...	Davie Sbdg. ...	18. 5.43	16.10.43	28. 5.44	Royal Canadian Navy, Esquimalt for disposal
DE.311	STETTLER	Canadian Vickers ...	31. 5.43	10. 9.43	7. 5.44	Royal Canadian Navy, Esquimalt for disposal

Machinery contracts: Antigonish and Beacon Hill engined by Dominion Engineering; Jonquiere, Lauzon, and Stettler by Canadian Vickers; and Ste. Therese by C.P.R. and Canadian Vickers.

Jonquiere

as ocean weather ships; one—GRANBY (ex-*Victoriaville*)—was converted to a support ship for divers; and thirty were scrapped.

Of the ten U.S. Navy vessels, two—Argentinian AZOPARDA (ex-*Hercules*, ex-U.S.N. *Asheville*, ex-R.C.N. *Nadur*, ex-*Adur*) and Dominican JUAN PABLO DUARTE (ex-U.S.N. *Natchez*, ex-R.C.N. *Annan*—since lost)—were sold, another unit was sold-out commercially, and the remaining seven were scrapped.

The vessels kept in service (including those later transferred to the Royal Norwegian Navy) were modernised in 1953–58 when the fo'c'sle deck was extended right to the stern, the bridge enlarged and funnel heightened, and a larger tripod foremast installed. The armament was re-distributed with a twin 4-inch A.A. mounting before the bridge, single 40mm. A.A. in each bridge wing and a twin 40mm. A.A. mounting abaft the funnel, and two A/S mortars in wells farther aft. Deckhouses were added abaft the funnel in ANTIGONISH, BEACON HILL, JONQUIERE, STE. THERESE and STETTLER while employed as training vessels.

Displacement: 1,570/2,360 tons.
Dimensions: 283(pp) $301\frac{1}{2}$(oa) $\times 36\frac{3}{4} \times 10/14\frac{3}{4}$ feet.
Machinery: Two Admiralty 3-drum boilers (235 lb/in²); two shafts; reciprocating (VTE—cyl. 16″:31″: $38\frac{1}{2}″ \times 30″$ stroke), I.H.P. 5,500 = 20/19 knots; O.F. 720 tons.
Armament: Two 4-inch A.A. (1×2), four 40mm. A.A. (1×2 and 2×1) guns; two A/S mortars (Squid).
Complement: 140.

Loch Fada

Pt. No.	Name	Builder	Laid down	Launched	Completed	Disposition
F.647	ALERT (ex-*Dundrum Bay*, ex-*Loch Scamadale*)	Blyth	28. 7.44	10. 7.45	24.10.46	Devonport for disposal
F.248	LOCH ALVIE	Barclay Curle... ...	31. 8.43	14. 4.44	21. 8.44	Singapore reserve and cannibalised for spares
F.390	LOCH FADA	Clydebank	8. 6.43	14.12.43	10. 4.44	Chatham for disposal
F.429	LOCH FYNE	Burntisland	8.12.43	25. 5.44	9.11.44	Devonport for disposal
F.628	LOCH KILLISPORT ...	Harland & Wolff ...	28.12.43	6. 7.44	9. 7.45	Portsmouth for disposal
F.437	LOCH LOMOND ...	Caledon	7.12.43	19. 6.44	16.11.44	Chatham for disposal
F.433	HANG TUAH (ex-*Loch Insh*)	Robb	17.11.43	10. 5.44	20.10.44	Royal Malaysian Navy (1964)

Machinery contracts: Loch Fyne engined by Rowan; *Loch Lomond* by Duncan Stewart; *Hang Tuah* by White's Marine Engineering; *Alert* by White; and others by builders.

"Loch" class: **ALERT, HANG TUAH, LOCH ALVIE, LOCH FYNE, LOCH KILLISPORT, LOCH LOMOND**

The pressing need to speed frigate building during the Second World War resulted in the "Loch/Bay" class, which were of prefabricated construction and so brought in the constructional steel firms to aid the traditional shipyards in rapid construction. To facilitate transport the prefabricated sections were limited to $29 \times 8\frac{1}{2} \times 8\frac{1}{2}$ feet in size, and $2\frac{1}{2}$ tons in weight to suit existing cranage at the shipyards.

Generally, the "River" class design was adhered to except that the hull form—especially above water—was revised to eliminate curves which were replaced by straight lines wherever possible. This was particularly noticeable in the sheer which was in three straight sections instead of the usual continious curve. As completed they emerged as two distinct sub-groups, primarily equipped as either anti-submarine ("Loch" class) or anti-aircraft ("Bay" class) escorts. The war terminated before the building programme was fully implemented so that some uncompleted hulls were adapted for other purposes. Four "Bay" class were completed as surveying vessels, and another pair as despatch vessels, while two "Loch" class were altered while building to depot ships for coastal forces.

All surviving units have had their single 4-inch gun forward replaced by a twin 4-inch A.A. mounting, and the original mixed light A.A. armament by a uniform 40mm. A.A. battery; and the HANG TUAH had a further twin 40mm. A.A. mounting and a helicopter landing pad added aft and the bridge built-up.

The class originally comprised one hundred and ten units of which half (fifty-four " Loch " and one " Bay " class) were cancelled; sixteen—the Finnish MATTI KURKI (ex-*Porlock Bay*, ex-*Loch Seaford*, ex-*Loch Muick*); Royal Malaysian Navy HANG TUAH (ex-*Loch Insh*); Royal New Zealand Navy HAWEA (ex-*Loch Eck*), KANIERE (ex-*Loch Achray*), PUKAKI (ex-*Loch Achanalt*), ROTOITI (ex-*Loch Katrine*), TAUPO (ex-*Loch Shin*), and TUTIRA (ex-*Loch Morlich*—all since scrapped); Persian BABR (ex-*Woodbridge Haven*, ex-*Loch Assynt*); Portuguese ALVARES CABRAL (ex-*Burghead Bay*, ex-*Loch Harport*), DON FRANCESCO DE ALMEIDA (ex-*Morecambe Bay,* ex-*Loch Heilen*), PACHECO PEREIRA (ex-*Bigbury Bay,* ex-*Loch Carloway*), and VASCO DA GAMA (ex-*Mounts Bay*, ex-*Loch Kilbernie*); and South African GOOD HOPE (F.432 ex-*Loch Boisdale*), NATAL (A.301 ex-*Loch Cree*), and TRANSVAAL (F.602 ex-*Loch Ard*) were sold, together with one " Loch " class sold out commercially; and twenty-eight (thirteen " Loch " and fifteen " Bay ") were scrapped including a despatch vessel and depot ship conversion.

Displacement: 1,575/2,400 tons.
Dimensions: 286(pp) 307(oa) $\times 38\frac{1}{2} \times 12/14\frac{3}{4}$ feet.
Machinery: Two Admiralty 3-drum boilers (225 lb/in²); two shafts; reciprocating (VTE—cyl. $18'':31'':38\frac{1}{2}''$ (2) $\times 30''$ stroke), I.H.P. $5,500 = 19\frac{1}{2}/18$ knots; O.F. 753 tons.
Armament: Two 4-inch A.A. (1×2), *Alert* two/others six/*Hang Tuah* eight 40mm. A.A. $(1/2 \times 2, 2/4 \times 1)$, four 3-pounder saluting (4×1) guns; two A/S mortars (Squid—not in *Alert*).
Complement: 140 except *Alert* 160.

ESCORT VESSELS

Pt. No.	Name	Builder	Laid down	Launched	Completed	Disposition
F.78	BLACKWOOD	Thornycroft	14. 9.53	4.10.55	22. 8.57	Rosyth reserve, for disposal
F.80	DUNCAN	Thornycroft	17.12.53	30. 5.57	21.10.58	Home
F.48	DUNDAS	White	17.10.52	25. 9.53	9. 3.56	2nd Training Squadron
F.84	EXMOUTH	White	24. 3.54	16.11.55	20.12.57	Chatham refitting
F.51	GRAFTON...	White	25. 2.53	13. 9.54	11. 1.57	Home
F.54	HARDY	Yarrow	4. 2.53	25.11.53	15.12.55	Gibralter reserve, for disposal
F.85	KEPPEL	Yarrow	27. 3.53	31. 8.54	6. 7.56	Home
F.88	MALCOLM	Yarrow	1. 2.54	18.10.55	12.12.57	Home
F.91	MURRAY	Stephen	30.11.53	25. 2.55	5. 6.56	2nd Training Squadron
F.94	PALLISER	Stephen	15. 3.55	10. 5.56	13.12.57	Portsmouth reserve
F.62	PELLEW	Swan Hunter	5.11.53	29. 9.54	26. 7.56	2nd Training Squadron, for disposal
F.97	RUSSELL	Swan Hunter	11.11.53	10.12.54	7. 2.57	Portsmouth reserve
F.149	KHUKRI	White	29.12.55	20.11.56	15. 7.58	Indian Navy
F.144	KIRPAN	Stephen	5.11.56	19. 8.58	00. 7.59	Indian Navy
F.146	KUTHAR	White	19. 9.57	14.10.58	00.11.59	Indian Navy

Machinery contracts: Grafton and Malcolm engined by Parsons; Pellew and Russell by Wallsend Slipway; all others by builders.

"Blackwood" class: **BLACKWOOD, DUNCAN, DUNDAS, EXMOUTH, GRAFTON, HARDY, KEPPEL, KHUKRI, KIRPAN, KUTHAR, MALCOLM, MURRAY, PALLISER, PELLEW, RUSSELL**

These vessels were built at the same time as the "Whitby" class, and solely incorporated the anti-submarine qualities of the larger vessels within the smallest possible hull.

This resulted in them being extreme examples of specialisation and they proved good A/S vessels and little else. They did, however, partly redress the numerical deficiency of the Royal Navy in this category by sacrificing some quality for quantity, and were known as the type 14 *utility* (less kindly as futility), while the "Whitby" class were rated as the type 12 *quality*, frigates. They were given the same steam turbine plant as the "Whitby" class, but as they only had a single shaft, they only had half the power, and were some 5 knots slower.

While the design had many shortcomings it was capable of development—especially in light of the continuous progress with more compact and weight saving equipment of all kinds—but after their construction Admiralty policy once again hardened towards quality from quantity, and they were dropped as soon as the planned programme was completed. They have, however, shown themselves to be excellent seaboats in adverse weather conditions while engaged in fishery protection duties off Iceland. Two banks of twin tubes for A/S torpedoes were later removed (where fitted) together with the 40mm. A.A. gun on the quarterdeck in Royal Navy vessels.

The EXMOUTH was taken in hand by H.M. Dockyard, Chatham, in 1966 to be re-engined solely with gas turbines. Main propulsion will be by a Rolls-Royce Olympus unit, installed in the former boiler room, developing S.H.P. 23,200, and two Proteus units for cruising, each rated at S.H.P. 4,250, installed in the engine room. The gas turbines will be coupled to the single shaft through gearing and the full utilisation of available power will be restricted.

This conversion is primarily a means of rapidly implementing the testing of this installation at sea, but will nevertheless still occupy two years to complete. In this particular instance the cruising turbines will not supplement the main unit for maximum power, but will be used independently as the hull could not absorb any large increase in power over that originally provided, while the increase in speed will be only marginal and it was not the purpose of the conversion to aim at greater speed.

Displacement: 1,180/1,535 tons.

Dimensions: 300(pp) 310(oa) $\times$ 33 $\times$ 11/15 feet.

Machinery: Two Babcock & Wilcox boilers (not in *Exmouth*); one shaft (c.p. propeller in *Exmouth* only); English Electric geared turbines, S.H.P. 15,000 $= 27\frac{3}{4}/24\frac{1}{2}$ knots except *Exmouth* S.H.P. 15,000/7,200 $= 28/22$ knots; O.F. 300 tons except *Exmouth* 325 tons.

Armament: Two except *Indian Navy vessels* three 40mm. A.A. $(2/3 \times 1)$ guns; two A/S mortars (Limbo).

Complement: 112 except *Indian Navy vessels* 140.

Prominent air intakes for the gas turbines have been added forward and abaft the re-modelled funnel in the *Exmouth,* and a controllable pitch propeller fitted as gas turbines are non-reversing. Bunker capacity was increased to compensate for higher fuel consumption of gas turbines. A speed of 16 knots was attained with one Proteus unit, 22 knots with both Proteus units, and 25 knots with the Olympus unit.

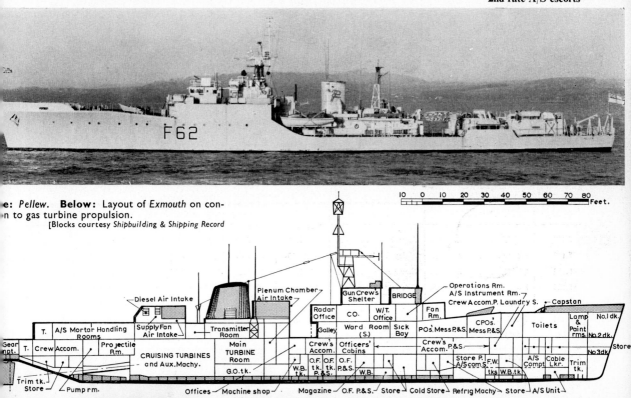

e: *Pellew.* **Below:** Layout of *Exmouth* on con-
n to gas turbine propulsion.
[Blocks courtesy *Shipbuilding & Shipping Record*

10 0 10 20 30 40 50 60 70 80
Feet.

ESCORT VESSELS

Ashanti.

Pt. No.	Name			Builder			Laid down	Launched	Completed	Disposition
F.117	ASHANTI	...	...	Yarrow	...	...	15. 1.58	9. 3.59	23.11.61	Portsmouth refitting
F.119	ESKIMO	...	...	White ...	...	...	22.10.58	20. 3.61	21. 2.63	Home
F.122	GURKHA	...	...	Thornycroft ...		...	3.11.58	11. 7.60	13. 2.63	Rosyth refitting
F.125	MOHAWK	...	...	Vickers-Armstrongs (Barrow)			23.12.60	5. 4.62	29.11.63	Home/Middle East
F.131	NUBIAN	...	...	H.M. Dockyard (Portsmouth)		...	7. 9.59	6. 9.60	9.10.62	Home/Middle East
F.133	TARTAR	...	...	H.M. Dockyard (Devonport)		...	22.10.59	19. 9.60	26. 2.62	Home/Middle East
F.124	ZULU	...	...	Stephen	...	...	13.12.60	3. 7.62	17. 4.64	Home/Middle East

Machinery contracts: Mohawk and *Nubian* engined by A.E.I. (steam and gas); *Tartar* by Vickers-Armstrongs (steam) and Yarrow (gas); *Zulu* by Parsons (steam) and Yarrow (gas); and others by builders.

"Tribal" class: **ASHANTI, ESKIMO, GURKHA, MOHAWK, NUBIAN, TARTAR, ZULU**

This class reversed the policy of the earlier specialised frigates and—to a lesser degree—combined their individual functions within a single, but dimensionally larger, hull. As the specialised frigates were intended for form mutually self-supporting groups, the "Tribal" class could individually be more flexibly employed, and were so more suitable to meet the varied demands of detached service abroad. A small Royal Marine detachment was included in their complement.

The fully automatic and weighty twin 4·5-inch turret was replaced by two lighter single mountings originally borne by war-built destroyers; only a single A/S mortar was carried in the well aft; and they had less complex radar and communications equipment than the A.D. frigates. They were, however, the first Royal Navy frigates designed to carry a helicopter, which enhanced their anti-submarine qualities as they were otherwise so slow to counter nuclear-powered submarines. Although intended to ship two quadruple Seacat launchers they were completed *pro tem* with two single 40mm. A.A. guns—except in the ZULU—which they have retained as more suitable for their peace-time employment, while the original provision to fit six fixed tubes for A/S torpedoes was not implemented. The ZULU only has been equipped with the Seacat system, together with their DCT's to port and starboard abreast the after funnel.

Departures from standard practice were the flush-decked hull; only a single boiler for the steam plant, while an auxiliary boiler was provided for harbour use; and the combined steam and gas turbine main propulsion, coupled through gearing to a single shaft, which permitted economies in machinery weights. They were the first operational vessels with COSAG propulsion while a similar twin-shaft installation had been simultaneously prepared for the "County" class (see p. 40-43) which came into service a little after them. A speed of $21\frac{1}{2}$ knots is attained with the gas turbine only, a speed of $24\frac{3}{4}$ knots with the steam turbine, and a speed of 28 knots with both turbines.

Displacement: 2,300/2,700 tons.

Dimensions: 350(pp) 360(oa) $\times 42\frac{1}{2} \times 11\frac{1}{4}/13\frac{1}{4}$ feet.

Machinery: One Babcock & Wilcox boiler (550 lb/in² at 850°F); one shaft (c.p. propeller); Metrovick single drum steam and A.E.I. gas geared turbines, S.H.P. 12,500+7,500=28 knots; O.F. .... tons.

Armament: Eight Seacat (2×4) G.W.S. in *Zulu* only; two 4·5-inch D.P. (2×1), two 40mm. A.A. (2×1—not in *Zulu*) guns; one A/S mortar (Limbo); one helicopter.

Complement: 253.

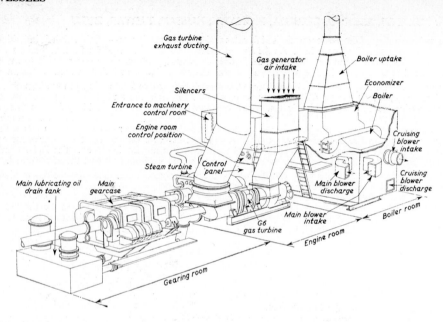

Gas turbine exhaust ducting

Gas generator air intake

Boiler uptake

Silencers

Economizer

Boiler

Entrance to machinery control room

Engine room control position

Cruising blower intake

Steam turbine

Control panel

Main lubricating oil drain tank

Main gearcase

Main blower discharge

Cruising blower discharge

G6 gas turbine

Main blower intake

Boiler room

Engine room

Gearing room

Engine room arrangement of "Tribal" class G.P. frigates showing single shaft layout of combined steam and gas turbine plant. A similar, but twin-shaft arrangement, was installed in the "County" class destroyers (see pp. 40-43).

[Block ourtesy *Shipbuilding & Shipping Record*

Above: *Nubian.*

Right: *Nigeria*, combined frigate and despatch vessel.

ESCORT VESSELS

[Block courtesy *Shipbuilding & Shipping Record*

Kromantse, Mk. I G.P. version of the Vickers/Vosper corvette.

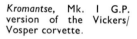

The 4-inch gun forward is an ex-submarine model, and a Squid A/S mortar is fitted aft.

Vosper/Vickers type: **KETA, KROMANTSE**

A private design of high merit to provide emergent Commonwealth—and other—navies with modern and relatively inexpensive vessels as opposed to the more complex designs which they could neither afford, or be able to efficiently maintain, during early stages of naval development.

Described as corvettes, they are diminutives of the more sophisticated frigates, and are largely fitted with standard up-to-date equipment of proven quality and reliability. They can undertake, with greater economy, most of the peace-time duties of frigates while at the same time provide realistic training. During war-time they could carry out many functions which would not fully utilise the capabilities of the more elaborate frigates. Their limitations, however, must clearly be recognised. They have barely sufficient speed to counter conventionally propelled submarines, but the provision of an A/S mortar enables them to deliver a lethal blow once contact is secured and held. The gun armament is defensive and sufficient to cope with most forms of attack likely to be directed against vessels of this type. Fin stabilised, they are able to face adverse weather conditions and still be able to effectively fight their armament.

These vessels were constructed to the builders' Mk. I general purpose design. Other designs include a gun version of the Mk. I with no anti-submarine equipment but the addition of three more 40mm. guns; a Mk. 2 design which incorporates a more sophisticated armament—including A.A. and A/S missiles—and a provision to ship a third engine raising the speed to 24 knots; and an enlarged and faster Mk. 3 design with a greater radius of action. A Mk. I gun version has been built for the Royal Libyan Navy but is powered by Davey Paxman diesel engines.

Displacement: 435/500 tons.
Dimensions: 160(pp) 177(oa) $\times 28\frac{1}{2} \times 9\frac{1}{2}/13$ feet.
Machinery: Two shafts; 16-cyl. Maybach diesel engines, B.H.P. 5,720=20/17 knots; O.F. 68 tons.
Armament: One 4-inch D.P., one 40mm. A.A. guns; one A/S mortar (Squid).
Complement: 51.

Pt. No.	Name	Builder	Laid down	Launched	Completed	Disposition
F.18	KETA	Vickers-Armstrongs (Tyne)	25.10.63	18. 1.65	4. 5.65	Ghanian Navy
F.17	KROMANTSE	Vosper	10.12.62	5. 9.63	27. 7.64	Ghanaian Navy

Machinery contracts: Both engined by Bristol Siddeley.

Vosper/Vickers type: **TWO** unnamed vessels.

The Mk. 3 design is a development of the Mk. 1 corvettes described on the previous page, and the principal advantages accruing from increased length were improved seaworthiness and higher speed, while—if desired—a more sophisticated armament could be carried.

The contracts for these vessels were finally placed after prolonged negotiations as the result of civil strife, and while the Nigerian Navy appreciated the advantages of greater size they preferred the simpler armament of the Mk. 1 design. With the larger hull internal arrangements could be advantageously modified. The officers' accommodation was moved to amidships and the stern compartment made available for more extensive A/S missile stowage; the auxiliary engine room was enlarged to accommodate a third main propulsion engine coupled to the centre shaft; and an extra compartment worked in for increased generator capacity and workshop facilities. Draught was decreased by 1 foot as screws of reduced diameter could be utilised.

Displacement: 500/575 tons.
Dimensions: 182(pp) 200(oa) $\times$ 268$\frac{1}{2}$ $\times$ .../12 feet.
Machinery: Three shafts; 16-cyl. Maybach diesel engines B.H.P. 8,580 = 25$\frac{1}{2}$/24 knots; O.F. 70 tons.
Armament: One 4-inch, one 40mm A.A. guns; one A/S mortar (Squid).
Complement: 63.

Pt. No.	Name	Builder	Laid down	Launched	Completed	Disposition
F.	Unnamed	Vosper Thornycroft (Portsmouth)	69	....	72	Building for Nigerian Navy.
F.	Unnamed	Vosper Thornycroft (Portsmouth)	69	....	72	Building for Nigerian Navy.

Machinery contracts: Engined by Maybach.

N.V.S.B. type: **NIGERIA**

The requirement of the Nigerian Navy for a less sophisticated frigate than those currently building in the United Kingdom led to this order being placed in the Netherlands, where the Netherlands Shipbuilding Bureaux—a consortium of four ship- and one engine-builder which undertake all Dutch naval work—modified a design project to suit Nigerian specifications. In the interim, while the vessel was under construction, the Royal Netherlands Navy co-operated by lending a former American PC boat to the Nigerian Navy for training purposes.

Designed to serve as a combination frigate/despatch vessel, considerable space was devoted to providing accommodation for official passengers with consequent less refinement to armament and control arrangements, warning radar, and anti-submarine equipment. There is an open twin 4-inch A.A. mounting forward, four single 40mm. A.A. guns mounted on the superstructure (two forward and two aft), an A/S mortar further aft, and a helicopter landing pad at the stern.

A similar, but slightly smaller and more combatant, vessel was built for the Ghanaian Navy (see following page) with an identical armament, and also intended to serve in the dual role of frigate/despatch vessel.

Displacement: 1,725/2,000 tons.
Dimensions: $341\frac{1}{4}$(pp) $360\frac{1}{4}$(oa) $\times 37 \times 10\frac{1}{2}/\dots$ feet.
Machinery: Two shafts; 16-cyl. M.A.N. diesel engines (two/shaft), B.H.P. 15,500=26 knots; O.F. 275 tons.
Armament: Two 4-inch A.A. (1$\times$2), four 20mm. A.A. (4$\times$1) guns; one A/S mortar (Squid).
Complement: 216.

Pt. No.	Name	Builder	Laid down	Launched	Completed	Disposition
F.87	NIGERIA	Wilton-Fijenoord ...	9. 4.64	29. 4.65	16. 9.65	Nigerian Navy

Machinery contract: Engined by M.A.N.

ESCORT VESSELS

Russian "Petya" class: **KADMATH, KAMORTA,** and **FOUR** unnamed

These units were scheduled for transfer to the Indian Navy from 1968, and belong to a class of standard escort vessels built since 1960. Main propulsion is by a CODOG machinery arrangement with a flat-sided, squat funnel amidships serving as an air intake and exhaust for the gas turbines.

The guns are mounted in twin turrets fore and aft, the torpedo tubes in a quintuple bank amidships, and the 12-barrelled rocket projectors are quadrantly disposed abaft each turret. The following legend details are approximately correct.

1,000/1,150 tons; 250(wl) $262\frac{1}{2}$(oa) $\times 32 \times 9\frac{1}{4}$ feet; two shafts, gas turbines and diesel engines S.H.P./B.H.P. 10,000/4,000 = 30/16 knots, O.F. ...tons; four 3-inch D.P. (2×2) guns, five 16-inch A/S (1×5) T.T., four (16b.) A/S rocket projectors; complement ....

The Ghanaian frigate is now laid-up awaiting sale.

Yarrow type: **ONE** unnamed vessel

Originally ordered by the Ghanaian Navy, the contract for this vessel was cancelled in 1966 and she consequently was not named when launched. On completion she was laid-up for sale, probably to a Commonwealth Navy. Generally similar to the diesel-engined frigates (types 41 and 61) except that the hull has been made flush-decked, the exhaust uptakes led to a single funnel and the enclosed mainmast, the superstructure extended to provide additional accommodation, and a modified and lighter armament was shipped.

An open twin 4-inch A.A. mounting replaced the turret forward and is controlled by a STD on the bridge; single 40mm. A.A. guns are mounted on the superstructure abreast the fore- and main-masts; the A/S mortar is in a well aft; and a helicopter landing pad provided. Also meant to double as a despatch vessel, special suites are provided for official passengers and in this, and other respects, she is very similar to the slightly larger NIGERIA built in the Netherlands for the Nigerian Navy.

Despite exaggerated accounts, extra accommodation is limited to that enclosed by the deckhouse abaft the bridge (dining/conference room, pantry, lobby, and two cabins) which has not been fitted out. This space is readily adaptable for command or training facilities, and there is a built-in provision to up-date the fire control system. Retractable fin stabilisers have been installed together with ABC defence measures but there is no pre-wetting system.

Displacement: 2,300/2,525 tons.

Dimensions: 330(pp) 344¾(oa) × 40 × 12/.. feet.

Machinery: Two shafts (c.p. propellers); 16-cyl. ASR.1 diesel engines (four/shaft), B.H.P. 16,000 at 920rpm = 24¾ knots; O.F. 230 tons (4,800 miles at 15 knots).

Armament: Two 4-inch A.A. (1 × 2), four 40mm. A.A. (4 × 1) guns; one A/S mortar (Limbo).

Complement: 227 + 19 spare.

Pt. No.	Name	Builder	Laid down	Launched	Completed	Disposition
F.	Unnamed	Yarrow	28.10.65	29.12.66	... 6.68	Laid-up Glasgow (Ghanian Navy)

Machinery contract: Engined by Vickers-Armstrongs (Barrow).

ESCORT VESSELS

Yarrow type: HANG JEBAT

A private design to provide a simplified frigate at 60 per cent of the cost of the larger units built for the Royal Navy, such as the "Leander" class.

The main feature of the design is diesel (for cruising) or gas turbine (for full speed) propulsion coupled, via gearing, to twin shafts fitted with controllable pitch propellers, and the general provision for standard and proven items of equipment. With 150 tons available for armament alternative designs include another general purpose frigate with modified armament, a general purpose frigate/despatch vessel, an anti-submarine frigate, or an anti-aircraft frigate. All manned spaces are fully air-conditioned, the hull fin stabilised to provide a steady weapon platform, and ABC defence measures incorporated.

The hull has a long fo'c'sle—with a helicopter landing deck at its after end—while the A/S mortar is offset to port on the main deck with its missile handling arrangements to starboard. In this mark of general purpose vessel there is a single 4·5-inch D.P. gun on the fo'c'sle in an open mounting; single 40mm. A.A. abreast the foremast to port and starboard; and a quadruple Seacat launchers close abaft mainmast. Radar control is provided for the guns, and the combined HA/LA.DCT aft can work with either the gun or missile armament. Warning, control, and navigational radar is carried on the tubular masts, and the usual whip aerials project from the aluminium superstructure. A low centre of gravity is constantly maintained by water displacement of oil fuel in the bunkers.

An order for another unit of this class has been placed by the Royal Thai Navy.

Displacement: .,.../1,550 tons.
Dimensions: 300(pp) 310(oa) × 34 × ../10 feet.
Machinery: Two shafts (c.p. propellers); 8-cyl. Pielstick diesel engine B.H.P. 4,000 = 16½ knots, and Bristol Siddeley gas turbine, S.H.P. 22,000 = 24 knots; O.F. ... tons.
Armament: Four Seacat (1×4) G.W.S.; one 4·5-inch D.P., two 40mm. A.A. (2×1) guns; one A/S mortar (Limbo); one helicopter.
Complement: 120.

Pt. No.	Name	Builder	Laid down	Launched	Completed	Disposition
F.24	HANG JEBAT	Yarrow	1. 6.67	18.12.67	... 8.69	Royal Malaysian Navy

Machinery contracts: Engined by Crossley (diesel) and Bristol Siddeley (gas turbines).

AMPHIBIOUS WARFARE VESSELS

"*Majestic*" *class:* **SYDNEY**

This former aircraft carrier, which was never modernised, was converted into a fast troop transport by the Royal Australian Navy during 1962–63. All capability for operating fixed-wing aircraft (catapults, arrester gear, etc.) was removed, the former hangar converted into troop space, and the flight deck used for vehicle stowage.

It should be borne in mind that the R.A.N. has comparatively few—which accentuates the problem of availability—mercantile vessels of comparable capacity and speed it could draw on in times of emergency for this purpose. Thus, it was eminently practicable to utilise a sound and fast hull, better able to withstand action damage than any merchant ship, which rapidly provided the R.A.N. with a type of vessel which is frequently required at short notice. The alteration was basically simple and inexpensive and should provide the SYDNEY with useful employment for some years.

Displacement: 14,380/19,550 tons.

Dimensions: 630(pp) 698(oa) $\times 80\frac{1}{4}$ ($112\frac{1}{2}$ across FD) $\times 21/25$ feet.

Machinery: Four Admiralty 3-drum boilers (400 lb/in^2 at 700°F); two shafts; Parsons geared turbines, S.H.P. 40,000 = $24\frac{3}{4}$ knots; O.F. 3,200 tons.

Armament: Four 40mm. A.A. (4×1) guns.

Complement: 544.

Pt. No.	Name	Builder	Laid down	Launched	Completed	Disposition
A.214	SYDNEY (ex-*Terrible*) ...	H.M. Dockyard (Devonport)	19. 4.43	30. 9.44	5. 2.49	Royal Australian Navy

Machinery contract: Engined by Parsons.

A.W. VESSELS

Albion

Pt. No.	Name	Builder	Laid down	Launched	Completed	Disposition
R.07	ALBION	Swan Hunter	23. 3.44	6. 5.47	26. 5.54	Far East
R.08	BULWARK	Harland & Wolff ...	10. 5.45	22. 6.48	4.11.54	Western Fleet.

Machinery contracts: Albion engined by Wallsend Slipway, and Bulwark by builders.

"Hermes" class: **ALBION, BULWARK**

These former aircraft carriers were converted to their present role at H.M. Dockyard, Portsmouth, in 1959–60 (BULWARK) and 1961–62 (ALBION).

While their fixed wing aircraft capability (angled deck, catapults, arrester gear, etc.) was removed, facilities for servicing the helicopters was retained so that all the hangar deck was not available for troop accommodation, and only a limited area of the flight deck for military behicles. They can at short notice, and using their own resources, convert the helicopters for anti-submarine purposes if required. The ALBION, the later modification, can accommodate 900 troops as opposed to 733 in the BULWARK, and both are provided with four LCA's suspended under davits on each quarter.

Although there were some initial misgivings over using modern carriers for this purpose, they belonged to a class least able to absorb the larger and heavier naval aircraft being brought into service owing to their limited hangar capacity (see notes on CENTAUR and HERMES), and have since ably demonstrated their ability to rapidly land, and re-embark, troops in troubled areas. The helicopters are fitted to carry ATS missiles to provide ground support after troops have been landed.

Displacement: 23,300/27,300 tons.

Dimensions: 650(pp) 737¼(oa) × 90 (123½ across FD) × 24/28 feet.

Machinery: Four Admiralty 3-drum boilers; two shafts; Parsons geared turbines, S.H.P. 80,000 = 27½ knots; O.F. 3,500 tons.

Protection: Flight deck 1 inch.

Armament: Eight 40mm. A.A. (4 × 2), four 3-pounder saluting (4 × 1) guns; twenty-two helicopters.

Complement: 1,035.

Fearless

[Block courtesy *Naval Record*

Pt. No.	Name	Builder	Laid down	Launched	Completed	Disposition
L.10	FEARLESS	Harland & Wolff ...	25. 7.62	19.12.63	25.11.65	Far East
L.11	INTREPID	Clydebank	10. 1.63	25. 6.64	11. 3.67	Far East

Machinery contracts: Both engined by English Electric.

"Fearless" class: **FEARLESS, INTREPID**

Developed from the LSD's built during the Second World War, these vessels were principally designed to transport military armour to a beachead and also to act as military and naval headquarters during all stages of a seaborne assault .

Unlike the LSD's—which were little more than a powered floating dock in which two loaded LCT's could be carried —the dock compartment is much smaller and can only accommodate four LCM(9)'s, and the balance of space is devoted to two vehicle decks which extend from below the bridge to the after end of the superstructure. Sixteen 50-ton tanks can be carried (eight on the upper vehicle deck and two in each LCM) while the number of military vehicles is very variable dependent on type and size. Up to six helicopters can be operated from the flight deck, arranged aft over the dock compartment, but none are actually borne. Consequently, the flight deck can also be used for the stowage of military vehicles—if needed—and is connected by a ramp at its fore end to the upper vehicle (tank) deck. A further ramp links the upper and lower vehicle decks, and vehicles stowed on the latter have first to pass-up to the former from where they can be run into the LCM's and ferried ashore. The four LCVP's, each stowed under patent gravity davits amidships, are fitted with a bow ramp and can carry a Land Rover towing a light gun as an alternative to 35 assault troops.

A troop of the Royal Corps of Signals are borne to man the military communications offices, a troop of the Corps of Royal Engineers to provide a beach unit, while the Royal Marine detachment supplies a further beach unit and the landing craft crews. In addition, there is accommodation in the dock walls for 370 troops which can be increased to 700 for short hauls.

Tankage is provided for over 7,000 tons of water ballast which can be pumped in/out at the rate of 10,000/5,000 tons/hour for a draught of $23\frac{1}{2}/32\frac{1}{2}$ feet forward/aft when flooded down.

Displacement: 10,550/12,500 tons (*ca.* 19,500 tons flooded down).

Dimensions: 500(pp) 520(oa) $\times$ 80 $\times$ 20$\frac{1}{2}$/25 feet.

Machinery: Two Babcock & Wilcox boilers (550 lb/in^2 at 950°F); two shafts; English Electric geared turbines, S.H.P. 22,000 = 21 knots; O.F. 2,250 tons.

Armament: Sixteen Seacat (4 $\times$ 4) G.W.S.; two 40mm. A.A. (2 $\times$ 1) guns.

Complement: 582.

The torpedo tubes amidships in *Delhi* have since been removed and the side plated over.

Old "Leander" class: DELHI

Outside of training duties, there is only a limited use for old gun-armed cruisers and destroyers other than supplying gunfire in support of sea-borne landing operations.

While both cruisers and destroyers can also provide anti-aircraft defence of varying degrees of effectiveness—depending to what extent their warning radar and gunnery control systems have been modernised—the latter can, in addition, furnish anti-submarine protection—again dependant on modernisation for effectiveness—to landing forces on passage to the beach head, and establish inshore patrols once these forces have been put ashore.

The DELHI belonged to a class of light cruiser which were the first to depart from Naval treaty limits of 10,000 tons and 8-inch guns: a lead soon followed by other countries. Of the eight ships originally comprising this class (three belonged to the Royal Australian Navy) three were war losses and four were scrapped. Wartime modifications included the provision of radar for warning and gunnery control purposes; the replacement of the pole masts by tripods; and the removal of "X" twin 6-inch gun turret together with aircraft and catapult to augment the mixed light A.A. armament which, post-war, was made a uniform tertiary battery of 40mm. guns. The T.T. were removed from the DELHI in 1958, and the side plating extended farther aft to provide additional accommodation.

Displacement: 7,114/9,740 tons.
Dimensions: 530(pp) 554½(oa) × 55¼ × 16/20 feet.
Machinery: Four Admiralty 3-drum boilers (300lb/in²); four shafts; Parsons geared turbines, S.H.P. 72,000 = 32/30½ knots; O.F. 1,800 tons.
Protection: Main belt 2-4 inches, deck 1¼ inches. Turrets 1 inch, magazines 2 (crown)-3½ (side) inches, DCT ½ inch.
Armament: Six 6-inch (3×2), eight 4-inch A.A. (4×2), fourteen 40mm. A.A. (4×2 & 6×1) guns.
Complement: 800.

Pt. No.	Name	Builder	Laid down	Launched	Completed	Disposition
C.70	DELHI (ex-*Achilles*) ...	Cammell Laird ...	11. 6.31	1. 9.32	10.10.33	Indian Navy (1948)

Machinery contract: Engined by builder.

Above: *Belfast.*

Right: Amidships detail showing eight HA.DCT's for heavy and light A.A. armament.

114

Improved "Southampton" class: **BELFAST**

Advantage was taken with these light cruisers of lapsed Naval limitation treaties to make improvements over the " Southampton " class (none of which now remain in service) which were basically enlarged " Leander " class with triple 6-inch gun turrets.   An extra section was worked into the hull abaft the bridge, which placed the machinery spaces in the after half length so that the fore funnel was well removed from the bridge and the mainmast stepped between the funnels; the heavy and light A.A. armaments were increased; and the armour belt was extended fore and aft to enclose the end barbettes, and protection and internal sub-division generally enhanced.

The BELFAST was heavily damaged early in the Second World War and spent a considerable time under repair. She emerged with her heavy A.A. armament slightly reduced and the light A.A. considerably increased; radar added for warning and gunnery control purposes; and externally bulged to improve stability and compensate for additional top-weight added.   Her sister ship EDINBURGH was a war loss.

During 1955–59 the BELFAST was extensively modernised when additions were made to the bridgework; the mixed light A.A. battery was replaced by twin 40mm. A.A. mountings; the original HA.DCT's were replaced by eight modern ones—one for each twin 4-inch A.A. mounting and one for each group of 40mm. A.A. guns; the torpedo tubes were removed; lattice replaced the tripod masts; and ABC defence measures were incorporated.

Displacement: 11,550/14,930 tons.
Dimensions: 579(pp) 613½(oa) × 63¼ (69 over bulges) × 19/21 feet.
Machinery: Four Admiralty 3-drum boilers; four shafts; Parsons geared turbines, S.H.P. 80,000 = 32 knots; O.F. 2,260 tons.
Protection: Main belt 3–4½ inches, deck 2 inches.   Turrets 1–2½ inches, barbettes 1 inch, DCT's ½ inch.   Externally bulged.
Armament: Twelve 6-inch (4 × 3), eight 4-inch A.A. (4 × 2), twelve 40mm. A.A. (6 × 2) guns.
Complement: 710.

Pt. No.	Name	Builder	Laid down	Launched	Completed	Disposition
C.35	BELFAST	Harland & Wolff ...	10.12.36	17. 3.38	3. 8.39	Portsmouth reserve

Machinery contract: Engined by builder.

115

Except for the modernisation of the light A.A. armament *Babur* has been little altered, and the twin 40mm. mountings are disposed abaft "B" turret and on each side amidships between the funnels, while the single mountings are in the bridge wings and abreast the after superstructure.

Pt. No.	Name	Builder	Laid down	Launched	Completed	Disposition
C.84	BABUR (ex-*Diadem*) ...	Hawthorn Leslie ...	15.12.39	26. 8.42	6. 1.44	Pakistani Navy (1956)

Machinery contracts: Engined by builder.

" *Dido* " class (second group): **BABUR**

This vessel formed one of the two groups of light cruisers authorised under the 1937 Re-armament and subsequent programmes, which comprised the larger "Fiji" class (see following page) and the smaller "Dido" class.

The "Dido" class were generally modelled on the "Arethusa" class (interposed between the "Leander" and "Southampton" classes) and sought to improve on the mixed calibres of the latter (six 6-inch L.A. and four 4-inch A.A. guns) by having a ten-gun D.P. main battery, and opinion was divided over whether, or not, they proved superior. Only the eleven units of the first group were designed to mount ten 5·25-inch guns and, of these, four were war losses, and the remainder were all scrapped.

The second group of five vessels omitted "Q" twin 5·25-inch turret and shipped a quadruple light A.A. mounting in lieu (a modification later extended to all surviving units of the first group during and after the war), and were easily distinguished by their upright masts and funnels, those in the first group being raked. Of the vessels of the second group one was a war loss and three (including two loaned to the Royal New Zealand Navy) were scrapped.

The BABUR has remained largely unaltered except that the former mixed light A.A. armament has been replaced by a uniform battery of 40mm. guns with local directors for the twin mountings.

Displacement: 5,900/7,560 tons.

Dimensions: 485(pp) 512(oa) × 50½ × 15/18½ feet.

Machinery: Four Admiralty 3-drum boilers; four shafts; Parsons geared turbines, S.H.P. 62,000 = 32 knots; O.F 1,100 tons.

Protection: Main belt ¾ (ends)–1 (over steering gear)–3 (amid) inches closed by bulkheads 1 inch, complete deck 1 (amid and over steering gear)–2 (abreast magazines) inches. Turrets 1–2 inches, barbettes ½–1 inch. DCT 1 inch.

Armament: Eight 5·25-inch D.P. (4×2), twelve 40mm. A.A. (3×2 & 6×1) guns; six 21-inch (2×3) T.T.

Complement: 588.

Mysore with new HA/LA.DCTs forward, lattice masts, remodelled bridge, former hangars cnt down, and removed. The cranes were previously stepped abreast the after funnel and stowed forward, but one was removed and the other repositioned on the centre line abaft the fore funnel and stowed aft, while the former flight deck is now used for boat stowage.

Pt. No.	Name	Builder	Laid down	Launched	Completed	Disposition
C.60	MYSORE (ex-*Nigeria*) ...	Vickers-Armstrongs (Tyne)	8. 2.38	18. 7.39	20. 9.40	Indian Navy (1957)

Machinery contracts: Engined by Parsons.

"Fiji" class: **MYSORE**

Further restrictive treaties limited these vessels to 8,000 tons and 6-inch guns, but they nevertheless emerged as most combatant diminutives of the "Southampton" class with a thinner but more extensive waterline belt and stronger deck protection. With them the box citadel protection of magazines was abandoned. The main belt was extended fore and aft to enclose the end barbettes, and the armoured deck was taken right across the hull over the magazines to join with the upper edge of the belt. Except for " Y " barbette (whose base was formed by the armoured deck) the remainder had 1-inch armoured bases connected by 1-inch armoured tubes to the crowns of the magazines.

While the first eight units were completed to the original design, this was modified for the last three which were completed without "X" turret or aircraft and an enhanced and built-in light A.A. armament; a modification later extended to the earlier vessels during, and after, the Second World War. Two vessels were war losses, two—the Peruvian Navy CORONEL BOLOGNESI (ex-*Ceylon*) and the ALMIRANTE GRAU (ex-*Newfoundland*)—were sold, and six (including one vessel transferred to the Royal Canadian Navy) were scrapped.

The MYSORE retained " X " turret until after the war when, in the course of a refit (1954-57), it was removed and the mixed light A.A. armament replaced by a uniform battery of 40mm. A.A. guns; additions were made to the bridge-work, the forebridge enclosed, and the hangars cut down in height; modern HA.DCT's replaced the original directors; the T.T. were removed; lattice replaced tripod masts; and ABC defence measures were incorporated.

Displacement: 8,700/11,040 tons.

Dimensions: 538(pp) 555½(oa) × 62 × 17½/21 feet.

Machinery: Four Admiralty 3-drum boilers; four shafts; Parsons geared turbines, S.H.P. 72,500=31½ knots; O.F, 1,620 tons.

Protection: Main belt 3¼–3½ (abreast magazines) inches closed by bulkheads 2 inches, complete deck 2 inches. Belt 1½ inches and deck 1¼ inches over steering gear. Turrets 1–2 inches, barbettes 1–2 inches, DCT ½ inch.

Armament: Nine 6-inch (3 × 3), eight 4-inch A.A. (4 × 2), twelve 40mm. A.A. (5 × 2 and 2 × 1) guns.

Complement: 800.

A.W. VESSELS

"R" class: RAJPUT, RANA, RANJIT

These standard destroyers have remained largely unaltered and outside of providing gunfire for troops ashore, could otherwise render little useful active service. They still possess a good turn of speed which could be utilised for tactical training or as fast transports for limited numbers of troops. Their T.T. were removed in 1963 and they are now too old for any modernisation to be put in hand.

Displacement: 1,725/2,425 tons.

Dimensions: $339\frac{1}{2}$(pp) $358\frac{1}{4}$(oa) $\times 35\frac{3}{4} \times 10/12$ feet.

Machinery: Two Admiralty 3-drum boilers; two shafts; Parsons geared turbines, S.H.P. $40,000 = 36\frac{3}{4}/31\frac{1}{4}$ knots; O.F. 490 tons.

Armament: Four 4·7-inch (4×1), four 2-pounder A.A. (1×4), four 40mm. A.A. (4×1) guns.

Complement: 240.

Pt. No.	Name	Builder	Laid down	Launched	Completed	Disposition
D.209	RAJPUT (ex-*Rotherham*) ...	Clydebank	10. 4.41	21. 3.42	16.11.42	Indian Navy (1949), 11th Destroyer Squadron
D.115	RANA (ex-*Raider*) ...	Cammell Laird ...	16. 4.41	1. 4.42	16.11.42	Indian Navy (1949), 11th Destroyer Squadron
D.141	RANJIT (ex-*Redoubt*) ...	Clydebank	19. 6.41	2. 5.42	1.10.42	Indian Navy (1949), 11th Destroyer Squadron

Machinery contracts: All engined by builders.

Finisterre (since scrapped) with twin STAAG mountings aft. Two twin 40mm. mountings between the T.T. had been removed and a single 40mm. gun on the quarterdeck replaced by an A/S mortar.

Camperdown with STAAG mountings replaced by twin 40mm. A.A. and type 283 radar. Originally a 4-inch HA/LA gun was mounted abaft the funnel, but was replaced by two 40mm. guns.

A.W. VESSELS

Anzac, without twin STAAG mountings aft and T.T., has since had the remaining 40mm. guns, "B" turret and the HA/LA.DCT removed as a training ship.

Pt. No.	Name	Builder	Laid down	Launched	Completed	Disposition
D.32	CAMPERDOWN	Fairfield	30.10.42	8. 2.44	18. 6.43	Devonport for disposal
D.84	SAINTES	Hawthorn Leslie ...	8. 6.43	19. 7.44	27. 9.46	Rosyth, static training ship
D.77	TRAFALGAR	Swan Hunter	15. 2.43	12. 1.44	23. 7.45	Portsmouth for disposal
161	BADR ... ... (ex-*Gabbard*)	Swan Hunter	2. 2.44	16. 3.45	10.12.46	Pakistani Navy (1957)
163	KHAIBAR (ex-*Cadiz*) ...	Fairfield	10. 5.43	16. 9.44	12. 4.46	Pakistani Navy (1957)
D.59	ANZAC	H.M.A. Dockyard (Williamstown)	23. 9.46	20. 8.48	22. 3.51	Royal Australian Navy
D.37	TOBRUK	Cockatoo	5. 8.46	20.12.47	8. 5.50	Royal Australian Navy
D.43	MATAPAN...	Clydebank	11. 3.44	30. 4.45	5. 9.47	Devonport reserve

Machinery contracts: Badr and Trafalgar engined by Wallsend Slipway; others by builders.

"Battle" class: First group **BADR, CAMPERDOWN, KHAIBAR, SAINTES, TRAFALGAR.** *Second group* **ANZAC, MATAPAN, TOBRUK.**

This class was a complete break from the standard war design. Intended for Pacific operations they were given a greater radius of action and a powerful light A.A. armament to supplement their main D.P. guns which were concentrated forward in two twin turrets.

The second group (twenty-four vessels) differed from the first group (sixteen vessels) in that: (*a*) they had a single 4·5-inch gun abaft the funnel instead of a 4-inch (later replaced by two single 40mm. A.A.) for starshell illuminants; (*b*) a more advanced mark of HA/LA.DCT was fitted on the bridge; (*c*) the single 40mm. A.A. guns before the bridge and on the quarterdeck were omitted, and only one twin 40mm. A.A. mounting was placed between the T.T.; and (*d*) had quintuple as opposed to quadruple T.T.

The Royal Australian Navy vessels also belonged to the second group, but had a deckhouse abaft the funnel with the 40mm. A.A. guns mounted over it (they never shipped the additional 4·5-inch gun), had their 4·5-inch guns in twin fully automatic turrets, and had funnel caps added. The ANZAC has had " B " turret, the DCT, all twin 40mm. mountings, and the T.T. removed as a training vessel, while temporary deckhouses have been added on the forward and after shelter decks.

Of the forty units of this class, sixteen were cancelled (all second group—of which nine had been launched); thirteen were scrapped (ten first and three second group); three of the first group—Pakistani Navy BADR (ex-*Gabbard*) and KHAIBAR (ex-*Cadiz*); and Iranian ARTEMIS (ex-*Sluys*)—were sold; and four (all second group) were converted to aircraft direction vessels (see p. 22).

Displacement: First group 2,325/3,360 tons except *R.A.N. vessels* 2,440/3,450 tons, *second group* 2,480/3,375 tons.

Dimensions: 355(pp) 379(oa) × 40¼ except *R.A.N. vessels* 41 × 10½/12¾ except *R.A.N. vessels* 13½ feet.

Machinery: Two Admiralty 3-drum boilers (400 lb/in²); two shafts; Parsons geared turbines, S.H.P. 50,000 = 35¾/31 knots; O.F. 680 tons.

Armament: Four except *Matapan* five 4·5-inch D.P. (2 × 2 and 1 × 1), *Matapan* eight/*first group* nine/*R.A.N. vessels* ten 40mm. A.A. (3 × 2 and 2 × 1: 2 × 2 and 5 × 1: 3 × 2 and 4 × 1) guns; eight except *second group* ten 21-inch (2 × 4/5) T.T.; one A/S mortar (Squid).

Complement: 247 except *Pakistani Navy vessels* 270, *R.A.N. vessels* 290, and *Matapan* 232.

A.W. VESSELS

Decoy fitted with Seacat launcher abaft second funnel (now removed), single 40 mm. A.A. in bridge wings, and new HA/LA. DCT on bridge.

Pt. No.	Name	Builder	Laid down	Launched	Completed	Disposition
D.108	DAINTY	White	17.12.45	16. 8.50	26. 2.53	Home
D.05	DARING	Swan Hunter	29. 9.45	10. 8.49	8. 3.52	Home, for disposal
D.106	DECOY (ex-*Dragon*) ...	Yarrow	22. 9.46	29. 3.49	28. 4.53	1st Division Western Fleet
D.114	DEFENDER (ex-*Dogstar*)...	Stephen	22. 3.49	27. 7.50	5.12.52	Far East
D.119	DELIGHT (ex-*Disdain*, ex-*Ypres*)	Fairfield	5. 9.46	21.12.50	9.10.53	1st Destroyer Squadron, for disposal
D.35	DIAMOND	Clydebank	15. 3.49	14. 6.50	21. 2.52	Home
D.126	DIANA (ex-*Druid*) ...	Yarrow	3. 4.47	8. 5.52	19. 3.54	Far East
D.154	DUCHESS	Thornycroft	2. 7.48	9. 4.51	23.10.52	Royal Australian Navy (1964), 2nd Destroyer Squadron
D.11	VAMPIRE	Cockatoo	1. 7.52	27.10.56	23. 6.59	Royal Australian Navy, 2nd Destroyer Squadron
D.08	VENDETTA	H.M.A. Dockyard (Williamstown)	4. 7.59	3. 5.54	26.11.58	Royal Australian Navy, 2nd Destroyer Squadron

Machinery contracts: Daring engined by Wallsend Slipway, all others by builders.

"Daring" class: **DAINTY, DARING, DECOY, DEFENDER, DELIGHT, DIAMOND, DIANA, DUCHESS, VAMPIRE, VENDETTA**

The last destroyers built for the Royal Navy, these vessels represented the culmination of development with this type, but their size and cost mitigated against their otherwise overall excellence.

All laid down after the Second World War as a further expansion of the "Battle" class, eight Royal Navy and one Royal Australian Navy units were cancelled, and another R.A.N. vessel—the VOYAGER—was lost by collision in 1964.

The design as cast included two banks of T.T. and five twin 40mm. A.A. mountings, but two of the latter—positioned at the fore end of the after shelter deck—were supressed at an early stage and replaced by an HA.DCT. The 4·5-inch guns were mounted in fully automatic twin turrets controlled by a radar-fitted combined HA/LA.DCT on the bridge. While four R.N. vessels had the usual 220V. d.c. electric supply, a 440V. a.c. supply was provided in DECOY, DIAMOND, DIANA, and DUCHESS, and the steam conditions were the highest used by the R.N. at the time.

The after bank of T.T. was removed from the R.N. vessels in 1958–59, and the after shelter deck extended forward, and the forward bank also from four units during 1963–64. It was originally intended in 1963 to fit the a.c. vessels with a quadruple Seacat launcher in place of the after twin 40mm. A.A. mounting—which was removed—but this modification was not finally implemented, and only the DECOY was so temporarily fitted.

The R.A.N. vessels were modified on generally similar lines to those in the R.N., except that the after shelter deck has also been extended aft to enclose the A/S mortar, and the bridge structure enlarged. It was intended to fit the Ikara A/S missile to these ships, which would have necessitated the removal of the after 4.5-inch turret, but the decision was subsequently reversed owing to the requirement to retain ships capable of providing gunfire support for troops ashore.

Displacement: 2,800/3,600 tons.

Dimensions: 366(pp) 390 except *R.A.N. vessels* 388½(oa) × 43 × 12¾/14½ feet.

Machinery: Two Foster Wheeler except *Daring, Decoy, Delight* and *Diana* Babcock & Wilcox boilers (650 lb/in² at 850°F); two shafts; Parsons except *Decoy, Diana* and *R.A.N. vessels* English Electric geared turbines, S.H.P. 54,000 = 34¾/30½ knots; O.F. 574 tons.

Armament: Six 4·5-inch D.P. (3 × 2), two except *Dainty, Daring, Defender, Delight, Vampire & Vendetta* six 40mm. A.A. (2 × 1: 3 × 2) guns; five 21-inch (1 × 5) T.T. (none in *Dainty, Daring, Defender* and *Delight*); one A/S mortar (Squid except *R.A.N. vessels* Limbo).

Complement: 295 except *Daring & Diamond* 308 and *R.A.N. vessels* 327.

Right: *Duchess* was transferred to the Royal Australian Navy to replace the lost *Voyager*. A new HA/LA. DCT has been fitted on the bridge, with only single 40 mm. A.A. guns in the wings.

Left: An additional HA. DCT has been added before the after funnel in *Vendetta* and there are now two twin 40 mm. A.A. mountings aft but only single guns in the bridge wings.   Compare original HA/LA. DCT on bridge with *Duchess* above.

A.W. VESSELS

The *Chiddingfold*—now the Indian *Ganga*—has been little altered since she was first completed for the Royal Navy except that single 40mm. A.A. have replaced the single 20mm. A.A. guns in the bridge wings, the searchlight removed, and altered pennant numbers have been painted-up together with squadron markings on the funnel.

Pt. No.	Name	Builder	Laid down	Launched	Completed	Disposition
D.94	GANGA (ex-*Chiddingfold*)	Scotts	1. 3.40	10. 3.41	16.10.41	Indian Navy (1953), 11th Destroyer Squadron
D.92	GODAVARI (ex-*Bedale*) ...	Hawthorn Leslie ...	25. 5.40	23. 7.41	9. 5.42	Indian Navy (1953), 11th Destroyer Squadron
D.93	GOMATI (ex-*Lamerton*) ...	Swan Hunter	10. 4.40	14.12.40	16. 8.41	Indian Navy (1953), 11th Destroyer Squadron

Machinery contracts: Gomati engined by Wallsend Slipway, others by builders.

"*Hunt*" *class* (*type II*): GANGA, GODAVARI, GOMATI

This class introduced the escort destroyer category to the Royal Navy and were basically small destroyers which sacrificed speed, radius, and torpedo tubes, and shipped an all-A.A. gun armament. They rendered sterling service during the Second World War providing anti-aircraft and anti-submarine cover for fleets and convoys, and anticipated—to a marked degree—the future trend of the fusion between fleet destroyers and escort vessels.

As completed they comprised four groups (types I–IV) with slight differences in armament, and both during and after the war proved popular with the smaller navies to which no less than thirty were transferred or sold. Of the twenty vessels of type I, four were war losses; four—Israeli Navy HAIFA (ex-Egyptian *Ibrahim-el-Awal*, ex-*Ali-el-Kebir*, ex-Chinese *Lin Fu*, ex-R.N. *Mendip*), Egyptian Navy ALI-EL-KEBIR (ex-*Ibrahim-el-Awal*, ex-*Cottesmore*), and Equadorian Navy PRESIDENTE VELASCO YBARRA (ex-*Meynell*) and PRESIDENTE ALFARO (ex-*Quantock*)—were sold; and eleven were scrapped and one wrecked en-route to the shipbreakers. Of the thirty-six vessels of type II eight were war losses (including one unit transferred to the Polish Navy); thirteen—Royal Norwegian Navy ARENDAL (ex-*Badsworth*—since scrapped), HAUGESUND (ex-*Beaufort*), and TROMSO (ex-*Zetland*); Royal Danish Navy ESBERN SNARE (ex-*Blackmore*), ROLF KRAKE (ex-*Calpe*), and VALDEMAR SEJR (ex-*Exmoor* (ii), ex-*Burton*—last two since scrapped); Royal Hellenic Navy AIGAION (ex-*Lauderdale*), KRITI (ex-*Hursley*), and THERMISTOKLES (ex-*Braham*—all since scrapped); West German Navy GNEISENAU (ex-*Oakley* (ii), ex-*Tickham*); and Indian Navy GANGA (ex-*Chiddingfold*), GODAVARI (ex-*Bedale*), and GOMATI (ex-*Lamerton*)—were sold; one—the BROCKELSBY—disarmed for service as a trials vessel is awaiting disposal; and fourteen were scrapped. Of the twenty-eight vessels of type III eleven were war losses (including three units transferred to the Royal Hellenic, Royal Norwegian, and French navies); eight—Royal Hellenic Navy ADRIAS (ex-*Tanatside*), HASTINGS (ex-*Catterick*), KANARIS (ex-*Hatherleigh*), MIAOULIS (ex-*Modbury*), and PINDOS (ex-*Bolebroke*—all since scrapped); Royal Norwegian Navy NARVIK (ex-*Glaisdale*—since scrapped); and West German Navy BROMMY (ex-*Eggesford*) and RAULE (ex-*Albrighton*)—were sold; and nine were scrapped. Both vessels of type IV were also scrapped.

Displacement: 1,050/1,610 tons.
Dimensions: 264¼(pp) × 282½(oa) × 31½ × 7¾/10 feet.
Machinery: Two Admiralty 3-drum boilers; two shafts; Parsons geared turbines, S.H.P. 19,000=25 knots; O.F. 280 tons.
Armament: Six 4-inch A.A. (3×2), four 2-pounder A.A. (1×4), two 40mm. A.A. (2×1) guns.
Complement: 191.

A.W. VESSELS

Minor landing craft: **TWO** LCA, **THIRTY-EIGHT** LCVP, **TWO** LCR, **ONE** LCN, **EIGHTEEN** LCP(L), **SEVENTEEN** LCM(6), **THREE** LCM(7), **ELEVEN** LCM(8), **FOURTEEN** LCM(9) and **TWELVE** RPL

While the bulk of minor landing craft are still composed of units constructed during the Second World War, a small amount of unreported new construction has also been undertaken.

The present British total is made-up of two LCA(1); thirty-eight LCA(2)—now classed as LCVP; two LCR and one LCN (all ex-LCA); one LCP(L)(1), one LCP(L)(2), and two LCP(L)(3); three LCM(7); and fourteen LCM(9). All craft except the LCM's are of wood construction, and post-war construction included the LCVP, LCP(L)(2) and (3), LCM(9) and the RPL for the British Army.

The LCVP are generally similar to the LCA(1) except that they have a bow ramp and have the coxun's position moved aft from the starboard side forward. Bullet-proof plating is fixed along the sides abreast the troop space and the engine room, on deck over the engine room, and completely encloses the coxun's shelter. No details are available for the LCP(L)(2) and (3) except that one unit is powered by a gas turbine. The LCM(9) were built for the assault ships FEARLESS and INTREPID, and have a bullet-proof wheelhouse, are equipped with radar, and fitted with Kort nozzle rudders to improve manoeuvrability. The RPL was built for cargo transfer from ship to shore, general harbour work, and limited coastal voyages. An accommodation block is provided aft for the crew which makes them more suitable for detached work than the naval LCM.

The production series of LCM(9) differ from the two prototypes in that the bow ramp was lengthened and modified resulting in the coxun's position being raised.

Post-war development with hydrofoil craft—which particularly lends itself to the fast approach now required by assault craft—has been completely neglected by the Royal Navy, but a combined services team is evaluating the hovercraft for amphibious warfare and other roles. In Australia there is considerable activity in minor landing craft both for their own account and the Royal Malaysian Navy. Planned new construction included fourteen LCP (all for the R.Mal.N.), seventeen LCM(6) (four for the R.Mal.N.), and eleven LCM(8), while an LCVP was purchased from Hong Kong in 1965.

The military loads are: *LCVP* one Land Rover and light gun or 36 troops; *LCM*(6) one 34-ton tank or 120 troops; *LCM*(7) one 35/40-ton tank; *LCM*(8) one 55-ton tank; *LCM*(9) two 50-ton tanks; and *RPL* one 55-ton tank.

LCA(1): 9/13½ tons; 38¾(pp) 41½(oa)×10×1/2¼ feet; two shafts; Ford petrol motors, B.H.P. 130=10/6 knots; complement 4+36 troops.

LCR and LCN: Generally similar to LCA(1) except in the matter of equipment.

LCVP: 11½/16½ tons; 40(pp) 43(oa)×10×1½/2½ feet; two shafts; 6-cyl. Foden diesel engines, B.H.P. 130=10/6 knots; complement 4+35 troops or Land Rover and light gun.

LCVP (R.A.N.): 3½ tons.

LCP(L)(1): 6½/10¾ tons; 36¾(oa)×10¾×2½/3½ feet; two shafts; Gray diesel engines, B.H.P. 225=12 knots; complement 3+25 troops.

LCP(L)(2) and (3): Generally similar to LCP(L)(1).

LCP (R.Mal.N.): 18½ tons; 48(oa)×14×3 feet; two shafts; Cummins diesel engines, B.H.P. 400=16 knots; one 20mm. A.A. gun; complment 4.

LCM(6) *(R.A.N.* and *R.Mal.N.):* 55½ tons; 56(oa)×14×3½/4½ feet; two shafts; 6-cyl. General Motors diesel engines, B.H.P. 330=9 knots; two 20mm. A.A. (2×1) guns; complement 4.

LCM(7): 28/63 tons; 51¾(pp) 60¼(oa)×16×3¾ feet; two shafts; Gray diesel engines, B.H.P. 290=9¾ knots; complement 6.

LCM(8) *(R.A.N.):* 60/115 tons; 73¾(oa)×21×5¼ feet; two shafts; 6-cyl. General Motors diesel engines, B.H.P. 680=9 knots; complement 8.

LCM(9): 75/176 tons; 85(oa)×21½×5½ feet; two shafts; 6-cyl. Davey Paxman diesel engines, B.H.P. 550=10 knots; complement 8.

RPL: 61¾/130½ tons; 62¼(pp) 72¼(oa)×20½×4¾/6¾ feet; two shafts, 6-cyl. Rolls-Royce diesel engines, B.H.P. 870=9 knots; complement ..

Left: A loaded LCM(9) about to enter the dock compartment of the *Fearless,* which is flooded down and trimmed for the operation.

Right: The *Medway* RPL 12 is launched. These craft are manned by the R.C.T. and are disposed three in the U.K., one at Hong Kong, two in the Persian Gulf, one at Malta, and five at Singapore.

A.W. VESSELS

Name	Disposition
WHIMBREL (ex-NSC(E).1012) ...	Experimental vessel
LCT(4).4294 (ex-1294)	Indian Navy (1949)
LOKOJA (ex-LCT(4).1312) ...	Nigerian Navy (1965)
MRC.1015...	For disposal
MRC.1023...	For disposal
MRC.1097...	For disposal
MRC.1098...	For disposal
MRC.1119...	For disposal

Name	Disposition
MRC.1120... ... ... MRC.1413 (ex-LCT(E).413) ...	Malta
CANNA (ex-MRC.1100) ... MEDWAY (ex-MRC.1109) ... SIMBANG (ex-MRC.1110) ...	Singapore reserve, for disposal Singapore R.N.A.S. Singapore
ASUANTSI (ex-MRC.1122) ...	Ghanaian Navy (1965)
LSM(R).1 ... ... LSM(R).2	Indian Navy Indian Navy

Name	Disposition
LCT.(7) (ex-U.S.N. LSM.315) ... LCT.(7) (ex-U.S.N. LSM.319) ...	Australian Army Australian Army

Name	Disposition
LCT.(7) (ex-U.S.N. LSM.477) ... LCT.(7) (ex-U.S.N. LSM.547) ...	Australian Army Australian Army

Name	Disposition
BASTION (ex-LCT(8).4040) ... CITADEL (ex-LCT(8).4038) ... PORTCULLIS (ex-LCT(8).4044)	Zambia Government Malta Malta
AACHEN (ex-LCT(8).4062) ... ABBEVILLE (ex-LCT(8).4041) ... AGEDABIA (ex-LCT(8).4085) ... AGHEILA (ex-LCT(8).4002) ...	Ministry of Defence (Army) Ministry of Defence (Army) Ministry of Defence (Army) Ministry of Defence (Army)

Name	Disposition
AKYAB (ex-Rampart, ex-LCT(8).4037)	Ministry of Defence (Army)
ANDALNES (ex LCT(8).4097) ...	Ministry of Defence (Army)
ANTWERP (ex-LCT(8).4074) ...	Ministry of Defence (Army)
ARAKAN (ex-LCT(8).4164) ...	Ministry of Defence (Army)
ARDENNES (ex-LCT(8).4073) ...	Ministry of Defence (Army)
ARREZZO (ex-LCT(8).4128) ...	Ministry of Defence (Army)
ARROMANCHES (ex-LCT(8).4086)	Ministry of Defence (Army)
AUDEMER (ex-LCT(8).4061) ...	Ministry of Defence (Army)

Major landing craft: **TWO** LCT(4). **FOUR** LCT(7), **FIFTEEN** LCT(8), **TWO** LSM(R)

No major landing craft have been built for the Royal Navy since the close of the Second World War, and the numbers retained steadily continue to decline annually.

At the present the total is made up of two LCT(4) and fifteen LCT(8), while ten of the former have been converted to maintenance and repair craft (MRC), and a further unit is used for trials purposes. In addition there are seven LCT(8) in the Canadian Coastguard employed as Artic supply vessels. In Australia landing craft are operated by the Army (and not the Navy), and it is planned to replace the existing LCT(7)—now classed as LSM—by a new series of 250-ton LSM(L)(2).

The LCT(4) has a hinged bow ramp, the bridge and machinery arranged aft, and can stow about 300 tons d.w., while ramps were provided fore and aft in the LCT(7) and the bridge offset to starboard. The larger LCT(8) were provided with bow doors enclosing the ramp forward but, like the earlier marks, the only weather protection to the open tank deck was by tarpaulins spread over bars.

The military loads are: LCT(4) six 40-ton tanks; LCT(7) three 40-ton tanks and 54 troops; LCT(8) eight 30-ton tanks and 42 troops. The ABBEVILLE, AYKAB, and BASTION now have lattice masts, ABBEVILLE and AYKAB have a deckhouse on the fo'c'sle to enclose a lengthened bow ramp, AACHEN has twin funnels set abreast abaft the bridge together with a tall tripod mast, and AGHEILA has gravity davits forward of the bridge for minor landing craft. A pole foremast has been added in all, while the bridgework has been built-up in most. This type of craft is illustrated on p. 105.

The Indian Navy took delivery of two Polish-built LSM(R) from the U.S.S.R. early in 1967, which had been adapted from the standard LSM design.

LCT(4): 200/586 tons; 171(pp) $187\frac{1}{4}$(oa) $\times 38\frac{3}{4} \times 3\frac{3}{4}/4\frac{1}{4}$ feet; two shafts; Davey Paxman diesel engines, B.H.P. 920=10 knots; two 20mm. A.A. (2×1) guns in *Lokoja* only; complement 12 except *Lokoja* 13.

LCT(7), LSM: 513/900 tons; 190(pp) $203\frac{1}{2}$(oa) $\times 34\frac{1}{2} \times 3\frac{1}{2}/7$ feet; two shafts; General Motors diesel engines, B.H.P. 2,800=$13\frac{1}{2}$ knots; six 20mm. A.A. (6×1) guns; complement 52.

LCT(8): 657/895 tons; 225(pp) $231\frac{1}{4}$(oa) $\times 39 \times 3\frac{3}{4}/5$ feet; two shafts; Davey Paxman diesel engines (two/shaft), B.H.P. 2,800=12 knots; complement 33/37.

LSM(L)(2): 250 tons.

LSM(R): 900 tons; ...(pp) 226 $\times 32\frac{1}{4} \times 8$ feet; two shafts, diesel engines B.H.P. 2,000=12 knots; two 57mm. A.A. (1×2) guns, rockets; complement ...

Above: *MRC.1015.* **Left:** *MRC.1098:* both former LCT(4) converted to maintenance and repair craft.

Right: LS(L) *Sir Bedivere* (top) and *Sir Tristram* (bottom).

[Blocks courtesy *Naval Record.*

A.W. VESSELS

Striker with additional LCAs forward and docking bridge at head of samson posts

Pt. No.	Name	Builder	Launched
L.3003	ANZIO	Vickers-Armstrongs (Tyne)	8. 6.45
L.3016	DIEPPE	Hawthorn Leslie ...	14.12.44
L.3043	MESSINA	Scotts	27. 4.45
L.3516	STRIKER	Canadian Yarrow ...	15. 2.45
L.3532	ZEEBRUGGE ...		00.00.45
L.3011	MAGAR	Harland & Wolff ...	12. 2.45
L.3009	REGINALD KERR...	Harland & Wolff ...	30.12.44
L.3525	EMPIRE GUILLEMOT (ex-*Walcheren*)	Davie Sbdg. ...	29. 8.45

Pt. No.	Name	Builder	Launched
L.3523	EMPIRE GULL ... (ex-*Trouncer*)	Davie Sbdg. ...	9. 7.45
L.3520	EMPIRE PETREL ... (ex-*Thruster*)	Canadian Vickers ...	1. 5.45
L.3033	EMPIRE SHEARWATER	Pickersgill	11. 2.45
L.3504	EMPIRE TERN ... (ex-*Pursuer*)	Canadian Vickers ...	3.11.44

Machinery contracts: Dieppe engined by North Eastern Marine; *Empire Guillemot* and *Empire Gull* by Canadian Pacific Railways; *Empire Shearwater* by George Clark, *Striker* by Dominion Bridge; *Messina* by Craigs; and others by builders.

138

LST(3): ANZIO, DIEPPE, MAGAR, MESSINA, STRIKER, ZEEBRUGGE

After early experience with mercantile conversions and a rather elaborate LST(1) in 1941–42, the Royal Navy prepared an outline plan of an Atlantic TLC which was modified and put into quantity production in the United States as the LST(2).

As the result of disagreement over the allocation of LST(2)'s between the Royal and United States navies, the former embarked on their own series—the LST(3)—which were generally similar to the LST(2) but slightly altered and enlarged to take standard steam reciprocating machinery as this was the only propulsion plant available in any quantity. The bridge and machinery were arranged aft—with the engine rooms forward of the boiler rooms—and forward was the tank deck closed by a bow ramp and doors. A further ramp connected the tank deck with the upper deck, aft of which was a hatch through which general cargo could be worked when tanks were not carried. The troop accommodation was arranged in wing compartments flanking the tank deck.

A total of one hundred and twenty-six LST(3)'s were planned: forty-five to be built in U.K. yards (numbered 3001 up), and seventy-one in Canadian yards (numbered 3501 up). Of these, forty-four were cancelled; ten were completed as mercnatile vessels or barges; ten—Royal Hellenic Navy ACHELOOS, ALFIOS, ALIAKMON, AXIOS, PINIOS and STRYMON (ex-Nos. 3503, 3020, 3002, 3007, 3506 and 3502—all since scrapped); Royal Australian Navy LABUAN, LAE and TARAKAN (ex-Nos. 3501, 3035 and 3017—all since lost or scrapped); and the Indian Navy MAGAR (ex-No. 3011)—were transferred, and seven others were sold-out commercially (four since scrapped); seven were transferred to the Ministry of Defence (Army) (three since scrapped and three sold-out commercially), while the Ministry of Transport undertook the management of a further twelve (seven since scrapped) on their behalf; and one was wrecked and sixteen scrapped.

Of the remaining vessels LOFOTEN was converted to a helicopter carrier, NARVIK and STALKER to submarine support vessels, and TRACKER to a boom and net carrier, and are listed on later pages. The ANZIO, MESSINA, and STRIKER are awaiting disposal at Portsmouth, DIEPPE is in reserve at Devonport, and ZEEBRUGGE—awaiting disposal—is used as an accommodation ship at Devonport.

The military load comprised fifteen 40-ton tanks in the tank deck, fourteen 3-ton lorries deck-stowed, and 168 troops. Post-war six LCA's each stowed under gravity davits, were added on the foredeck, and two additional LCA's replaced the boats originally carried abreast the funnel.

2,140/4,820 tons except *Messina* 2,255/4,930 tons; 330(pp) 345¾(oa × 54 × 8¼ feet; two Admiralty 3-drum boilers (225 lb/in²); two shafts; reciprocating (VTE—cyl. 18½″:31″:38½″(2) × 30″ stroke), I.H.P. 5,500 = 13 knots; O.F. 1,400 tons. Four except *Magar* two 40mm. A.A. (2/4 × 1), six 20mm. A.A. (2 × 2 and 2 × 1—in *Magar* only) guns; complement 105 except *Magar* 180.

A.W. VESSELS

LS(L) *Sir Lancelot* is managed by the British India Steam Navigation Co. for the Ministry of Transport. She is painted in traditional troopship colours: white hull with blue band; and buff funnel, masts, and cranes.

Pt. No.	Name	Builder	Laid down	Launched	Completed	Disposition
	SIR LANCELOT	Fairfield	29. 6.62	25. 6.63	18. 1.64	Ministry of Defence (Army)
	SIR BEDIVERE	Hawthorn Leslie ...	28.10.65	20. 7.66	17. 5.67	Ministry of Defence (Army)
	SIR GALAHAD	Stephen	22. 2.65	19. 4.66	00.11.66	Ministry of Defence (Army)
	SIR GERAINT	Stephen ...	21. 2.65	26. 1.67	12. 7.67	Ministry of Defence (Army)
	SIR PERCIVALE	Hawthorn Leslie ...	27. 7.66	4.10.67	22. 3.68	Ministry of Defence (Army)
	SIR TRISTRAM	Hawthorn Leslie ...	14. 3.66	12.12.66	00. 9.67	Ministry of Defence (Army)

Machinery contracts: All engined by Mirrlees National except *Sir Lancelot* by Denny.

LS(L)s

M.O.D. (Army) type: **SIR BEDIVERE, SIR GALAHAD, SIR GERAINT, SIR LANCELOT, SIR PERCIVALE, SIR TRISTRAM**

Multi-purpose vessels designed to replace the ageing LST(3)'s used by the Ministry of Defence (Army) for inter-theatre movements of freight, vehicles, and troops.

As military cargoes are not necessarily restricted to the commercial trade routes with port facilities they were required to be able to beach. The tank deck runs the whole length of the hull and is closed at both ends by ramps. Forward of the bridge the tank deck is twice as wide as the section running to the stern, and the crown of the deck projects above the upper deck forming a trunk between the poop and fo'c'sle. The trunk deck area is increased by extensions on each side so that greater parking space is available for deck-stowed vehicles, and is connected by two ramps to the tank deck.

Four 39-ton pontoons measuring $60 \times 24 \times 4\frac{3}{4}$ feet (each made up of nine sections) are normally carried, vertically stowed two a side, and can carry 68 tons d.w. Four Harbourmaster outboard units are provided enabling two to be powered, if so required, or the pontoons can be joined end-to-end to provide a causeway up to 240 feet long between ship and shore enabling non-waterproofed behicles to be landed.

The military load is composed of sixteen 50-ton tanks, twenty-five 3-ton and six $\frac{1}{4}$-ton lorries, 402 troops, 60 tons of cargo, 50 tons of petrol, 50 tons of aircraft fuel, and 30 tons of ammunition. A landing pad is provided aft for helicopters, which can also fly-off from the forward deck park. The load is, of course, infinitely variable, and the height of the tank deck is sufficient to accommodate such bulky military items as radar trailers, mobile cranes, helicopters, etc. If not used for vehicles the deck park can accommodate six LCA's and/or additional pontoon sections. To aid beaching there is a 400 S.H.P. electric powered bow thrust unit, and the water ballast—totalling 1,200 tons—is handled by pumps totalling 560 tons/hour capacity. The last five have flush upper decks to facilitate handling vehicles.

Although not normally armed, two Army type mobile 40mm. A.A. guns can be shipped on platforms forward. While these vessels are not warships they would provide valuable re-inforcement to amphibious warfare forces in times of emergency in the follow-up role once the initial assault has been mounted.

Displacement: 5,560 tons (*ca.* 6,760 tons ballasted down).
Dimensions: $366\frac{1}{4}$(pp) $412\frac{3}{4}$(oa) $\times 58 \times 12\frac{3}{4}$ feet.
Machinery: Two shafts; 10-cyl. Mirrlees diesel engines, B.H.P. 9,400, except *Sir Lancelot* 12-cyl. Sulzer diesel engines, B.H.P. 8,250=17 knots; O.F. 600 tons.
Armament: Two 40mm. A.A. (2×1) guns.
Complement: 69+402 troops.

141

MINESWEEPING & SURVEYING VESSELS

" *Bathurst* " *class:* INVERELL, KIAMA, STAWELL, WAGGA

This class was the Australian variant of the British "Bangor" class (which received either turbine, reciprocating, or diesel machinery) and were primarily intended for wire sweeping. All the Australian-built vessels were, however, reciprocating engined and were frequently used—and fitted—as an'i-submarine escorts.

Of the original sixty-three units in this class, three were cancelled (all for the Royal Indian Navy); four were war losses; twenty—the Royal Indian Navy BENGAL, BOMBAY, MADRAS and PUNJAB (all since scrapped); the Royal New Zealand Navy ECCHUCA (since scrapped), INVERELL, KAIMA and STAWELL; Turkish Navy ALANYA (ex-*Broome*), AMASRA (ex-*Pirie*), ANTALYA (ex-*Geraldton*), AYANCIK (ex-*Launceston*), and AYVALIK (ex-*Gawler* —the last two since scrapped); and the Royal Netherlands Navy BATJAN (ex-*Lismore*), BOEROE (ex-*Toowoomba*), CERAM (ex-*Burnie*), TIDORE (ex-*Tamworth*—all since scrapped), while the AMBON (ex-*Cairns*), BANDA (ex-*Wollongong*), MOROTAI (ex-*Ipswich*) and TERNATE (ex-*Kalgoorlie*) later became the Indonesian Navy BANTENG, RADJAWALI (both since scrapped), HANG TUAH (since lost) and PATTI UNIS respectively—were sold, together with a further five sold-out commercially; twenty-seven were scrapped; and one has been immobilised as a training ship and another converted to a tank cleaning vessel.

Displacement: 815/1,025 tons.
Dimensions: 162(pp) 186(oa) × 31 × 8¼/9½ feet.
Machinery: Two Admiralty 3-drum boilers; two shafts; reciprocating (VTE—cyl. 13″:21″:34″ except *Stawell* 14″: 24″:37¾″×21″ stroke), I.H.P. 1,800=15½ knots; O.F. 170 tons.
Armament: One 4-inch, one 40 mm. A.A. gun.
Complement: 85.

Pt. No.	Name	Builder	Laid down	Launched	Completed	Disposition
M.233	INVERELL	Morts Dock	6.12.41	2. 5.42	22. 9.42	Royal New Zealand Navy (1952)
M.353	KIAMA	Evans Deakin	26.11.42	9. 7.43	26. 1.44	Royal New Zealand Navy (1952)
M.348	STAWELL	H.M.A. Dockyard (Williamstown)	18. 6.42	3. 4.43	23. 8.43	Royal New Zealand Navy (1952)
M.183	WAGGA	Morts Dock	9. 3.42	5. 7.42	23.12.42	Royal Australian Navy, for disposal

Machinery contracts: Stawell engined by Perry Engineering; others unknown.

MINESWEEPING & SURVEYING VESSELS

Typical of the "Algerine" class is the *Parakrama* (since scrapped) which was transferred to Ceylon. In some units an A/S mortar replaced the 4-inch gun forward.

Pt. No.	Name	Builder	Laid down	Launched	Completed	Disposition
M.229	COCKATRICE	Fleming & Ferguson ...	29.12.41	27.10.42	10. 4.43	Barrow for disposal
M.446	PLUTO	Port Arthur	18. 1.44	21.10.44	19. 4.45	Barrow for disposal
M.304	WATERWITCH	Lobnitz	15. 8.42	22. 4.43	6. 8.43	Barrow for disposal
M.106	ACUTE (ex-*Alert*)... ...	Harland & Wolff ...	24. 7.41	14. 4.42	30. 7.42	For disposal
M.298	RECRUIT	Harland & Wolff ...	20. 4.43	26.10.43	14. 1.44	Barrow for disposal
M.299	RIFLEMAN...	Harland & Wolff ...	20. 4.43	25.11.43	11. 2.44	Barrow for disposal

Machinery contracts: All engined by builders.

"*Algerine*" *class: First group*—**COCKATRICE, PLUTO, WATERWITCH.** *Second group*—**ACUTE, RECRUIT, RIFLEMAN**

These vessels followed the "Bangor" and "Bathurst" classes, and were enlarged so that they could accommodate sweep gear for both moored and influence mines. They proved most successful in service and were often used as anti-submarine escorts during the Second World War. Construction was carried out in both U.K. and Canadian yards, and while those built in the latter were all reciprocating engined, the former received either turbine or reciprocating machinery.

Of the one hundred and twenty-five units (twelve were retained by the Royal Canadian Navy) comprising this class, fifteen were cancelled; nine were war losses; nine were built for the United States Navy and were subsequently transferred to the Royal Navy; seventeen—Royal Belgian Navy ADRIEN DE GERLACHE (ex-*Liberty*—now hulked), DE BROUWER (ex-*Spanker*), DE MOOR (ex-*Rosario*), DUFOUR (i) (ex-*Fancy*—now hulked as NZADI), DUFOUR (ii) (ex-R.C.N. *Winnipeg*), GEORGES LECOINTE (i) (ex-*Cadmus*—now scrapped), GEORGES LECOINTE (ii) (ex-R.C.N. *Wallaceburg*) and JAN VAN HAVERBEKE (ex-*Ready*—now scrapped); Burmese YAN MYO AUNG (ex-*Mariner*, ex-*Kincardine*); Imperial Iranian Navy PALANG (ex-*Fly*); Italian ALABARDA (ex-*Eritrea*, ex-*Ammaraglio Magnahi*, ex-*Larne*—now scrapped); Nigerian Navy NIGERIA (ex-*Hare*—now scrapped); Singhalese Navy PARAKRAMA (ex-*Pickle*) and VIJAYA (ex-*Flying Fish*, ex-*Tillsonburg*—both since scrapped); South African Navy BLOEMFONTEIN (ex-*Rosamund*—expended as target) and PIETERMARITZBURG (ex-*Pelorus*—now used for training); and Royal Thai Navy PHOSAMPTON (ex-*Minstrel*)—were sold, together with a further two sold-out commercially (including one R.C.N.); four (all R.C.N.) were converted to surveying vessels and are listed on a later page; one (R.C.N.) was lost and sixty-three (including six R.C.N.) were scrapped.

The nine United States Navy vessels were returned to them at the end of the war, and of these five—Royal Hellenic Navy ARMATOLOS (ex-*Aries*), MACHITIS (ex-*Postillion*), NAVMACHOS (ex-*Lightfoot*), POLEMISTIS (ex-*Gozo*), and PYRPOLITIS (ex-*Arcturus*)—were sold, another was sold-out commercially, and the remaining three scrapped.

Post-war the 4-inch gun forward was replaced by an A/S mortar in some Royal Navy vessels so that they could still serve in the dual role as 'sweeper and escort.

Displacement: *First group* 1,040/1,335 tons, *second group* 1,000/1,245 tons.

Dimensions: 212½(pp) 225(oa) × 35½ × 11½ (*first group*) or 10½ (*second group*) feet.

Machinery: Two Admiralty 3-drum boilers (235 lb/in²); two shafts; *first group* reciprocating (VTE—cyl. 15″:25″:40″ × 24″ stroke, *second group* Parons geared turbines, I.H.P./S.H.P. 2,400/2,000 = 16½ knots; O.F. 235 tons.

Armament: One 4-inch (not in *Recruit, Rifleman* and *Waterwitch*), four 40mm. A.A. (4 × 1) guns; one A/S mortar (Squid—in *Recruit, Rifleman* and *Waterwitch* only).

Complement: 95.

MINESWEEPING & SURVEYING VESSELS

Pt. No.	Name	Builder	Launched
M.1104	ALVERTON* (ex-*Thames*, ex-*Alverton*)	Camper & Nicholson	18.11.52
M.1106	APPLETON ...	Goole Sbdg. ...	4. 9.52
M.1198	ASHTON* (ex-*Cheriton*)	White	5. 9.56
M.1149	BADMINTON (ex-*Ilston*)	Camper & Nicholson	14 10.54
M.1107	BEACHAMPTON*	Goole Sbdg. ...	29. 6.53
M.1199	BELTON*	Doig	3.10.55
M.1110	BILDESTON ...	Doig	9. 6.52
M.1112	BOULSTON* (ex-*Warsash*, ex-*Boulston*)	Richards I.W. ...	6.10.52
M.1132	BLAXTON... ...	Thornycroft ...	21. 6.55
M.1113	BRERETON* ...	Richards I.W. ...	14. 3.55
M.1114	BRINTON	Cook, Welton & Gemmell	8. 8.52
M.1116	BURNASTON* ...	Fleetlands	18.12.52
M.1117	BUTTINGTON* (ex-*Thames*, ex-*Buttington*, ex-*Venturer*, ex-*Buttington*)	Fleetlands	11. 6.53
M.1118	CALTON	Wivenhoe	24.10.53
M.1119	CARHAMPTON ...	Wivenhoe	21. 7.55
M.1120	CAUNTON ...	Montrose	20. 2.53
M.1209	CHAWTON* ...	Fleetlands	24. 9.57
M.1122	CHILCOMPTON ...	Herd & McKenzie...	23.10.53

Pt. No.	Name	Builder	Launched
M.1123	CLARBESTON ...	Richards I.W. ...	18. 2.54
M.1101	CONISTON ...	Thornycroft ...	9. 7.52
M.1125	CUXTON	Camper & Nicholson	9.11.53
M.1203	DARTINGTON* ...	Philip	2.10.56
M.1128	DERRITON (ex-*Killiekrankie*, ex-*Deriton*)	Thornycroft ...	22.12.53
M.1145	DUFTON	Goole Sbdg. ...	13.11.54
M.1206	FISKERTON* ...	Doig	12. 4.57
M.1137	FLOCKTON ...	White	3. 6.54
M.1140	GAVINTON ...	Doig	27. 7.53
M.1141	GLASSERTON ...	Doig	3.12.53
M.1130	HIGHBURTON* ...	Thornycroft ...	2. 6.54
M.1211	HOUGHTON ...	Camper & Nicholson	22.11.57
M.1150	INVERMORISTON	Dorset Yacht ...	2. 6.54
M.1153	KEDLESTON (ex-*Burnicia*, ex-*Kedleston*)	Pickersgill ...	21.12.53
M.1154	KELLINGTON ...	Pickersgill ...	12.10.54
M.1156	KEMERTON ...	Harland & Wolff ...	27.11.53
M.1162	KILDARTON (ex-*Liston*)	Harland & Wolff ...	23. 5.55
M.1158	LALESTON ...	Harland & Wolff ...	18. 5.54

" –ton " class: **M.16, 1101-1107, 1109, 1110, 1112-1130, 1132-1134, 1136, 1137, 1139-1141, 1143, 1145-1147, 1149-1170, 1172-1175, 1177, 1179-1183, 1185, 1187-1206, 1208, 1209, 1211, 1216, MCB.149, 154, 159-164**

The Second World War saw the large scale introduction of the influence mine with which the conventional wire 'sweepers could not cope. The initial threat was the magnetic mine, and while immunity through de-gaussing was rapidly secured, the LL sweep took longer to perfect.

As the influence mine was more often ground-sown in shallow water than moored in deep water, the Royal Navy's initial countermeasure was a small wooden 'sweeper (the MMS) based on the commercial motor fishing vessel (MFV). With the entry of the United States into the war they rapidly designed and mass produced a versatile wooden 'sweeper on more orthodox warship lines (the YMS—units built for the Royal Navy were correspondingly designated BYMS) which met all requirements. To the later introduction of the acoustic and combination magnetic/acoustic mines with period delay mechanisms, the MMS and YMS quickly adapted themselves by the provision of an acoustic hammer.

After the war it was recognised that the emphasis on mining had shifted from the deep-laid moored mines to the ground mines laid in the shallow water approaches to ports and harbours. As a result the large steel-built ocean mine-sweepers were phased-out as a large programme of wooden coastal minesweepers (CMS) came into service. The CMS proved as ubiquitous as its American predecessor, the YMS, and has been largely copied abroad. As completed they had open bridges, tripod masts with forward leading struts, and Mirrlees diesel engines. The HIGHBURTON was the first unit to receive Napier Deltic diesel engines, which was then adopted for future construction and back-fitted to most earlier units. Later, the bridge was closed-in, a lattic replaced the tripod mast, and fin stabilisation added.

In 1964 the KIRKLISTON was the first unit converted to a minehunter when the LL sweep gear was removed, minehunting sonar installed, active rudders fitted, and the complement augmented by four divers. Eight further units have since been similarly modified. Auxiliary diesel-hydraulic propulsion was fitted to the SHOULTON in 1965-66.

Twenty-five units have been transferred to Commonwealth navies: six to the Royal Australian Navy, one to the Ghanaian Navy (whose pennant number was changed from M.1171 to M.16), four to the Indian Navy, six to the Royal Malaysian Navy, and eight—EAST LONDON (ex-*Chilton*—M.1215), JOHANNESBURG (ex-*Castleton*—M.1207), KAPSTAAD (ex-*Hazleton*—M.1142), KIMBERLEY (ex-*Stratton*—M.1210), MOSSELBAA (ex-*Oakington*—M.1213), PORT ELIZABETH (ex-*Dumbleton*—M.1212), PRETORIA (ex-*Dunkerton*—M.1144), and WALVISBAAI (ex-*Pack-ington*—M.1214)—to the South African Navy who also had two additional units—DURBAN (M.1499) and WIND-HOEK (M.1498)—built for their own account. A further six units—BEVINGTON (M.1108), HICKLETON (M.1131), ILMINGTON (M.1148), RENNINGTON (M.1176), SANTON (M.1178), and TARLTON (M.1186)—were sold to the Argentine Navy. Eleven CMS's are attached to the R.N.R. training divisions and two others, the EDDERTON (M.1111) and SULLINGTON (M.1184) have been converted to surveying vessels and renamed MYRMIDON and MERMAID respectively, while the FENTON (M.1135) and FLORISTON (M.1138) have been scrapped.

A very similar series was constructed in Canada for the Royal Canadian Navy. Six were later sold to the French Navy—LA BAYONNAISE (ex-*Chignecto*), LA DIEPPOISE (ex-*Chaleur*), LA DUNKERQUOISE (ex-*Fundy*), LA

MINESWEEPING & SURVEYING VESSELS

Pt. No.	Name	Builder	Launched
M.1159	LANTON	Harland & Wolff ...	30. 7.54
M.1160	LETTERSTON ...	Harland & Wolff ...	26.10.54
M.1161	LEVERTON* ...	Harland & Wolff ...	2. 3.55
M.1208	LEWISTON* ...	Herd & McKenzie...	3.11.59
M.1164	MADDISTON ...	Harland & Wolff ...	27. 1.56
M.1202	MARYTON* ...	Montrose	3. 4.58
M.1155	MONKTON* (ex-Kelton)	Herd & McKenzie...	30.11.55
M.1129	OULSTON... ...	Thornycroft ...	20. 7.54
M.1169	PENSTON	Cook, Welton & Gemmell	9. 5.55
M.1170	PICTON	Cook, Welton & Gemmell	20.10.55
M.1174	PUNCHESTON* ...	Richards I.W. ...	20.11.56
M.1167	REPTON (ex-Ossington)	Harland & Wolff ...	1. 5.57
M.1177	RODINGTON ...	Fleetlands	24. 2.55
M.1179	SEFTON	White	15. 9.54
M.1180	SHAVINGTON* ...	White	25. 4.55
M.1200	SOBERTON* ...	Fleetlands	20.11.56
M.1204	STUBBINGTON*	Camper & Nicholson	8. 8.56
M.1187	UPTON*	Thornycroft ...	15. 3.56
M.1188	WALKERTON* ...	Thornycroft ...	21.11.56

Pt. No.	Name	Builder	Launched
M.1189	WASPERTON* ...	White	28. 2.56
M.1192	WILKIESTON* ...	Cook, Welton & Gemmell	26. 6.56
M.1205	WISTON*	Wivenhoe	3. 6.58
M.1193	WOLVERTON* ...	Montrose	22.10.56
M.1195	WOTTON* ...	Philip	24. 4.56
M.1196	YARNTON* ...	Pickersgill	26. 3.56
M.1105	CLYDE* (ex-Amerton, ex-Mersey, ex-Amerton)	Camper & Nicholson	16. 3.53
M.1136	CURZON* (ex-Fittleton)	White	3. 2.54
M.1109	KILLIEKRANKIE* (ex-Bickington, ex-Curzon, ex-Bickington)	White	14. 5.53
M.1103	KILMOREY* (ex-Alfriston, ex-Warsash, ex-Alfriston)	Thornycroft ...	29. 4.53
M.1173	MERSEY* (ex-Pollington)	Camper & Nicholson	10.10.57
M.1126	MONTROSE* (ex-Dalswinton)	White	24. 9.53
M.1175	NORTHUMBRIA* (ex-Quainton)	Richards I.W. ...	10.10.57
M.1124	ST. DAVID* (ex-Crichton, ex-Clyde, ex-Crichton)	Doig	17. 3.53

LORIENTAISE (ex-*Miramichi*), LA MALOUINE (ex-*Cowichan*), and LA PAIMPOLAISE (ex-*Thunder*)—and their names were reallocated to replacement vessels, four more were sold to the Turkish Navy—TEKIRDAG (ex-*Ungava*), TERME (ex-*Trinity*), TIREBOLU (ex-*Comox*) and TRABZON (ex-*Gaspe*)—but without replacement, and two others were sold-out commercially.

The coastal minesweepers are disposed as follows, those marked* being earmarked for disposal: 1*st Mine Countermeasures Squadron:* BILDESTON, BRONINGTON, IVESTON, LEWISTON, MONKTON, NURTON, UPTON, WOOLVERTON. 3*rd Mine Countermeasures Squadron:* GLASSERTON, HIGHBURTON, LALESTON, SHOULTON. 4*th Mine Countermeasures Squadron:* KEDLESTON, KELLINGTON. 6*th Mine Countermeasures Squadron:* BOSSINGTON, HOUGHTON, HUBBERSTON, MAXTON, SHERATON. 7*th Mine Countermeasures Squadron:* ASHTON, CROFTON, LEVERTON, SHAVINGTON, STUBBINGTON, WALKERTON. 8*th Mine Countermeasures Squadron:* DARTINGTON, WILKIESTON. 9*th Mine Countermeasures Squadron:* APPLETON, BEACHAMPTON, BRERETON, BRINTON, BURNASTON, CHAWTON, GAVINGTON, KIRKLISTON, PUNCHESTON, WISTON, YARNTON. 10*th Mine Countermeasures Squadron* (*R.N.R. Divisions*): CLYDE (Clyde), CURZON (Sussex), *DUFTON, KILLIEKRANKIE (Forth), KILMOREY (Ulster), MERSEY (Mersey), MONTROSE (Tay), NORTHUMBRIA (Tyne), ST. DAVID (South Wales), THAMES (Thames), VENTURER (Severn), WARSASH (Solent). 16*th Minesweeping Squadron* (*R.A.N.*): CURLEW, GULL, HAWK, IBIS, SNIPE, TEAL. 18*th Minesweeping Squadron* (*Indian Navy*): CANNAMORE, CUDDALORE, KAKINADA, KARWAR. *Royal Canadian Navy:* CHALEUR, CHIGNECTO, COWICHAN, FUNDY, MIRAMICHI, *QUINTE, *RESOLUTE, THUNDER. *Ghanaian Navy:* EJURA. *Royal Malaysian Navy:* BRINCHANG, JERAI, KINABALU, LEDANG, MAHAMIRU, TAHAN. *Fishery Protection Squadron:* BELTON, CHILCOMPTON, LETTERSTON, SOBERTON, WASPERTON, WOTTON. *Chatham:* *CALTON, *SEFTON. *Devonport:* *CARHAMPTON, *CLARBESTON. *Gibraltar:* ALVERTON, BLAXTON, CUXTON, MADDISTON, OULSTON, REPTON, *RODDINGTON. *Hythe:* CONISTON, *DERRITON, *KILDARTON, *PENSTON. *Milford:* INVERMORISTON (R.F.A. manned). *Portsmouth:* BADMINTON, CAUNTON, FISKERTON, *FLOCKTON, *KEMERTON, LANTON, *MARYTON, *PICTON, WOOLASTON.

Displacement: 360/425 tons except *Royal Canadian Navy* vessels 390/412 tons.
Dimensions: 140(pp) 152(oa) × 28¾ except *Royal Canadian Navy vessels* 28 × 8¼ except *Royal Canadian Navy vessels* 7¾ feet.
Machinery: Two shafts; ..-cyl. Mirrlees diesel engines B.H.P. 2,500, or 12-cyl. G.M. diesel engines B.H.P. 2,400 (in *Royal Canadian Navy vessels*), or 18-cyl. Napier Deltic diesel engines B.H.P. 3,000 (in vessels marked *) = 15 knots; O.F. 45 tons except *Royal Canadian Navy vessels* 52 tons.
Armament: One except *Royal Australian Navy vessels* and *minehunters* two 40mm. A.A. (1/2 × 1), two 20mm. A.A. (1 × 2—not in *Royal Australian* and *Royal Canadian navies vessels* or *minehunters*) guns.
Complement: 27 except *minehunters* 31, *Royal Canadian Navy vessels* 38, and *Indian Navy vessels* 40.

MINESWEEPING & SURVEYING VESSELS

Pt. No.	Name	Builder	Launched
M.1194	THAMES* (ex-Woolaston)	Herd & McKenzie...	6. 3.58
M.1146	VENTURER* (ex-Hodgeston, ex-Northumbria, ex-Hodgeston)	Fleetlands	6. 4.54
M.1216	WARSASH* (ex-Crofton)	Thornycroft ...	7. 3.58
M.1121	CURLEW* (ex-Chediston, ex-Montrose, ex-Chediston)	Montrose	6.10.53
M.1185	GULL* (ex-Swanston)	Doig	1. 7.54
M.1139	HAWK* (ex-Somerleyton, ex-Gamston)	Richards I.W. ...	17. 9.55
M.1183	IBIS* (ex-Singleton)	Montrose	18.11.55
M.1102	SNIPE* (ex-Alcaston)	Thornycroft ...	5. 1.53
M.1152	TEAL* (ex-Jackton)	Philip	28. 2.55
M.16	EJURA (ex-Aldington, ex-Pittington)	Camper & Nicholson	15. 9.55
M.1191	CANNAMORE* (ex-Whitton)	Fleetlands	30. 1.56
M.1190	CUDDALORE* (ex-Wennington)	Doig	6. 4.55

Pt. No.	Name	Builder	Launched
M.1201	KAKINADA* (ex-Durweston)	Dorset Yacht ...	18. 8.55
M.1197	KARWAR* (ex-Overton)	Camper & Nicholson	28. 1.56
M.1172	BRINCHANG (ex-Thankerton)	Camper & Nicholson	4. 9.56
M.1168	JERAI (ex-Dilston, ex-Pilston)	Cook, Welton & Gemmell	15.11.54
M.1134	KINABALU (ex-Essington)	Camper & Nicholson	00. 9.54
M.1143	LEDANG (ex-Hexton)	Cook, Welton & Gemmell	00.00.54
M.1127	MAHAMIRU (ex-Darlaston)	Cook, Welton & Gemmell	25. 9.53
M.1163	TAHAN (ex-Lullington)	Harland & Wolff	31. 8.55
M.1133	BOSSINGTON* (ex-Embleton)	Thornycroft ...	2.12.55
M.1115	BRONINGTON*	Cook, Welton & Gemmell	19. 3.53
M.1147	HUBBERSTON* ...	Camper & Nicholson	14. 9.54
M.1151	IVESTON*	Philip	1. 6.54
M.1157	KIRKLISTON* (ex-Kilmorey, ex-Kirkliston)	Harland & Wolff ...	18. 2.54

Pt. No.	Name		Builder	Launched
M.1165	MAXTON*	...	Harland & Wolff ...	24. 5.56
M.1166	NURTON* (ex-*Montrose*, ex-*Nurton*)		Harland & Wolff ...	22.10.56
M.1181	SHERATON*	...	White	20. 7.55
M.1182	SHOULTON*	...	Montrose	10. 9.54
MCB.164	CHALEUR ...	...	Marine Industries ...	11. 5.57

Pt. No.	Name		Builder	Launched
MCB.160	CHIGNECTO	...	G. T. Davie ...	17.11.56
MCB.162	COWICHAN	...	Canadian Yarrow ...	26. 2.57
MCB.159	FUNDY ...	...	Davie Sbdg. ...	14. 6.56
MCB.163	MIRAMICHI	...	Victoria M.D. ...	22. 2.57
MCB.149	QUINTE ...	...	Port Arthur ...	8. 8.53
MCB.154	RESOLUTE	...	Kingston	20. 6.53
MCB.161	THUNDER...	...	Port Arthur ...	27.10.56

Machinery contracts: Early *Royal Navy vessels* and *Royal Malaysian vessels* engined by Mirrlees, Bickerton & Day; later *Royal Navy vessels*, *Royal Australian vessels*, and *Indian Navy vessels* by Napier; *Royal Canadian Navy vessels* by General Motors.

Teal with closed-in bridge and tripod mast, a modification extended to most CMS, and with additional 40mm. gun added aft.

MINESWEEPING & SURVEYING VESSELS

General arrangement of CMS.

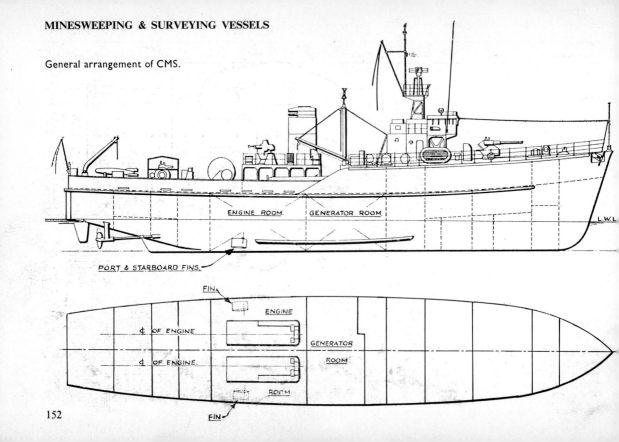

ENGINE ROOM. GENERATOR ROOM.

L.W.L.

PORT & STARBOARD FINS.

FIN.

ENGINE

℄ OF ENGINE

GENERATOR

℄ OF ENGINE.

ROOM

ROOM

FIN.

Right: *Highburton* as completed with open bridge and lattice mast. She was the first CMS to be fitted with Deltic diesel engines.

Right: *Thunder*, and other Royal Canadian Navy units, had a smaller bridge than the Royal Navy CMS's.

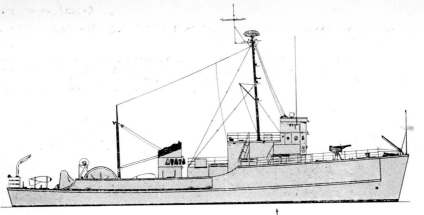

"MSC.60" class.

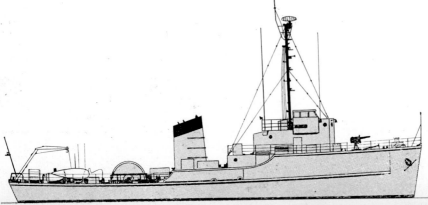

"MSC.209" class.

[Drawings courtesy *United States Naval Institute.*

Ex-U.S.N. "MSC.60" class: **MAHOOD, MUBARAK, MUHAFIZ, MUJAHID, MUKHTAR, MUNSIF.** *Ex-U.S.N. "MSC.209" class:* **MOMIN, MOSHAL**

Wooden vessels generally similar to, but slightly smaller than, the "–ton" class, from which they are easily distinguished by their tall pole foremast and short funnel. Taller funnels were fitted in the last two units, which have their sweep generator powered by a gas turbine. In addition to the above eight vessels turned over to the Pakistani Navy between 1955-62, a further one hundred and sixty-three have been transferred by the United States Navy to other navies under the terms of MDAP.

"MSC.60" class
320/370 tons; 138(pp) 144(oa) × 28 × 8½ feet; two shafts; 6-cyl. G.M. diesel engines, B.H.P. 880 = 13 knots; O.F. 25 tons; one 20mm. A.A. gun; complement 39.

"MSC.209" class
360/400 tons; 138(pp) 145½(oa) × 26½ × 7 feet; two shafts, 6-cyl. Harnischfeger diesel engines (two/shaft) B.H.P. 1,000 = 13 knots; O.F. 25 tons; one 20mm. A.A. gun; complement 39.

Pt. No.	Name	Builder	Launched	Pt. No.	Name	Builder	Launched
160	MAHOOD (ex-U.S.N. MSC.267)	Quincy Adams ...	00.00.57	165	MUKHTAR (ex-U.S.N. MSC.274)	Bellingham	20. 6.58
162	MUBARAK (ex-U.S.N. MSC.262)	Hodgson	00.00.56	166	MUNSIF (ex-U.S.N. MSC.273)	Bellingham	00.00.58
163	MUHAFIZ (ex-U.S.N. MSC.138)	Bellingham	5. 3.54	161	MOMIN (ex-U.S.N. MSC.293)	Peterson	00.00.61
164	MUJAHID (ex-U.S.N. MSC.261)	Hodgson	00.00.55	167	MOSHAL (ex-U.S.N. MSC.294)	Peterson	00.00.62

Machinery contracts: All engined by General Motors except *Momin* and *Moshal* by Harnischfeger.

MINESWEEPING & SURVEYING VESSELS

"*Black Swan*" *class:* **JUMNA, SUTLEJ**

Former escort sloops converted into surveying vessels in 1955 (SUTLEJ) and 1957 (JUMNA) when all armament was removed and survey launches added aft. Of nine similar vessels (three "Egret" and six "Black Swan" classes), three were war losses, one—West German GRAF SPEE (ex-*Flamingo*)—was sold, one—WESSEX (ex-*Erne*)—was converted into a stationary R.N.R. training ship, and one was scrapped. With eight 4-inch A.A. (4×2) guns (except that the Indian Navy vessels were never designed to ship "Y" mounting, and later Royal Navy units shipped a quadruple 2-pounder A.A. in lieu of "Y" mounting) they were the heaviest gun-armed sloops ever built for the Royal Navy.

1,300/1,735 tons; 282(pp) 299½(oa)×37½×8½/11½ feet; two Admiralty 3-drum boilers; two shafts; Parsons geared turbines, S.H.P. 3,600=19½ knots; O.F. 370 tons; complement 220.

Pt. No.	Name	Builder	Laid down	Launched	Completed	Disposition
F.11	JUMNA	Denny...	20. 2.40	16.11.40	13. 5.41	Indian Navy
F.95	SUTLEJ	Denny...	4. 1.40	1.10.40	23. 4.41	Indian Navy

Machinery contracts: Both engined by builders.

Robb type: **TUI**

Former anti-submarine trawler converted for surveying duties, when the fo'c'sle was extended aft to the bridge, a lattice replaced the pole foremast, and a deckhouse was added aft. Sister ships MOA was a war loss and KIWI was scrapped.

600/825 tons; 150(pp) 156(oa)×30×14 feet; one cylindrical S.E. boiler; one shaft; reciprocating (VTE—cyl. ..":..":.."×.." stroke), I.H.P. 1,000=14 knots; O.F. ... tons; complement 55.

P.33	TUI	Robb	19. 3.40	26. 8.41	5.12.41	Royal New Zealand Navy

Machinery contract: Engined by Plenty.

"Flower" class: SACKVILLE

The corvette design was based on the mercantile whalecatcher SOUTHERN PRIDE, and by largely adopting commercial practices their construction was mainly undertaken by yards which did not specialise in Admiralty work. The initial order for fifty-six was placed before the war and was large by peace-time standards, while subsequent war programme orders—placed in U.K. and Canadian yards—increased this total to two hundred and seventy-six, in addition to twenty-two ordered by the French Navy (sixteen in U.K. and six in French yards).

Of this total, thirteen were cancelled; thirty-five (including two transferred to the Royal Norwegian Navy and two to the French Navy) were war losses; and forty-nine were transferred to Commonwealth and Allied navies (Royal Canadian Navy four, in addition to one hundred and three ordered for their own account; Royal Indian Navy four; Royal Netherlands Navy one; Royal New Zealand Navy two; Royal Norwegian Navy six; Royal Yugoslavian Navy one; and United States Navy eighteen) during the war, while seven units ordered by the United States Navy were transferred to the Royal Navy. After the war one hundred and eleven were sold-out commercially and at least seven (Argentine Navy one, Communist Chinese Navy three, Israeli Navy one, Portuguese Navy one, and Saudi-Arabian Coast Guard one) later reverted to warships; twenty-four were sold to other navies (Chilean Navy three, Nationalist Chinese Navy one, Royal Danish Navy one, Dominican Navy five, Irish Navy three, Israeli Navy one, South African Navy one, and Venezuelan Navy seven) of which three were later sold-out commercially, while a further four (Egyptian Navy one, Italian Navy, and Royal Thai Navy two) changed flags on transfer from Commonwealth and Allied navies; and sixty-seven were scrapped, but the machinery of some was retained for installation in new- or re-engined existing, mercantile tonnage.

The seven vessels built for the United States Navy were returned to them post-war, when one was sold to the Argentine Navy, three were sold-out commercially, and the remainder scrapped. Of the twenty-two vessels ordered by the French Navy fourteen were cancelled, and the only one completed (in a U.K. yard) under the French flag was precipitately lost while running trials. The remaining seven under construction (three in U.K. four in French yards) were respectively acquired by the Royal Navy and the German Navy after the French surrender in 1940. Of these four

Pt. No.	Name	Builder	Laid down	Launched	Completed	Disposition
AGOR.113	SACKVILLE	St. John D.D... ...	28. 5.40	15. 5.41	30.12.41	Royal Canadian Navy

Machinery contract: Engined by Dominion Engineering.

MINESWEEPING & SURVEYING VESSELS

were lost (one Royal Navy and three German Navy); two were sold-out commercially, one still incomplete at a French yard at the end of the war, while the other later reverted to a warship in the Royal Hellenic Navy; and one was scrapped.

From the above it will be noted that the "Flower" class corvettes experienced a diversity of service unequalled by any other single class of warship. The sole survivor in the Commonwealth navies, the SACKVILLE, was first converted post-war into a cable layer, was later designated a loop layer; and is now employed as a surveying vessel. A deckhouse has been added aft with a tripod mainmast stepped on it, but she is otherwise little altered.

1,085/1,177 tons; 190(pp) 205(oa) × 33 × 12/00 feet; two cylindrical S.E. boilers (225 lb/in²); one shaft; reciprocating (VTE—cyl. 16″:31″:38½″(2) × 30″ stroke), I.H.P. 2,750 = 16 knots; O.F. 232 tons; complement 38.

Pt. No.	Name	Builder	Laid down	Launched	Completed	Disposition
F.243	INVESTIGATOR (ex-*Khukri*, ex-*Trent*)	Hill	31. 1.42	10.10.42	27. 2.43	Indian Navy (1946)
262	ZULFIQUAR (ex-*Dhanush*, ex-*Deveron*)	Smiths Dock	16. 4.42	12.10.42	2. 3.43	Pakistani Navy (1945)
F.175	BARCOO	Cockatoo	21.10.42	26. 8.43	17. 1.44	Royal Australian Navy
F.377	DIAMANTINA	Walkers	12. 4.43	6. 4.44	27. 4.45	Royal Australian Navy
F.354	GASCOYNE	Morts Dock	4. 6.42	20. 2.43	20.12.43	Royal Australian Navy
F.364	LACHLAN	Morts Dock	00.00.00	25. 3.44	00.00.00	Royal New Zealand Navy (1948)

Machinery contracts: Investigator engined by Bellis & Morcom, Zulfiquar by builders, and all Australian-built vessels by sub-contractors except Barcoo by builders.

"*River*" class: **BARCOO, DIAMANTINA, GASCOYNE, INVESTIGATOR, LACHLAN, ZULFIQUAR**

Former frigates converted to surveying vessels. The Royal Australian Navy vessels were modified during 1959–60 when the BARCOO and DIAMANTINA had a deckhouse and a pole mainmast added aft, while the GASCOYNE was little altered except for the provision of a helicopter landing pad aft. The LACHLAN was altered on generally similar lines to the BARCOO except that the side plating was also extended aft to abaft the deckhouse and a helicopter landing deck was added aft. Of the twenty-two Australian-built "River" class, ten were cancelled, one was converted to a depot ship for minesweepers, one—the LACHLAN—was transferred to the Royal New Zealand Navy, and the remainder scrapped.

Of the fifty-seven British built vessels of this class, six were war losses; twenty—Burmese Navy MAYU (ex-*Fal*); Royal Danish Navy HOLGAR DANSKE (ex-*Monnow*), and NIELS EBBESEN (ex-*Annan*—both since scrapped); Egyptian Navy ABIKIR (ex-*Usk*), DOMIAT (ex-*Nith*—both since lost), and RASHEED (ex-*Spey*); French CROIX DE LORRAINE (ex-*Strule*, ex-*Glenarm*), L'AVENTURE (ex-*Braid*), L'ESCARMOUCHE (ex-*Frome*), LA SUPRRISE (ex-*Torridge*), LE DECOUVERTE (ex-*Windrush*), and TONKINOIS (ex-*Moyola*—all since scrapped); Indian Navy INVESTIGATOR (ex-*Khukri*, ex-*Trent*), NEZA (ex-*Test*—since scrapped), and TIR (ex-*Bann*); Royal Netherlands Navy JOHANN MAURITS VAN NASSAU (ex-*Ribble*—since scrapped); Pakistani Navy SHAMSHER (ex-*Nadder*—since scrapped), and ZULFIQUAR (ex-*Dhanush*, ex-*Deveron*); and Portugese Navy DIOGO GOMES (ex-*Awe*), and NUNA TRISTAO (ex-*Avon*)—were sold, together with another unit sold-out commercially; and one was wrecked and twenty-nine scrapped.

The INVESTIGATOR was altered in 1951 when the bridge was completely remodelled, a lattice replaced the former tripod foremast, and a long deckhouse added abaft the bridge extending to the break in fo'c'sle deck level. Little alterations were effected in the ZULFIQUAR, only part of the armament was removed, and a small deckhouse added forward of the bridge.

All these vessels had motor survey launches added, stowed under heavy radial davits in the Royal Australian Navy vessels and the ZULFIQUAR, and under luffing davits—with their heads joined by a boom—in LACHLAN and INVESTIGATOR.

Investigator 1,460/1,930 tons, *Zulfiquar* 1,490/2,215 tons, *Royal Australian Navy vessels* 1,489 except *Barcoo* 1,477/2,200 tons, *Lachlan* 1,460/1,930 tons; 283(pp) 301¼(oa) × 36¾ × 12/14 feet; two Admiralty 3-drum boilers (225 lb/in²); two shafts; reciprocating (VTE—cyl. 18½":31":38½"(2) × 30" stroke), I.H.P. 5,500 = 20 knots; O.F. 640 tons; one 4-inch in *Zulfiquar* only, *Royal Australian Navy vessels* one/*Zulfiquar* two/others nil 40mm. A.A. (1/2 × 1) guns; complement 150 except *Royal Australian Navy vessels* 183 and *Lachlan* 140.

MINESWEEPING & SURVEYING VESSELS

Pt. No.	Name	Builder	Laid down	Launched	Completed	Disposition
AGOR.170	FORT FRANCES	Port Arthur	11. 5.43	30.10.43	21.11.44	Royal Canadian Navy
FSE.171	KAPUSKASING	Port Arthur	19.12.43	22. 7.43	17. 8.44	Royal Canadian Navy, loaned to Department of Mines & Technical Surveys
AGOR.168	NEW LISKEARD	Port Arthur	8. 7.43	14. 1.44	21.11.44	Royal Canadian Navy
AGOR.174	OSHAWA	Port Arthur	18.11.42	6.10.43	6. 7.44	Royal Canadian Navy

Machinery contracts: All engined by Montreal Loco. Works.

Pt. No.	Name	Builder	Laid down	Launched	Completed	Disposition
A.307	COOK (ex-*Pegwell Bay*, ex-*Loch Mochrum*)	Pickersgill	30.11.44	1. 9.45	20. 7.50	Completed H.M. Dockyard, Devonport; for disposal
A.303	DAMPIER (ex-*Herne Bay*, ex-*Loch Eil*)	Smiths Dock	7. 8.44	15. 5.45	6. 6.48	Completed H.M. Dockyard, Chatham
A.311	OWEN (ex-*Thurso Bay*, ex-*Loch Muick*)	Hall Russell	30. 9.44	19.10.45	23. 9.49	Completed H.M. Dockyard, Chatham

Machinery contracts: Cook engined by George Clark, and others by builders.

Pt. No.	Name	Builder	Laid down	Launched	Completed	Disposition
A.200	VIDAL	H.M. Dockyard (Chatham)	5. 7.50	31. 7.51	29. 3.54	

Machinery contract: Engined by builder.

"Algerine" class: **FORT FRANCES, KAPUSKASING, NEW LISKEARD, OSHAWA**

These former minesweepers were converted in 1959 and were little altered structually except that deckhouses were added forward (before the bridge) and aft at the break in fo'c'sle deck level. Their designation was changed from AGH to AGOR in 1964, and NEW LISKEARD was placed in reserve on the completion of ENDEAVOUR (see p. 165).

1,040/1,265 tons; $212\frac{1}{2}$(pp) 225(oa)$\times 35\frac{1}{2}\times 7\frac{1}{2}$/00 feet; two Admiralty 3-drum boilers (235 lb/in²); two shafts; reciprocating (VTE—cyl. 15″:25″:40″$\times$24″ stroke), I.H.P. 2,000$=16\frac{1}{2}$ knots; O.F. 235 tons; complement 51.

"Loch/Bay" class: **COOK, DAMPIER, OWEN**

The Royal Navy vessels of this class were incomplete at the end of the Second World War, and they were finally completed in the Royal dockyards as surveying vessels with considerable addition to the superstructure, rigged with a lattice foremast and pole mainmast, and with survey launches stowed under boom-headed luffing davits. The DAMPIER was provided with an enclosed bridge in 1961, and a fourth unit—Portuguese Navy AFONSO DE ALBUQUERQUE (ex-*Dalrymple*, ex-*Luce Bay*, ex-*Loch Glass*)—was sold.

1,640/2,330 tons; 286(pp) 307(oa)$\times 38\frac{1}{2}\times 12\frac{3}{4}$/$14\frac{1}{4}$ feet; two Admiralty 3-drum boilers (225 lb/in²); two shafts; reciprocating (VTE—cyl. $18\frac{1}{2}$″:31″:$38\frac{1}{2}$″(2)$\times$30″ stroke), I.H.P. 5,500$=19\frac{1}{2}$/18 knots; O.F. 580 tons; complement 149.

Admiralty type: **VIDAL**

Designed for both hydrographic survey work and chart production, the VIDAL was the first post-war surveying vessel for the Royal Navy. On dimensions approximating the "Loch/Bay" class she retained a warship hull form, while the installation of diesel engines was an innovation—in the Royal Navy—for a vessel of her type. A hangar for a helicopter was provided at the after end of the superstructure, aft of which is the landing deck extending nearly to the stern. Rigged with a lattice foremast and pole mainmast and a short funnel set aft of amidships, the VIDAL is readily distinguishable. Her survey launches are stowed under boom-headed luffing davits, and she was fitted with an enclosed bridge in 1961.

1,940/2,173 tons; 297(pp) 315(oa)$\times 40\times 12$/00 feet; two shafts; 12-cyl. ASR.1 diesel engines (two/shaft), B.H.P. 4,200$=15$ knots; O.F. ... tons; four 3-pounder saluting (4×1) guns, one helicopter; complement 164.

Moresby perpetuates a traditional surveying service name in the Royal Australian Navy.

[Block courtesy *Shipbuilding Shipping Record*

Indian Navy type: **DARSHAK**

Generally similar to, but dimensionally larger than, the VIDAL, the Indian Navy DARSHAK is easily distinguished by the large boat crane abaft the bridge, while the funnel is sited more amidships and there is no mainmast. All the boats are handled by the crane except for the aftermost survey launches on each side, which are stowed under boom-headed luffing davits.

2,790/.,... tons; 300(pp) 319(oa) × 49 × 28¾d./15 feet; two shafts; diesel engines and electric motors, B.H.P./S.H.P. 5,000/3,000 = 16 knots; O.F. ... tons; one helicopter; complement 150.

Pt. No.	Name	Builder	Laid down	Launched	Completed	Disposition
A.	DARSHAK...	Hindustan D.Y. ...	....	2.11.59	28.12.64	Indian Navy

Machinery contract:

R.A.N. type: **MORESBY**

Slightly smaller than the VIDAL, the Royal Australian Navy MORESBY is distinctive by the gunwhale bounding the fo'c'sle deck forward, a larger bridge structure, and a short funnel placed well aft. She is rigged with a tubular foremast and pole mainmast and has a helicopter landing deck at the stern. The survey launches are stowed under boom-headed gravity davits, and a crane is stepped abaft the bridge. Each of the diesel engines powers a 1,330kW. generator supplying current at 600V. to the propulsion motors.

2,000/2,500 tons; 284¼(pp) 303(oa) × 42 × 15 feet; two shafts; three 16-cyl English Electric diesel engines and two electric motors, B.H.P./S.H.P. 5,934/5,000 = 16 knots; O.F. ... tons; two 40mm. A.A. (2 × 1) guns, one helicopter; complement 130.

AGS.73	MORESBY	Newcastle State D.Y.	I. 6.62	7. 9.63	6. 3.64	Royal Australian Navy

Machinery contract: Engined by English Electric.

MINESWEEPING & SURVEYING VESSELS

Hydra typifies the modern surveying vessel in adopting a mercantile form hull for improved seaworthiness and greater internal capacity.

Pt. No.	Name	Builder	Laid down	Launched	Completed	Disposition
A.137	HECATE	Blythswood	26.10.64	31. 3.65	19.12.65	Completed Yarrow
A.133	HECLA	Blythswood	6. 5.64	21.12.64	8. 9.65	Completed Yarrow
A.144	HYDRA	Yarrow	14. 5.64	14. 7.65	4. 5.66	

Machinery contracts: All engined by Davey Paxman (diesel engines) and A.E.I. (electric motors).

R.C.N. type: **ENDEAVOUR**

A mercantile hull form to provide the best seakeeping qualities in the shortest length was adopted for this Royal Canadian Navy vessel, with a raised fo'c'sle and a long bridge extending well aft. A 5-ton crane with an articulated jib is stepped at the fore end of the well deck forward, together with two 9-ton telescopic cranes positioned fore and aft respectively. The ENDEAVOUR is rigged with a light tripod mast on the fo'c'sle, and a tubular mast abaft the bridge with an enclosed crow's nest at its head. Aft of the short, domed-top funnel is a telescopic hangar and landing deck for a helicopter. Specially designed for anti-submarine research projects, she is civilian-manned.

1,560/0,000 tons; 215(pp) 235¾(oa) × 38½ × 13 feet; two shafts; 9-cyl. Fairbanks-Morse diesel engines and G.E.C. electric motors, B.H.P./S.H.P. 3,440/2,960 = 16 knots; O.F. ... tons; one helicopter; complement 37 + 13 scientific staff.

Pt. No.	Name	Builder	Laid down	Launched	Completed	Disposition
AGOR.171	ENDEAVOUR	Canadian Yarrow ...	4. 9.63	4. 9.64	9. 3.65	Royal Canadian Navy, Atlantic

Machinery con'(acts: Engined by Canadian Locomotive (diesel engines) and Canadian General Electric (electric motors).

"Hecla" class: **HECATE, HECLA, HYDRA**

With this class the warship form hull was abandoned in favour of the more functional mercantile hull form, and in many respects they are markedly similar to the Royal Research ship DISCOVERY which preceded them. They are the first Royal Navy surveying vessels to be built on purely commercial lines without a supplemental naval function, a factor which enabled them to have a fuller form and less speed than the VIDAL, where space is lost by the finer form naval hull and the power required for speed in excess of surveying requirements. In view of the large electrical load diesel-electric propulsion was provided, but in this respect they were anticipated by the DARSHAK and MORESBY (see above). Each of the three diesel engines drives a 610kW. main and 200kW. auxiliary generator, the former supplying the power to a single electric propulsion motor. A hangar and landing deck for a helicopter is provided aft, a garage for a Land Rover forward, and the survey launches are stowed under gravity davits.

1,915/2,733 tons; 235 (pp) 260(oa) × 49 × 11¼/14¾ feet; one shaft; 12-cyl. Davey Paxman diesel engines and A.E.I. electric motor, B.H.P./S.H.P. 3,570/2,000 = 14 knots; O.F. 450 tons; one helicopter; complement 116 + 6 scientific staff.

165

Pt. No.	Name	Builder	Laid down	Launched	Completed	Disposition
—	QUADRA	Burrard	... 2.65	4. 7.66	...3.67	Canadian Coast Guard, Pacific.
—	VANCOUVER	Burrard	... 2.65	29. 6.65	4. 7.66	Canadian Coast Guard, Pacific.

Machinery contracts: Both engined by Canadian Westinghouse.

Below: Profile of C.C.G. weather ships.   **Right:** Conspicious features of the *Vancouver* are the meteorlogical radar enclosed in a spherical weather screen and the telescopic hangar abaft the funnel for the helicopter.

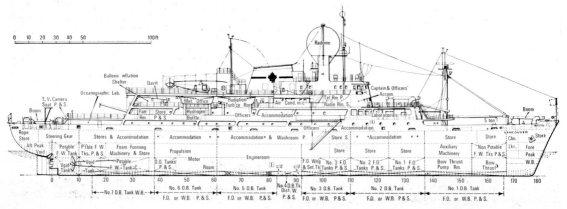

C.C.G. type: **QUADRA, VANCOUVER**

These vessels were designed as replacements for the "River" class frigates *St. Catherine, St. Stephen* and *Stonetown* employed on weather service duties in the Pacific.

While on station they will undertake oceanographic work in addition to meteorlogical observations; and to ensure quiet operation, slow speed to maintain station, and high speed for search and rescue missions turbo-electric propulsion was selected. The heavy electric load is supplied by two 2,900kW. turbo-alternators for main propulsion, three 650kW. turbo alternators for ship's services, three 100kW. back pressure turbo-alternators for weather and research services, and two 180kW. diesel alternators for harbour and emergency purposes.

5,600 tons; $361\frac{1}{4}$(pp) $404\frac{3}{4}$(oa) $\times$ 50 $\times$ 30$\frac{1}{2}$d./17$\frac{1}{2}$ feet; two Babcock & Wilcox boilers, two shafts, Westinghouse turbines and electric motors S.H.P. 7,500 = 18 knots, O.F .,... tons, one helicopter; complement 86+14 scientific staff.

Left: *Bulldog*

Below: *Vidal*

Right: *Bulldog*

Right: *Bulldog*

Below: *Endeavour*

Official sketch of the Canadian research vessel *Quest*. Designed for near silent operation the immersed hull is specially sheathed for sound insulation and is sub-divided by transmission loss bulkheads and acoustic decks. When operating in the silent mode the electric propulsion motors are powered by gas turbine generator.

R.C.N. type: **QUEST**

Generally similar and slightly enlarged edition of the ENDEAVOUR, and similarly intended for anti-submarine research work. The hull is strengthened for work in heavy ice, and the mast is faired into the fore end of the funnel casing.

2,130/.,... tons; 235(pp) 253(oa)×42×21d./15 feet; two shafts; Fairbanks Morse diesel engines and Canadian-G.E. electric motors, B.H.P./S.H.P. .,.../2,900=16 knots; O.F. ... tons; one helicopter; complement 39+15 scientific staff.

Pt. No.	Name	Builder	Laid down	Launched	Completed	Disposition
AGOR.172	QUEST	Burrard D.D. ...	....	9. 7.68	....	Building for Royal Canadian Navy, Pacific

Machinery contracts: Fairbanks Morse (diesel engines) and Canadian General Electric (electric motors).

"Bulldog" class: **BEAGLE, BULLDOG, FAWN, FOX**

Although designed for world-wide operation the size of these vessels was limited so that they could work inshore. Two further projected units were cancelled.

1,000/1,088 tons; 168½(pp) 189½(oa)×37½×19¾d./11½ feet; two shafts (Bamford c.p. propellers), 8-cylinder Lister Blackstone diesel engines (two/shaft) B.H.P. 2,640=15 knots, O.F. 98 tons; two 20mm. A.A. (2×1) guns; complement 41.

Pt. No.	Name	Builder	Laid down	Launched	Completed	Disposition
A.317	BEAGLE	Brooke Marine ...	15.11.66	7. 9.67	23. 3.68	
A.319	BULLDOG	Brooke Marine ...	15.11.66	12. 7.67	9. 5.68	
A.320	FAWN	Brooke Marine ...	21.12.66	29. 2.68	3.10.68	
A.335	FOX	Brooke Marine ...	21.12.66	6.11.67	11. 7.68	

Machinery contracts: All engined by Lister Blackstone.

Left: *Challenger*, Nigerian Navy Customs cruiser and surveying vessel.

Below: *Pathfinder*, coastal surveying vessel for Nigerian Navy.

Ex-CMS: MERMAID, MYRMIDON

Former coastal minesweepers converted to surveying vessels in 1964 when all armament and sweeping gear was removed. A chartroom has been added abaft the enclosed bridge and a pole mainmast stepped aft, but they still retain their tripod foremasts and the davits at the stern. With the completion of the first two units of the "Bulldog" class (see p. 171) they were placed on the disposal list and MYRMIDON was sold to the Royal Malaysian Navy in 1968.

355/420 tons; 140(pp) 152(oa)×28¾×8¼ feet; two shafts; Mirrlees diesel engines, B.H.P. 2,500=15 knots; O.F. 15 tons; complement 15.

Pt. No.	Name	Builder			Launched
A.154	MERMAID (ex-*Sullington*)	Doig	...	...	7. 4.54
A.151	MYRMIDON (ex-*Edderton*)	Doig	...	...	1.11.52

Machinery contracts: Engined by Mirrlees, Bickerton & Day.

White type: PATHFINDER

Designed for coastal survey work the Nigerian Navy PATHFINDER is flush-decked, has a prominent bridge structure, and a long boat deck extending to the stern. She is rigged with pole masts, has a small hold forward served by two derricks, and a noticeable funnel cap. Provision is made to ship a 40mm. A.A. gun if required.

544 tons *gross*; 145¼(pp) ...(oa)×27×11 feet; two cylindrical boilers; one shaft; reciprocating (VTE—cyl. 10½″:17½″:27½″×18″ stroke), I.H.P. 200=8 knots; complement 42.

Pt. No.	Name	Builder			Launched
P.06	PATHFINDER ...	White	...	...	23.10.53

Machinery contract: Engined by Plenty.

Aldous type: CHALLENGER

Sea-going craft for service as a survey or preventitive launch with the Nigerian Navy. The hull has a half-raised fo'c'sle forward of the machinery space, and the detatched superstructures are joined by a low engine room casing on which the short—and rather inconspicious—funnel is mounted. A pole mast is stepped abaft the upper open bridge, and provision is made to ship a 40mm. A.A. gun forward if required.

114 tons *gross*; 110½(pp) ...(oa)×18½×5 feet; ...... shafts; Gleniffer diesel engines, B.H.P. ...=13 knots; complement 12.

Pt. No.	Name	Builder			Launched
P.10	CHALLENGER ...	Aldous	...	...	55

Machinery contract: Engined by Glenifer.

Echo running trials with 40 mm. A.A. gun shipped forward.

Below: The British coastal surveying craft *Waterwitch* (ex-*Powderham*) following her conversion from an inshore minesweeper.
[*Photographs C. F. Foss*

Ex-minelayer: **BLUETHROAT**

Former controlled minelayer, modified as a cablelayer in 1959, and then as a research vessel for coastal work with the Royal Canadian Navy.

785/870 tons; 150¾(pp) 157(oa)×33×10 feet; two shafts; 4-cyl. Fairbanks-Morse diesel engines, B.H.P. 1,200=13 knots; O.F. ... tons; complement 25.

Pt. No.	Name	Builder	Launched
AGOR.114	BLUETHROAT ...	G. T. Davie ...	15. 9.55

Machinery contract: Engined by Canadian Locomotive.

"Echo" class: **ECHO, EGERIA, ENTERPRISE.** *Ex-ISMS:* **WATERWITCH, WOODLARK**

These coastal craft were based on the inshore mine-sweeper hull but were fitted with engines of reduced power and controllable pitch propellers. The super-structure is more extensive than in the ISMS's and the sounding launch, stowed on the after deck, is handled by a boat derrick. Although not normally armed, provision was made for shipping a 40mm A.A. gun forward, which was carried only during trials. The WATERWICH and WOODLARK were converted from ISMS's to surveying duties in 1964.

120/160 tons; 100(pp) 106¾ except *Waterwitch* 106½ and *Woodlark* 107½(oa)×21¾×5 except *Waterwitch* and *Woodlark* 5¾ feet; two shafts; 8-cyl. Davey Paxman diesel engines, B.H.P. 700 except *Waterwitch* and *Woodlark* 12-cyl. Davey Paxman diesel engines, B.H.P. 1,100=13 knots; O.F. ... tons; complement 18.

Pt. No.	Name	Builder	Launched
A.70	ECHO	White	1. 5.57
A.72	EGERIA	Weatherhead	13. 9.58
A.71	ENTERPRISE ...	Blackmore ...	30. 9.58
A.	WATERWITCH (ex-*Powderham*)	White	27.11.58
A.	WOODLARK (ex-*Yaxham*)	... ...	21. 1.58

Machinery contract: All engined by Davey Paxman.

Aldous type: **PENELOPE**

Steel-built survey and boarding launch of robust con-struction for harbour and esturial duties with the Nigerian Navy. Despite her limited dimensions, the PENELOPE made the delivery passage from the U.K. to West Africa under her own power.

79 tons *gross*; 77(pp) 79½(oa)×17×4½ feet; two shafts; 6-cyl. Gardner diesel engines, B.H.P. 216=10 knots; O.F. 4½ tons; complement 16.

Pt. No.	Name	Builder	Launched
P.11	PENELOPE... ...	Aldous	59

Machinery contract: Engined by Gardner.

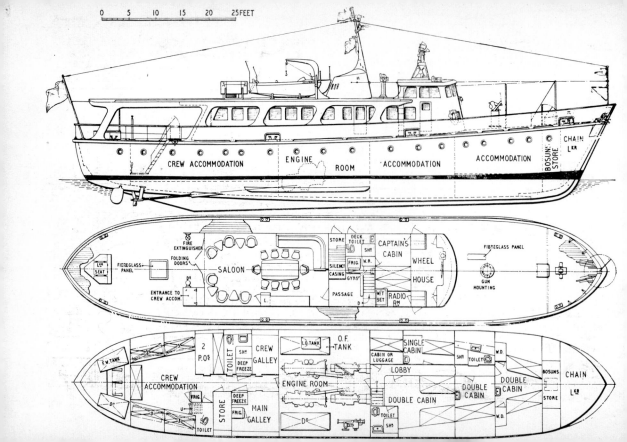

0 5 10 15 20 25 FEET

CREW ACCOMMODATION   ENGINE   ROOM   ACCOMMODATION   ACCOMMODATION   BOSUN'S STORE   CHAIN LKR

FIRE EXTINGUISHER
FOLDING DOORS
FIBREGLASS PANEL
LKR SEAT
SALOON
ENTRANCE TO CREW ACCOM
STORE   DECK TOILET
SILENCER
CASING
GYRO
PASSAGE
W/T SET
RADIO RM
CAPTAIN'S CABIN
SH.
FRIG.
W.R.
WHEEL HOUSE
FIBREGLASS PANEL
GUN MOUNTING

F.W. TANK
CREW ACCOMMODATION
2 P.O's
TOILET
SH.
DEEP FREEZE
CREW GALLEY
FRIG.
DEEP FREEZE
FRIG.
STORE
MAIN GALLEY
TOILET
L.O. TANK
O.F. TANK
ENGINE ROOM
TOILET
SH.
CABIN OR LUGGAGE
SINGLE CABIN
LOBBY
DOUBLE CABIN
DOUBLE CABIN
SH.
TOILET
W.D.
DOUBLE CABIN
W.D.
BOSUNS STORE
CHAIN LKR

Thornycroft type: **MUTIARA**

Combined surveying and despatch vessel, and the first
ship built for the Royal Malaysian Navy as all earlier
units had been acquired from the Royal Navy. Accommodation is provided for eight official passengers (in
addition to the ship's complement) in three double and
two single cabins forward, while a large deck saloon is
arranged aft of the funnel.

95/100 tons; 91(pp) 98(oa) × 19 × 5½ feet; two shafts;

. .-cyl. Thorncroft diesel engines, B.H.P. 400=12 knots;
O.F. 7½ tons; one 20mm. A.A. gun; complement 16.

Pt. No.	Name	Builder	Launched
P.3504	MUTIARA	Thornycroft (Singapore)	17. 1.61

Machinery contract: Engined by builder.

Left: General arrangement *Mutiara*.

COASTAL CRAFT

Fairmile "B" type: **CALABAR**

Former wooden motor launch (MLs) converted into minesweeper (MSML) after the Second World War.

This series originally comprised nearly six hundred units (Nos. 112–311, 336–500, 511–600, 801–1000, 4001–4004, and R.C.N. 050–129) built between 1940–45 in boatyards in the U.K., Dominions, Colonies, and also in the United States and Egypt, of which about seventy were ultimately cancelled.

Intended for general patrol work, they proved most versatile craft and practically did everything and went everywhere. While there was less private demand for them post-war as pleasure craft (they were a little large for this use and petrol-engined), nearly fifty were purchased by foreing navies, in addition to eighty-seven (R.A.N. thirty-five, R.I.N. twenty-four, R.N.Z.N. twelve, and S.A.N. sixteen) were allocated to Commonwealth navies, and eight to the United States Navy, during the war, while the Royal Canadian Navy built eighty for their own account.

85 tons; 112(oa) × 18¼ × 3¾ feet; two shafts; Hall Scott petrol motors, B.H.P. 1,200 = 20/16 knots, petrol .. tons; two 20mm. A.A. (1 × 2) guns; complement 16.

+1·4·05 in

Pt. No.	Name	Builder	Disposition
P.08	CALABAR (ex-*ML.223*)	Robertson	Nigerian Navy (1959)

U.S. Navy "PC" type: **OGOJO**

This steel-hulled former American sub-chaser was transferred to the Nigerian Navy in 1963 by the Royal Netherlands Navy for training purposes after the order for the frigate NIGERIA (see p. 101) had been placed with a Netherlands yard.

This series originally comprised four hundred and nineteen craft of which forty-three were cancelled, twenty-four converted to PGN's and thirty-five to PCC's, and forty-one (Brazil eight, France twenty-nine, and the R.H.N. R.N.N., R.Neth.N. and Uruguay one each) were transferred to Allied navies during the Second World War.

320/413 tons; 165(pp) 173¾(oa) × 26 × 6½/7½ feet; two shafts; Fairbanks diesel engines, B.H.P. 2,880 = 20 knots; O.F. 60 tons; one 3-inch, one 40mm. A.A., five 20mm. A.A. (5 × 1) guns; complement 70.

Pt. No.	Name	Builder	Launched
	OGOJO (ex-R.Neth.N. *Queen Wilhelmina*, ex-U.S.N. *PC.468*)	Geo. Lawley ...	30. 4.42

Name	Builder	Disposition
SDB.1321 (ex-*HDML.1321*)	Purdom & Featherstone	Royal Australian Navy
SDB.1324 (ex-*HDML.1324*)	MacFarlane	Royal Australian Navy
SDB.1325 (ex-*HDML.1325*)	E. Jack	Royal Australian Navy
SDML.3517 (ex-*HDML.1261*)	Bombay	Pakistani Navy
SDML.3520 (ex-*HDML.1266*)	Bombay	Pakistani Navy
SDML.3502 (ex-*HDML.1105*)	African Marine & General Eng.	Royal Malaysian Navy
SDML.3506 (ex-*HDML.1334*)	Frederick Nicol ...	Royal Malaysian Navy
SDML.3507 (ex-*HDML.1335*)	Frederick Nicol ...	Royal Malaysian Navy
SPC.3110 (ex-*HDML.1110*)	H. Mohatta	Indian Navy
SPC.3112 (ex-*HDML.1112*)	Calcutta	Indian Navy
SPC.3117 (ex-*HDML.1117*)	Bombay	Indian Navy
SPC.3118 (ex-*HDML.1118*)	Calcutta	Indian Navy
IRIRANGI (ex-*HDML.1192*)	Grays Harbour Shpg.	Royal New Zealand Navy
MAKO (ex-*HDML.1183*)	Madden & Lewis ...	Royal New Zealand Navy

Name	Builder	Disposition
MANGA (ex-*HDML.1185*)	Madden & Lewis ...	Royal New Zealand Navy
NGPONA (ex-*HDML.1193*)	Grays Harbour Shpg.	Royal New Zealand Navy
OLPHERT (ex-*HDML.1190*)	Everett Marine ...	Royal New Zealand Navy
PAEA (ex-*HDML.1184*)	Madden & Lewis ...	Royal New Zealand Navy
PEGASUS (ex-*HDML.1348*)	Ackerman Boat ...	Royal New Zealand Navy
TAKAPU (ex-*HDML.1188*)	Everett Marine ...	Royal New Zealand Navy
TAMAKI (ex-*HDML.1191*)	Grays Harbour Shpg.	Royal New Zealand Navy
TARAPUNGA (ex-*HDML.1187*)	Everett Marine ...	Royal New Zealand Navy
TOROA (ex-*HDML.1350*)	Ackerman Boat ...	Royal New Zealand Navy
WAKEFIELD (ex-*HDML.1194*)	Grays Harbour Shpg.	Royal New Zealand Navy

Pt. No.	Name	Pt. No.	Name
P.3551	MAKO	P.3562	OLPHERT
P.3552	PAEA	P.3563	PEGASUS
P.3553	TAMAKI	P.3564	TOROA
P.3554	IRIRANGI	P.3565	WAKEFIELD
P.3555	NGPONA	P.3566	TARAPUNGA
P.3556	TAKAPU	P.3567	MANGA

Admiralty type: **SDB.1321, 1324, 1325. SDML.3502, 3506, 3507, 3517, 3520, 3551-3556, 3562-3567. SPC.3110, 3112, 3117, 3118**

Former harbour defence motor launches (HDML's) which were re-classed as seaward defence motor launches (SDML's) and re-numbered after the Second World War.

This series originally comprised six hundred units (Nos. 1001–1600) built between 1940–44 in boatyards in the U.K., Dominions and Colonies, and also in the United States, of which about one hundred were ultimately cancelled.

Primarily intended for anti-submarine duties off ports and harbours, they proved such robust and seaworthy units that their operationa scope was much windened. Post-war large numbers passed into private ownership as pleasure craft (they were of a suitable size and diesel-engined), and nearly one hundred were purchased by foreign navies for patrol work, in addition to eighty-seven (R.A.N. twenty-four, R.I.N. twenty, R.N.Z.N. sixteen, and S.A.N. sixteen) allocated to Commonwealth navies during the war. Craft in the Royal Australian Navy were lengthened by about 8 feet and re-engined post-war.

46/54 tons except *R.A.N. craft* 47/58 tons; 70(pp) 72(oa) except *R.A.N. craft* 78(pp) $80\frac{1}{4}$(oa) × 16 × $5\frac{1}{2}$ feet; two shafts; Geniffer except *Pakistan Navy craft* Gardner and *R.A.N. craft* Buda diesel engines, B.H.P. 320/300/390 = 12 knots; O.F. ... tons; *R.A.N. craft* one 40mm. A.A. gun, *Pakistan Navy craft* one 3-pounder and one 20mm. A.A. guns, *Indian Navy craft* two/*R.N.Z.N. craft* one 20mm. A.A. (1/2 × 1) guns; complement 14 except *R.A.N.* and *R.N.Z.N. craft* 12.

Lengthened Australian HDML with bridge closed in and cabin added aft.

181

COASTAL CRAFT

Pt. No.	Name	Builder	Launched
M.2603	ARLINGHAM ...	Camper & Nicholson	1. 4.53
M.2605	BASSINGHAM ...	Vosper	24. 6.42
M.2614	BUCKLESHAM ...	Ardrossan D.Y. ...	26. 8.53
M.2617	CHILLINGHAM ...	McLean	19.12.52
M.2618	COBHAM	Fairlie	14. 5.53
M.2629	DAMERSHAM ...	Brooke Marine ...	15. 6.53
M.2619	DARSHAM... ...	Jones	19.11.52
M.2620	DAVENHAM ...	Weatherhead ...	23. 9.53
M.2621	DITTISHAM ...	Fairlie	23.10.53
M.2622	DOWNHAM ...	White	1. 9.55
M.2626	EVERINGHAM ...	Philip	4. 3.54
M.2628	FLINTHAM ...	Bolson	10. 3.55
M.2630	FRITHAM	Brooke Marine ...	24. 9.53
M.2631	GLENTHAM ...	Ardrossan D.Y. ...	29. 4.57
M.2635	HAVERSHAM ...	McLean	3. 6.54
M.2637	HOVINGHAM ...	Fairlie	24. 5.56
M.2601	INGLESHAM ...	White	23. 4.52
M.2636	LASHAM	Weatherhead ...	31. 5.54

Pt. No.	Name	Builder	Launched
5010	Unnamed (ex-Bottisham)	Ailsa Sbdg. ...	16. 2.53
5011	Unnamed (ex-Chelsham)	Jones	9. 7.52
5012	Unnamed (ex-Halsham)	Jones	... 9.53
M.2609	JERONG (ex-Boreham)	Brooke Marine ...	21.10.52
M.2606	LANGA SUKA (ex-Bedham)	Bolson	29. 7.53
M.2602	SRI JOHORE (ex-Altham)	Camper & Nicholson	2.12.52
M.2604	SRI PERLIS (ex-Asheldham)	Philip	30. 9.52
M.2612	TEMASEK (ex-Brantingham)	Ailsa Sbdg. ...	4.12.53
M.2627	TODAK (ex-Felmersham)	Camper & Nicholson	24. 9.53

Machinery contracts: Engined by Davey Paxman.

Pt. No.	Name	Builder	Launched
M.2717	FORDHAM (ex-Pavenham)	Jones	25. 7.56

"-ham" class (first series): **M.2601-2606, 2610, 2612, 2614, 2617-2622, 2626-2631, 2635-2637, Nos. 5010-5012**

The marked development made during the Second World War with influence mines considerably increased the mining potential in shallow waters, and greatly increased the mining hazard in approaching ports and harbours.

During the war the threat was countered by wooden motor minesweepers, while post-war some of the surviving Fairmile "B" motor launches were converted to this role. The inshore minesweepers were developed from the mine-sweeping motor launches, were also of wood construction, and were fitted for magnetic, acoustic, and wire 'sweeping. The parent firm supervising construction was White.

Six craft—JERONG, LANGA SUKA, SRI JOHORE, SRI PERLIS, TEMASEK, and TODAK—were sold to the Royal Malaysian Navy in 1958-59 and had their 'sweeping gear removed and two 20mm. A.A. (2×1) guns added; two others—ZUARA (ex-*Greetham*—M.2632) and BRAK (ex-*Harpham*—M.2634)—were sold to the Royal Libyan Navy in 1963; three were transferred to the Royal Air Force—Nos. *5010* (ex-*5000*, ex-*Bottisham*—M.2611), *5011* (ex-*5001*, ex-*Chelsham*—M.2616), and *5012* (ex-*5002*, ex-*Halsham*—M.2633)—in 1965-66; and a further three—BLUNHAM (M.2608), BODENHAM (M.2609), and ELSENHAM (M.2624)—were sold to the South Arabian Navy in 1967; and BISHAM (M.2607), BRIGHAM (M.2613), CARDINGHAM (M.2615, ELDINGHAM (M.2623), and ETCHINGHAM (M.2625) have been discarded.

The remaining craft are disposed as follows, those marked thus * being earmarked for disposal: *Clyde:* ARLING-HAM (PAS), EVERINGHAM (PAS). *Hythe:* *INGLESHAM. *Portsmouth:* DITTISHAM (TRV), FLINTHAM (TRV), FRITHAM (TRV), HAVERSHAM (TRV). *Singapore:* *COBHAM, *DAMERSHAM, *DARSHAM, *DAVENHAM, *GLENTHAM, *HOVINGHAM. *Disposition unknown:* *BASSINGHAM, BUCKLESHAM (TRV), *CHILLINGHAM, DOWNHAM (TRV), LASHAM (TRV).

120/159 tons; 100(pp) 106½(oa)×21×5½ feet; two shafts; 12-cyl. Davey Paxman diesel engines, B.H.P. 1,100=14 knots; O.F. 15 tons; one 20mm. or 40mm. A.A. gun; complement 15.

" -ham " class (second series): **M.12, 2705-2708, 2712-2714, 2716, 2717, 2722, 2723, 2726-2729, 2733, 2735, 2737**

The next series of inshore minesweepers were also of wood construction and were similar to the initial series from which they were practically indistinguishable except for a prominent rubbing strake round the hull. The REEDHAM was fin stabilised, a modification back-fitted to most of these craft brought out of reserve for active employment.

Under the MDAP agreement fifteen craft of this series—FRETTENHAM (M.2702), WEXHAM (M.2738), MERSHAM (M.2709), ISHAM (M.2703), KINGHAM (M.2704), STEDHAM (M.2730), RENDLESHAM (M.2724), PETERSHAM (M.2718), MILEHAM (M.2711), TIBENHAM (M.2734), SPARHAM (M.2731), WHIPPINGHAM

COASTAL CRAFT

Pt. No.	Name	Builder	Launched
M.2706	LEDSHAM	Bolson	30. 6.54
M.2708	LUDHAM	Fairlie	16. 6.54
M.2713	NETTLEHAM ...	White	19.12.56
M.2714	OCKHAM	Ailsa Sbdg.	12. 5.59
M.2716	PAGHAM	Jones	4.10.55
M.2722	RACKHAM ...	Saunders-Roe	27. 4.56
M.2723	REEDHAM... ...	Saunders-Roe	19. 8.58
M.2727	SAXLINGHAM ...	Berthon Boat	17.10.55
M.2726	SHIPHAM	Brooke Marine ...	14. 7.55
M.2728	SHRIVENHAM ...	Bolson	28. 3.56
M.2729	SIDLESHAM ...	Harris	25. 3.55
M.2733	THAKEHAM ...	Fairlie	9. 9.57
M.2735	TONGHAM	Miller	30.11.55
M.2737	WARNINGHAM ...	Thornycroft (Hampton)	23. 4.54
M.2712	.... (ex-*Neasham*)	White	14. 3.56
M.12	AFADZATO (ex-*Ottringham*)	Ailsa Sbdg.	22. 1.58

Machinery contracts: All engined by Davey Paxman.

Pt. No.	Name	Builder	Launched
M.2707	BASSEIN (ex-*Littleham*)	Brooke Marine ...	4. 5.54
M.2705	BIMLIPATAN (ex-*Hildersham*)	Vosper	5. 2.54
M.2002	AVELEY	White	16. 2.53
M.2003	BREARLEY... ...	White	16. 6.53
M.2004	BRENCHLEY ...	Saunders-Roe	19. 7.54
M.2005	BRINKLEY... ...	Saunders-Roe	14. 9.54
M.2009	CHAILEY	Saunders-Roe	12.11.54
M.2010	CRADLEY (ex-*Isis*, ex-*Cradley*)	Saunders-Roe ...	24. 2.55

Machinery contracts: All engined by Davey Paxman.

Pt. No.	Name	Builder	Launched
M.2787	ABBOTSHAM ...	Blackmore	16.12.55
M.2785	BIRDHAM	Taylor	19. 8.55
M.2788	GEORGEHAM ...	Harris	14. 2.57
M.2783	ODIHAM	Vosper	21. 7.55
M.2781	PORTISHAM ...	Dorset Yacht ...	3.11.55
M.2784	PUTTENHAM ...	Thornycroft (Hampton)	25. 6.56

(M.2739), SULHAM (M.2732), RIPLINGHAM (M.2725) and PINCHAM (M.2719)—were built for the French Navy and re-numbered M.771–776 and M.781–789 respectively on transfer. The BASSEIN and BIMLIPATAN were sold to the Indian Navy in 1955; the AFADZATO to the Ghanaian Navy in 1959, when her pendant number was changed from M.2715 to M.12; the POWDERHAM (M.2720) was converted into an inshore surveying vessel in 1964 and re-named WATERWITCH; NEASHAM was transferred to the Royal Australian Navy; and CRANHAM (M.2701), MICKLEHAM (M.2710), PULHAM (M.2721), and TRESHAM (M.2736) have been discarded.

The remaining craft are disposed as follows, those marked thus * being earmarked for disposal: *Clyde:* LEDSHAM (RNR), RACKHAM (RNXS), SIDLESHAM (PAS). *Chatham:* THAKEHAM (RNXS). *Devonport:* FORDHAM (TRV). *Hythe:* OCKHAM, *REEDHAM. *Portsmouth:* WARNINGHAM (DGV). *Rosyth:* TONGHAM (PAS). *Disposition unknown:* LUDHAM (PAS), *NETTLEHAM, PAGHAM (RNXS), SAXLINGHAM (RNXS), SHIPHAM (RNXS), *SHRIVENHAM.

120/159 tons; 100(pp) 106$\frac{1}{2}$)oa)$\times 21\frac{3}{4}\times 5\frac{3}{4}$ feet; 12-cyl. Davey Paxman diesel engines, B.H.P. 1,100=14 knots; O.F. 15 tons; one 20mm. or 40mm. A.A. gun (not in *port auxiliary craft*); complement 15.

" *-ley* " class: **M.2002-2005, 2009, 2010**

These craft were generally similar to the initial series of inshore minesweepers except that they were of composite construction with alloy frames and wood skin, and now fitted as minehunters they have no 'sweeping gear and more extensive superstructure. A further unit—the EDGLEY (M.2011)—was cancelled, and the parent firm supervising construction was White.

The BROADLEY (M.2006), DINGLEY (M.2001), SQUIRREL (ex-*Burley*—M.2008), and WATCHFUL (ex-*Broomley*—M.2007) have been discarded, and the remaining craft are disposed as follows, those marked thus * being earmarked for disposal: *Devonport:* AVELEY, BEARLEY. *Hythe:* CRADLEY. *Portsmouth:* *CHAILEY. *Rosyth:* *BRENCHLEY, *BRINKLEY.

123/164 tons; 100(pp) 106$\frac{3}{4}$(oa)$\times 21\frac{3}{4}\times 5\frac{1}{2}$ feet; two shafts; 8-cyl. Davey Paxman diesel engines, B.H.P. 700=13 knots; O.F. 15 tons; one 20mm. or 40mm. A.A. gun; complement 15.

Altham, ISMS of the first series and armed with a single 40 mm. A.A. gun forward.

Rackham, ISMS of the second series and distinguishable from the first series by conspicuous rubbing strake round hull.

Cardingham (since scrapped) also belonged to the first series of ISMS and shipped a 20mm. A.A. gun forward.

The Indian ISMS *Bhaktal* is a unit of the third series and is armed with a 20mm A.A. gun.

COASTAL CRAFT

" -ham " class (*third series*): **M.11, 89, 2777-2779, 2781-2788, 2790, 2791, 2793,** and **ONE** unnamed

The final series of inshore minesweepers also adhered to wood construction with a promiment rubbing strake round the hull. The YOGADA was transferred to the Ghanaian Navy in 1959 when her pennant number was changed from M.2789 to M.11; two—OTTER (ex-*Popham*) and SEAL (ex-*Wenbringham*)—were transferred to the Royal Australian Navy for employment as diving tenders; the YAXHAM (M.2780) was converted into a surveying vessel in 1964 and renamed WOODLARK; and the POLSHAM (M.2792) has been discarded.

They are disposed as follows, those marked * being earmarked for disposal: *Gareloch:* *SANDRINGHAM. *Hythe:* *RAMPISHAM, *WRENTHAM. *De-gaussing vessel:* THATCHAM. *Port auxiliary service:* BIRDHAM, ODIHAM, PORTISHAM, PUTTENHAM, *WOLDINGHAM. *Disposition unknown:* *ABBOTSHAM, *GEORGE-HAM, *THORNHAM.

120/159 tons; 100(pp) 107½(oa) × 22 × 5¾ feet; two shafts; 12-cyl. Davey Paxman diesel engines, B.H.P. 1,100=14 knots; O.F. 15 tons; one 20mm. A.A. gun (not in *port auxiliary service craft*); complement 15.

Pt. No.	Name	Builder	Launched
M.2786	RAMPISHAM ...	Bolson	I. 5.57
M.2791	SANDRINGHAM ...	McLean	16. 4.57
M.2790	THATCHAM ...	Jones	25. 9.57
M.2793	THORNHAM ...	Taylor	18. 3.57
M.2778	WOLDINGHAM ...	White	30.11.55
M.2779	WRENTHAM ...	Dorset Yacht ...	8. 2.55
M.11	YOGADA (ex-*Malham*)	Fairlie	29. 8.58
M.89	BHAKTAL	Mazagon Dock ...	... 4.67
M.	A	Mazagon Dock ...	....

Pt. No.	Name	Builder	Launched
M.2782	OTTER (ex-*Popham*)	Vosper	II. 1.55
M.2777	SEAL (ex-*Wintringham*)	White	24. 5.55

Machinery contracts: All engined by Davey Paxman or licencees.

P.1109	DARK CLIPPER ...	Vosper	9. 2.55
P.1113	DARK FIGHTER ...	Taylor	4.10.55
P.1114	DARK GLADIATOR	Taylor	5.12.56
P.1115	DARK HERO ...	McGruer	16. 3.57

Machinery contracts: All engined by Napier.

"*Dark*" *class:* DARK CLIPPER, DARK FIGHTER, DARK GLADIATOR, DARK HERO

The first Royal Navy motor torpedo boats (MTB's) to be diesel engined, their merit over preceding types is not readily apparent unless the advantage of diesel propulsion—which considerably reduced the fire hazard under which the earlier boats laboured for so long, besides extending the radius of action—are fully appreciated. Of composite construction— alloy framing and deck and wood skin—they were designed as interchangable gun- or torpedo-boats, or to act as mine-layers. The parent firm supervising construction was Saunders-Roe, who also built five similar craft for the Burmese Navy and two for the Finnish Navy. Of the 19 units originally comprising this class one was cancelled; eight were sold to the Italian Customs; six others scrapped including DARK SCOUT (all alloy); the remainder is earmarked for disposal.

50/64 tons; 67(pp) 71¼(oa)×19½×5 feet; two shafts; 18-cyl. Napier Deltic diesel engines, B.H.P. 5,000=40/36 knots; O.F. 8 tons; one 4·5-inch D.P. and one 40mm. A.A. guns (as MGB's), or one 40mm. A.A. gun and four 21-inch (4×1) T.T. (as MTB's) or six mines (as MML's); complement 15.

COASTAL CRAFT

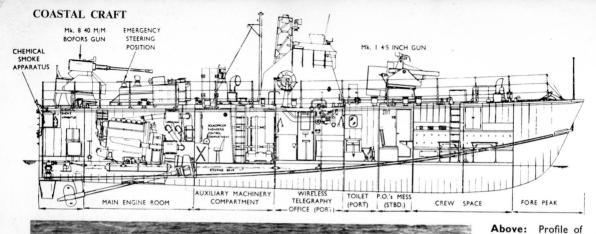

CHEMICAL SMOKE APPARATUS

Mk. 8 40 M/M BOFORS GUN

EMERGENCY STEERING POSITION

Mk. I 4·5 INCH GUN

SQUADRON ENGINEERS CONTROL COMPARTMENT

STEERING GEAR

| MAIN ENGINE ROOM | AUXILIARY MACHINERY COMPARTMENT | WIRELESS TELEGRAPHY OFFICE (PORT) | TOILET (PORT) | P.O.'s MESS (STBD.) | CREW SPACE | FORE PEAK |

Above: Profile of "Dark" class gun/torpedo boat.
[Courtesy *Motor Ship*

Left: *Shalford* fitted with a squid A/S mortar aft.

General arrangement of " -ford " class SDB.

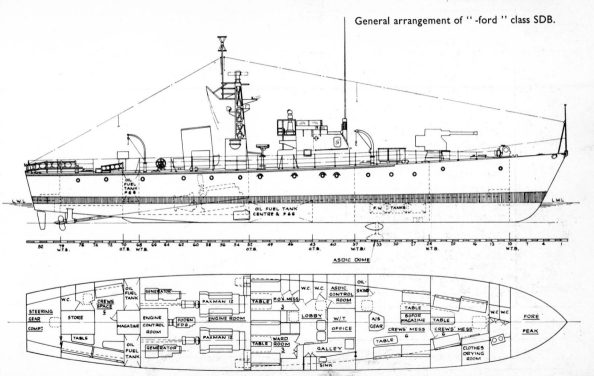

COASTAL CRAFT

Pt. No.	Name	Builder	Launched
P.3104	BECKFORD ...	Simons	27. 4.55
P.3107	CAMBERFORD ...	Vosper	28. 7.53
P.3113	DROXFORD (ex-Dee, ex-Droxford)	Pimblott	28. 1.54
P.3109	GREATFORD ...	White	29. 1.53
P.3116	ICKFORD	Rowhedge I.W. ...	17. 6.54
P.3121	KINGSFORD ...	Rowhedge I.W. ...	24. 3.55
P.3122	MARLINGFORD ...	Yarwood	17. 6.64
P.3114	MAYFORD... ...	Richards I.W. ...	30. 9.54
P.3101	SHALFORD ...	Yarrow	29 10 51
P.3123	TILFORD	Vosper	21.11.56
P.3102	NYATI (ex-Aberford)	Yarrow	22. 9.52
P.3115	BENIN (ex-Hinksford)	Richards I.W.	4.10.55

Pt. No.	Name	Builder	Launched
P.3119	BONNY (ex-Dubford)	White	2. 3.53
P.12	ENUGU	Camper & Nicholson	30. 6.61
P.3124	IBADAN (ex-Montford)	Pimblott	10.10.57
P.3103	KADUNA (ex-Axford)	Simons	30. 9.54
P.3111	SAPELE (ex-Gifford)	Scarr	30. 6.54
P.3106	.... (ex-Bryansford)	Inglis	2. 4.54
P.13	ELMINA	Yarrow	15. 6.62
P.14	KOMENDA ...	Yarrow.	17. 5.62
SPC.3135	ABHAY	Hooghly Dock ...	61
SPC.3134	AJAY	Garden Reach ...	60
SPC.3136	AKSHAY	Hooghly Dock ...	61

Machinery contracts: Engined by Davey Paxman.

"-ford" class: **P12-14, 3101-3107, 3109, 3111, 3113-3116, 3119, 3121-3124, SPC.3134-3136**

This class was developed from the war-built HDML's but with dimensions enlarged to that of contemporary ML's, and were designed to detect and engage submarines in the approaches to ports and harbours. In harbours lacking fixed anti-submarine defences (such as those infrequently used in peace-time), or freshly established beachheads, they can establish immediate offshore anti-submarine protection until more permanent measures are adopted. They also have a limited application with emergent Commonwealth (and other) navies for initial anti-submarine training.

Of steel construction, the main propulsion is to the wing shafts with auxiliary drive only to the centre shaft. The lead craft—the SHALFORD—was fitted with a Squid A/S mortar aft, but later units were provided with two throwers and two racks over the stern for depth charges. A single 40mm. A.A. gun is mounted forward, two rocket flare projectors abreast the bridge, and they are distinctively rigged with a lattice mast and twin funnels set abreast. The parent firm supervising construction was Yarrow.

The missing numbers P.3110, 3112, 3117 and 3118 were not allocated because they were already borne by Indian Navy craft, while SPC.3128–3133 are held by Indian Navy craft not belonging to this class. The GELDERLAND (ex-*Brayford*—P.3105) and NAUTILUS (ex-*Glassford*—P.3120) were transferred to the South African Navy in 1954–55; KOTIYA (ex-*Desford*—P.3108) to the Singhalese Navy in 1955, and was wrecked at Colombo on 22/12/64; NYATI to the Kenyan Navy in 1964; and BENIN, BONNY, IBADAN, KADUNA and SAPELE to the Nigerian Navy in 1967, and BRYANSFORD in 1968. In addition six units—South African Navy, HAERLEM (P.3126), COSTERLAND (P.3127) and RIJGER (P3125); Ghanian Navy ELMINA and KOMMENDA; and Nigerian Navy ENEGU—were ordered directly by Commonwealth navies and were all fitted with fin stabilisation, while a further three units (ABHAY, AJAY, and AKSHAY) were locally-built for the Indian Navy.

They are disposed as follows: *Barrow:* MAYFORD. *Portsmouth:* DROXFORD. *Singapore:* CAMBERFORD, GREATFORD, ICKFORD, MARLINGFORD, SHALFORD, TILFORD. *R.N.R.:* BECKFORD (Mersey Division), KINGSFORD (Clyde Division).

120/160 tons except Indian Navy *Abhay* and *Akshay* 150 tons and *Ajay* 145 tons; 110(pp) $117\frac{1}{4}$(oa) $\times 20 \times 5$ feet; three shafts; 12-cyl. Davey Paxman diesel engines (wing shafts), B.H.P. 1,100 = 18/15 knots + 6-cyl. Foden diesel engine (centre shaft—removed in Nigerian craft), B.H.P. 100 = 8 knots; O.F. 23 tons; one 40mm. A.A. gun, one A.S mortar (Squid—*Shalford only*); complement 19 except *Indian vessels* 24 and *Enugu* 26.

"*Bird*" *class:* BLUE HERON, CORMORANT, LOON, MALLARD

Reduced editions of the Royal Navy's "–ford" class and intended for similar duties with the Royal Canadian Navy but of composite construction. They are armed with a single 20mm. A.A. gun abaft the funnel, a split Hedgehog A/S mortar on the foredeck, and depth charge racks aft, and are rigged with a conspicious tripod mast. Four further units—the ARCTIC TERN, HERRING GULL, KINGFISHER and SANDPIPER—were cancelled. The BLUE HERON was loaned to the marine division of the Royal Canadian Mounted Police in 1956-68, who also had a steel-built version—the VICTORIA (Canadian Yarrow 1955)—built for their own account.

55/66 tons; 92(pp) . .(oa)×17×5¼ feet; two shafts; diesel engines, B.H.P. 1,200=14 knots; O.F. . . tons; one 20mm. A.A. gun, one A/S mortar (Hedgehog); complement 21.

Pt. No.	Name	Builder	Launched
PCS.782	BLUE HERON ...	Hunter Boat ...	7. 5.56
PCS.781	CORMORANT ...	Midland	15. 5.56
PCS.780	LOON	Taylor	4.10.54
PCS.783	MALLARD	Grew Boats ...	30. 4.56

Machinery contract: Engined by

194

R.Mal.N. type: PANGLIMA

Built as a training tender for the Royal Malaysian Navy Reserve, the PAGLIMA had a similar hull to the Royal Navy's "–ford" class and also had two funnels set abreast. The superstructure was more extensive and comprised a full-height deckhouse forward of the funnels, with an open bridge superimposed at its fore end. She was transferred to the Singapore Navy in 1967.

119/131 tons; 110(pp) 117(oa)×20×6 feet; two shafts; 12-cyl. Davey Paxman diesel engines, B.H.P. 1,000=14½ knots; O.F. 15 tons; one 40mm. A.A. gun; complement 15.

Pt. No.	Name	Builder	Launched
P.48	PANGLIMA ...	United Engineers (Singapore)	14. 1.56

Machinery contract: Engined by Davey Paxman.

"*Brave*" *class:* BRAVE BORDERER, BRAVE SWORDSMAN

Following experience with experimental craft fitted with gas turbines, and the resulting prototypes BOLD PATHFINDER and BOLD PIONEER (since scrapped), the original design of this class was cast round a fully automatic 3·3-inch gun, gas turbine propulsion, a hull of composite construction (alloy frames, bulkheads, and deck and wood skin), and a sustained sea speed of 44 knots for a 10-hour patrol. There was no staff require-

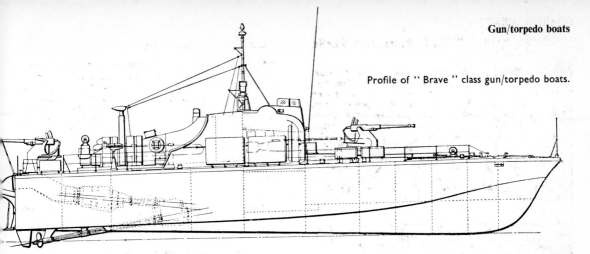

Profile of '' Brave '' class gun/torpedo boats.

ment for cruising and consequently auxiliary diesel propulsion was not incorporated. In the final outcome the 3·3-inch gun proved too weighty and, positioned amidships, cramped arrangements aft. A special feature was their ability to rapidly convert to any of several roles, such as a *torpedo boat* (one 40mm. gun and four torpedoes), *torpedo/gunboat* (two 40mm. guns and two torpedoes), *gunboat* (two 40mm. guns), *minelayer* (one 40mm. gun and ten ground mines), or *raiding craft* (one 40mm. gun, two outboard powered Gemini inflatable dinghies, and raiding party). Side launching gear in lieu of conventional tubes were provided for the torpedoes, and a similar vessel—the STRAHL—was built for the West German Navy by Vosper.

75/114 tons; 90(pp) $98\frac{3}{4}$(oa) $\times 25\frac{1}{2} \times 6$ feet; three shafts; Bristol Siddeley gas turbines, S.H.P. 10,500 = 50/44 knots; O.F. 25 tons; two 40mm. A.A. (2×1) guns and two 21-inch torpedoes or one 40 mm.A.A. gun and four 21-inch torpedoes; complement 20.

Pt. No.	Name	Builder	Launched
P.1011	BRAVE BORDERER	Vosper	7. 1.58
P.1012	BRAVE SWORDSMAN	Vosper	22. 5.58

Machinery contracts: Both engined by Bristol Siddeley.

Brave Borderer armed as a gun/torpedo boat.

Note the differences in bridge work and extra fuel tanks on the deck.

Brave Swordsman armed as a torpedo boat.

Malaysian *Perkasa* armed as a torpedo boat.

Unlike the "Brave" class these craft have cruising diesel engines coupled to the wing shafts.

Quarter view of *Perkasa* showing air intake for gas turbines.

U.S.S.R. type: **FOUR** craft (names not advised)

Steel patrol boats acquired by the Ghanian Navy from the U.S.S.R. during 1967.

86 tons (91 tons full load); 98(pp) . . .(oa) × 15 × 4¾ feet; two shafts, type M.50-3 diesel engines B.H.P. 1,200 (at 1,600 r.p.m.) = 18 knots, O.F. 9¼ tons (460m. at 17k); two 14.5mm. (1 × 2) machine guns; complement 16.

Pt. No.	Name			Builder			Launched
P.20	A	..	..	..	..	..	63
P.21	B	..	..	..	..	..	63
P.22	C	..	..	..	.;	..	63
P.23	D	..	..	..	..	..	63

Machinery contracts: Engined by

U.S.S.R. type: **SIX** craft (names not advised)

100-ton patrol boats scheduled for transfer to the Indian Navy 1967-68 from the U.S.S.R.

Vosper type: **GEMPITA, HANDALAN, PENDEKAR, PERKASA,** and **PAHLAWAN**

A private design in which Vosper incorporated some of their own special features. The hull was of wood construction throughout with all members bonded together, and diesel engines were coupled to the wing shafts only to extend the radius of action. The builder's private specualtion prototype—the FEROCITY, a diminutive of the "Brave" class—only had twin-screw propulsion, and a similar vessel—the PFEIL—was built for the West German Navy. These craft, the first four for the Royal Malaysian Navy and the remaining unit for the Sultan of Brunei, were slightly enlarged to ship an additional gas turbine but are otherwise generally similar to the six units built for the Royal Danish Navy (two by Vosper and four under licence by the Royal Dockyard at Copenhagen).

95/114 tons; 90(wl) 99¾(oa) × 24 × 3¾/7 feet; three shafts; Bristol Siddeley gas turbines, S.H.P. 12,750 = 54 knots, 6-cyl. G.M. diesel engines, B.H.P. 380 = 10 knots; O.F. 24¼ tons; two 40mm. A.A. (2 × 1) except *R.Mal.N. craft* one 40mm. A.A. and one 20mm. A.A. guns, four 21-inch (4 × 1—*R.Mal.N. craft* only) T.T.; complement 24.

Pt. No.	Name		Builder			Launched
P.	GEMPITA	...	Vosper	...	...	6. 4.66
P.	HANDALAN	...	Vosper	...	...	18. 1.66
P.	PENDEKAR	...	Vosper	...	...	24. 6.66
P.	PERKASA	...	Vosper	...	...	26.10.65
P.	PAHLAWAN	...	Vosper	...	...	5.12.66

Machinery contracts: All engined by Bristol Siddeley (gas turbines) and General Motors (diesel engines).

R.C.N. type: **BRAS D'OR**

The Royal Canadian Navy evinced an early interest in hydrofoil craft as a most suitable type for anti-submarine warfare. A small 17½-ton craft with fixed ladder foils— also named BRAS D'OR—was built for them by Saunder Roe in 1957 for exploratory research in this field, and the final outcome is the present craft of this name. Intended to cruise as a displacement hull and become foil-borne when high speed was required, the BRAS D'OR is bold in concept and may well influence the trend of future anti-submarine vessels. It should be noted that the prime advantage of the hydrofoil is not pure speed, but its ability to maintain speed in adverse weather conditions when compared with displacement craft of similar size. When hull-borne the BRAS D'OR is propelled by a diesel engine, boosted by a gas turbine, with propulsion nacelles fixed high on the main foil which are lifted clear of the water when foil-borne. In the latter condition she is supported by a bow foil together with a main foil farther aft with propulsion nacelles fixed lower on the foil, and is powered by a gas turbine. In both conditions the drive is through a single input/twin output gearbox, using controlable pitch propellers when hull-borne, and fixed pitch when foil-borne. The hull and superstructure is of all-welded aluminium construction. The design contract for this craft was awarded to the De Havilland Aircraft of Canada.

180/200 tons; 146½(wl) 151½(oa) × 21½ (66 across foil base) × 7½ (foil-borne)/23 (hull-borne) feet; two shafts; 16-cyl. Davey Paxman diesel engine and Pratt & Whitney gas turbine, B.H.P. 2,000+390=18 knots (hull-borne), Pratt & Whitney gas turbine, S.H.P. 22,000=60 knots (foil-borne); O.F. .. tons; twelve 12-inch A/S (4×3) T.T.; complement 20.

Pt. No.	Name		Builder	Launched
FHE.400	BRAS D'OR	...	Marine Industries ...	00.00.66

Machinery contracts: Davey Paxman (diesel engines) and Pratt & Whitney (gas turbines).

Vosper type: **P.34, 36-39, 40-47, 49, 3110, 3112, 3117, 3138-3143, CG.1 and 2**

A private design, and worthy successors to the war-built Fairmile "B" ML's, these craft incorporated accumulated post-war technical development in material, propulsion, and equipment. The hull is of all-welded steel construction with aluminium superstructure, combined with a high standard of habitability. All spaces except the engine room (not normally manned) are air-conditioned which, while contributing to crew comfort, effectively controlled corrosion problems which would otherwise have arisen in view of their employment in the tropics. Similarly, fin stabilisation—which also adds to crew comfort—made them a stable weapon platform from which the armament could be effectively fought in weather conditions which would normally render craft of this size not so fitted inoperative. The original order for six craft (P.3138–3143) by the Royal Malaysian Navy was followed by repeat orders for a further four (P.3144–3147) and then another fourteen (P.3148–3161). Except that they do not ship the after 40mm. A.A. gun and are

199

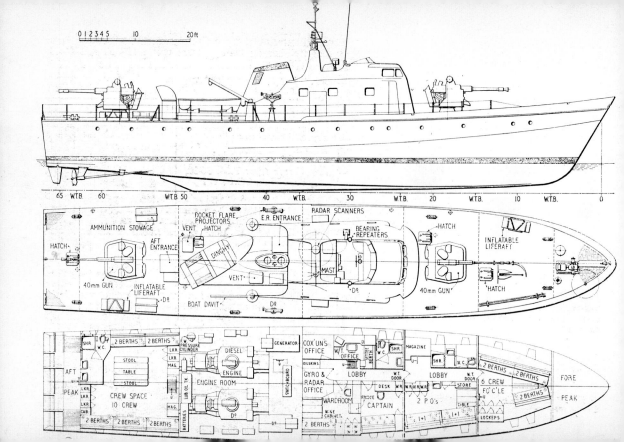

0 1 2 3 4 5   10   20 ft

65 W.T.B.   60   W.T.B. 50   40   W.T.B.   30   W.T.B.   20   W.T.B.   10   W.T.B.   0

AMMUNITION STOWAGE

ROCKET FLARE
PROJECTORS
VENT   HATCH

E.R. ENTRANCE

RADAR SCANNERS

BEARING
REPEATERS

HATCH

INFLATABLE
LIFERAFT

HATCH·

AFT
ENTRANCE

DINGHY

MAST

Dº

HATCH

40mm GUN

INFLATABLE
LIFERAFT

40mm GUN

VENT ·

Dº

BOAT DAVIT·

Dº

SHR.

W.C.

2 BERTHS   2 BERTHS

F.W.
PRESSURE
CYLINDER

LKR.
LKR.
MAG.

DIESEL
ENGINE

GENERATOR

COX'UNS
OFFICE

W/T
OFFICE

BERTHS

SHR.

W.C.

MAGAZINE

SHR.

W.C.

2 BERTHS   2 BERTHS

AFT

PEAK

LKR.
LKR.
LKR.
CAB.

STOOL

TABLE

STOOL

CREW SPACE
10 CREW

LUB OIL TK.

ENGINE ROOM

SWITCHBOARD

OILSKINS

GYRO &
RADAR
OFFICE

WARDROOM

LOBBY

W.T. DOOR

DESK

W.R.

CAPTAIN

FR'CE

W.T. DOOR

LOBBY

W.R.W.R.W.R.

STORE

W.T.
DOOR

6 CREW

2 PO's

FORE

FC'C'LE

PEAK

WINE CABINET.

2 BERTHS   2 BERTHS

BATTERIES

MAG.

Dº

2 BERTHS

LOCKERS

2 BERTHS

Left: General arrangement of Malaysian patrol boats.

Above: Bridge details.
[Blocks courtesy *Shipbuilding & Shipping Record.*

Top right Trinidad and Tobago *Trinity*.

Right: Kenyan *Simba*.
[Blocks courtesy *Naval Record.*

Pt. No.	Name	Builder	Launched
P.3138	SRI KEDAH ...	Vosper	4. 6.62
P.3142	SRI KELANTAN ...	Vosper	8. 1.63
P.3147	SRI MELAKA ...	Vosper	25. 2.64
P.3146	SRI NEGRI SEMBILAN	Vosper	17. 2.64
P.3141	SRI PAHANG ...	Vosper	15.10.62
P.3140	SRI PERAK ...	Vosper	30. 8.62
P.3144	SRI SABAH ...	Vosper	30.12.63
P.3145	SRI SARAWAK ...	Vosper	20. 1.64
P.3139	SRI SELANGOR ...	Vosper	17. 7.62
P.3143	SRI TRENGGANU ...	Vosper	12.12.62
P.37	BADEK	Vosper	8. 5.66
P.44	BELEDAU	Vosper	11. 1.67
P.45	KELEWANG ...	Vosper	31. 1.67
P.43	KERAMBIT ...	Vosper	30.11.66
P.34	KRIS	Vosper	11. 3.66
P.40	LEMBING	Vosper	22. 8.66
P.42	PANAH	Vosper	14.10.66
P.38	RENCHONG ...	Vosper	22. 6.66
P.46	RENTAKA ...	Vosper	15. 3.67
P.41	SERAMPANG ...	Vosper	14. 9.66

Pt. No.	Name	Builder	Launched
P.49	SRI JOHOR ...	Vosper	22. 6.67
P.47	SRI PERLIS ...	Vosper	26. 5.67
P.36	SUNDANG ...	Vosper	22. 5.66
P.39	TOMBAK ...	Vosper	20. 6.66
CG.2	COURLAND BAY	Vosper	20. 5.64
CG.1	TRINITY ...	Vosper	14. 4.64
P.3112	CHUI	Vosper	25.11.65
P.3110	SIMBA	Vosper	9. 9.65
P.3117	NDOVU (ex-*Twiga*)	Vosper	22.12.65

Machinery contracts: All *Royal Malaysian Navy* craft engined by Bristol Siddeley, and all *Trinidad and Tobago Coast Guard* and *Kenyan Navy* craft engined by Davey Paxman.

powered by diesel engines of slightly less power, the craft for the Trinidad and Tobago Coast Guard (CG. 1 and 2) and the Kenyan Navy are generally similar. Six slightly larger multi-purpose craft (110 feet) were delivered to the Peruvian Navy in 1965.

109/130 tons; 95(pp) 103(oa) × 19½ × 5½ feet; two shafts; 12-cyl. Maybach diesel engines, B.H.P. 3,550= 27 knots except *Trinidad & Tobago Coast Guard* and *Kenyan Navy* craft 12-cyl. Davey Paxman diesel engines, B.H.P. 2,400=24 knots; O.F. 20 tons; two except *Trinidad & Tobago Coast Guard* craft one 40mm. A.A. (1/2×1) guns; complement 23 except *Kenyan craft* 24.

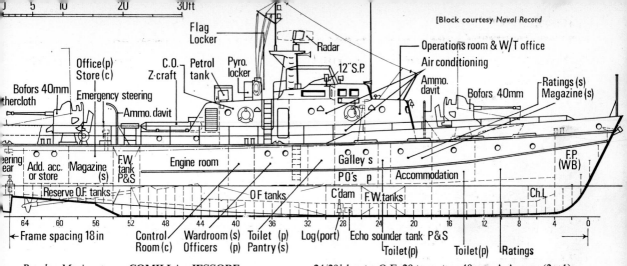

Labels on diagram:

Flag Locker

Radar

Operations room & W/T office
Air conditioning

C.O. Petrol
Store (c) tank

Pyro. locker

12" S.P.

Ammo. davit

Ratings (s)
Magazine (s)

Office (p)
Store (c)

Bofors 40mm
therplate

Emergency steering

Ammo. davit

Bofors 40mm

F.P. (WB)

eering
ear

Add. acc.
or store

Magazine
(s)

F.W.
tank
P&S

Engine room

Galley s

PO's p

Accommodation

Reserve O.F. tanks

O.F tanks

C'dam

F.W. tanks

Ch.L.

64 60 56 52 48 44 40 36 32 28 24 20 16 12 8 4 0

← Frame spacing 18 in

Control
Room (c)

Wardroom (s)
Officers   (p)

Toilet (p)
Pantry (s)

Log (port)

Echo sounder tank P&S

Toilet (p)

Toilet (p)

Ratings

Brooke Marine type: COMILLA, JESSORE, RAJSHAHI, SYLHET

Although rather similar to the Vosper series, these craft are an entirely independent design built for the Pakistan Navy. As the design parameters for these and the Vosper craft were nearly the same, externally similar vessels are bound to result. They have steel hulls, aluminium superstructure, a compound system of framing, and are rigged with a short tubular mast abaft the half-raised enclosed bridge.

115/143 tons; 100(pp) 107(oa) × 20 × 5 feet; two shafts; 12-cyl. Maybach diesel engines, B.H.P. 3,600/3,000 = 24/20½ knots; O.F. 20 tons; two 40mm. A.A. guns (2 × 1); complement 19.

Pt. No.	Name		Builder		Launched
P.142	COMILLA	...	Brooke Marine	...	20. 1.65
P.141	JESSORE	...	Brooke Marine	...	17. 2.65
P.140	RAJSHAHI	...	Brooke Marine	...	28. 6.65
P.143	SYLHET	...	Brooke Marine	...	26. 7.65

Machinery contracts: All engined by Bristol Siddeley.

203

Sri Kedah, lead ship of the series for the Royal Malaysian Navy.

Patrol boat *Comilla* for the Pakistan Navy.

[Block courtesy *Naval Record*

Sewart type: **DISCOVERY BAY, HOLLAND BAY, MANATED BAY**

All-aluminium patrol boats built in the United States for Jamaican Defence Force Coast Guard.

60 tons; 85(pp) ...(oa) × 18¾ × 6 feet; two shafts, 16-cyl. General Motors type V71N diesel engines B.H.P. 700 = 21 knots, O.F. 13 tons (500m. at 12k.); one ·5-inch machine gun; complement 10.

Pt. No.	Name	Builder	Launched
P.4	DISCOVERY BAY	Sewart Seacraft ...	... 8.66
P.5	HOLLAND BAY ...	Sewart Seacraft ...	67
P.6	MANATEE BAY ...	Sewart Seacraft ...	68

Machinery contracts: Engined by General Motors.

R.A.N. type: **ACUTE, ADROIT, ADVANCE, ARCHER, ARDENT, ARROW, ASSAIL, ATTACK, AWARE, BANDOLIER, BARBETTE, BARRICADE, BAYONET, BOMBARD, BUCCANEER, AITAPE, LADAVA, LAE, MADANG, SAMARAI**

These Royal Australian Navy craft, now building, will be generally similar to the Brooke patrol boats and have steel hulls and aluminium superstructure. The first fifteen ("A" and "B" names) will be locally employed in Australian Home waters, and the last five in the New Guinea area.

100/125 tons; 100(pp) 107(oa) × 20 × 5 feet; two shafts; 16-cyl. Davey Paxman diesel engines, B.H.P. 3,460 = 27 knots, O.F. 20 tons; one 40mm. A.A., two ·5-inch A.A. (2 × 1) guns; complement 19.

Pt. No.	Name	Builder	Launched
P.81	ACUTE	Evans Deakin ...	28. 6.67
P.82	ADROIT	Evans Deakin ...	3. 2.68
P.83	ADVANCE... ...	Walkers	16. 8.67
P.86	ARCHER	Walkers	2.12.67
P.87	ARDENT	Walkers	27. 4.68
P.88	ARROW	Walkers	17. 2.68
P.89	ASSAIL	Evans Deakin ...	18.11.67
P.90	ATTACK	Evans Deakin ...	8. 4.67
P.91	AWARE	Evans Deakin ...	7.10.67
P.95	BANDOLIER ...	Walkers	2.10.68
P.97	BARBETTE ...	Walkers	10. 4.68
P.98	BARRICADE ...	Evans Deakin ...	29. 6.68
P.101	BAYONET ...	Walkers	6.11.68
P.99	BOMBARD ...	Walkers	6. 7.68
P.100	BUCCANEER ...	Evans Deakin ...	14. 9.68

Official sketch of the Canadian anti-submarine hydrofoil *Bras d'Or* which has the gas turbine on deck.

Australian patrol boat *Attack*.

Pt. No.	Name	Builder	Launched
P.84	AITAPE	Walkers	6. 7.67
P.92	LADAVA	Evans Deakin ...	11. 5.68
P.93	LAE...	Walkers	5.10.67
P.94	MADANG	Evans Deakin ...	10. 8.68
P.85	SAMARAI	Evans Deakin ...	14. 7.67

Machinery contracts: All engined by Davey Paxman.

P.	INDEPENDENCE	Vosper Thornycroft (Portsmouth)	15. 7.69
P.	B	Vosper Thornycroft (Portsmouth)	....
P.	C	Vosper Thornycroft (Singapore)	....
P.	D	Vosper Thornycroft (Singapore)	....
P.	E	Vosper Thornycroft (Singapore)	....
P.	F	Vosper Thornycroft (Singapore)	....

Machinery contracts: Engined by Maybach.

Vosper type: **INDEPENDENCE** and **FIVE** unnamed craft

Following the acquisition of the training tender PANG-LIMA from Malaysia, in 1967, Singapore ordered six patrol boats in 1968 from Vosper Thornycroft of their standard 110-foot design, of which six were delivered to Peru in 1965. These craft are closely similar to the 103-foot type and the additional length is nearly all absorbed by the engine room to provide higher powered machinery for increased speed, and a third engine can be incorporated if required.

100 tons (130 tons full load); 103(wl) 109¾(oa)×21× 10½d/6 feet; two shafts, Maybach diesel engines B.H.P. 6,000 =30 knots, O.F. ... tons; two 40mm. A.A. (2×1) guns; complement 25.

Vosper type: **CUTLASS, SABRE, SCIMITAR**

These craft will act as targets to provide defensive training in attacks by fast light naval craft. While generally adhering to the standard Vosper all-wood design, they will be unarmed and have only two screws with CODOG arrangement of machinery.

90/ ... tons; 90(wl) 99¾(oa)×24×3½/7 feet; two shafts, Rolls-Royce gas turbines, S.H.P. 8,500 =40 knots, 6-cyl. Foden diesel engines B.H.P. 240 =9 knots, O.F. ... tons; complement ...

Pt. No.	Name	Builder	Launched
P.	CUTLASS	Vosper Thornycroft (Portsmouth)	69
P.	SABRE	Vosper Thornycroft (Portsmouth)	69
P.	SCIMITAR	Vosper Thornycroft (Portsmouth)	69

Machinery contracts: Engined by Rolls-Royce (gas turbines) and Foden (diesel engines).

Seal prototype long-range weapon recovery and support craft for the Royal Air Force.

R.A.F. type: **SEAL** and **TWO** unnamed boats

These craft are employed to recover the costly weapons and other equipment used by maritime aircraft of the Royal Air Force at far greater distances offshore than was previously permissible. Prior to their introduction this task was undertaken by R.A.F. marine craft primarily designed for inshore work, so that maritime aircraft had to exercise within an arbitarily limited radius—if weapon recovery was involved—rather than in their true environment over the open sea.

The weapon recovery compartment is located at the stern, and the compartment is opened to the sea by door—hinged at its foot—over which weapons are hauled in by an electric/hydraulic winch. As an alternative there is a 1-ton davit plumbing a hatch on the after deck and two small hatches in the casing roof; and also the inflatable Z-boat, powered by an outboard motor, which is used to assist with recovery from the sea. As recovery is accomplished at slow speed, or stopped, active fin stabilisation would be of no use, while a passive system to be effective would have to be installed high, so that weatherly qualities were secured by a carefully designed hull.

This hull form proved successful, and was adopted by Brooke Marine—who constructed the prototype on a design-and-build contract—for their 120ft. fast patrol boat of which four are building for the Royal Libyan Navy.

It is estimated that up to ten such craft are required by the R.A.F., and in addition to their main function they are also utilised for support functions, target towing, rescue work, and other general duties. Stowage space is provided for nine short and four long torpedoes.

125/158 tons; 110(pp) $120\frac{1}{4}$(oa) $\times 23\frac{1}{2} \times 14\frac{1}{2}$d/$5\frac{1}{2}$ feet; two shafts, 16-cyl. Davey Paxman diesel engines B.H.P. 4,000 (at 1,485 r.p.m.) =25 knots, O.F. 31 tons; complement 17.

Pt. No.	Name	Builder	Launched
	SEAL	Brooke Marine ...	11. 5.67
	A	Fairmile	69
	B	Fairmile	69

Machinery contracts: Engined by Davey Paxman.

Vosper Thornycroft Uniteers type: **SRI GUMANTONG** and **ONE** more unnamed

These craft were ordered by the Sabah Government in 1968-69 and belong to a standard series of which sixteen have been delivered to the Royal Malaysian Police (PX.1-16) while a further two are building for the Philippine Navy.

85 tons; ...(pp) $87\frac{1}{2}$(oa) $\times 19 \times 4\frac{3}{4}$ feet; two shafts, 12-cyl. Mercedes-Benz type MB.820Db turbocharged diesel engines B.H.P. 2,700=25 knots, O.F. $10\frac{3}{4}$ tons; two 20mm A.A. (2×1) guns; complement 15.

Pt. No.	Name	Builder	Launched
PX.17	SRI GUMANTONG	Vosper Thornycroft Uniteers (Singapore)	69
PX.18	SRI	Vosper Thornycroft Uniteers (Singapore)	69

Machinery contracts: Both engined by Maybach Mercedes-Benz.

FLEET TRAIN

For nuclear submarines: FORTH, MAIDSTONE

Modified to support nuclear submarines by H.M. Dockyards, Portsmouth (MAIDSTONE—1958–62) and Chatham (FORTH—1962–66) when the twin 4·5-inch D.P. and quadruple 2-pounder A.A. mountings were removed; additions made to the superstructures forward and aft; and a lattice replaced the pole foremast. The light cranes amidships were replaced by heavier units and an additional crane added on the quaterdeck, while a prominent hinged exhaust (horizontally stowed when not in use) for the gas turbine generator was sited before the bridge.

10,000/14,000 tons; 497(pp) 531(oa)×73×20/21¼ feet; four Admiralty 3-drum boilers; two shafts; Brown-Curtis *Forth*/Parsons *Maidstone* geared turbines, S.H.P. 7,000=16 knots; O.F. 2,300 tons; five 40mm. A.A. (5×1) guns; complement 1,590.

For destroyers: TYNE

The TYNE has been little altered except that the former mixed light A.A. armament has been replaced by 40mm. guns. Like the ADAMANT below—but to a greater extent—she can only now provide limited support facilities, outside of accommodation and victualling, for modern flotilla vessels. A sister ship, the HECLA, was a war loss.

11,000/14,600 tons; 585(pp) 621(oa)×66×20¼ feet; four Admiralty 3-drum boilers; two shafts; Parsons geared turbines, S.H.P. 7,500=17 knots; O.F. 1,400 tons; eight 4·5-inch D.P. (4×2), seven 40mm. A.A. (2×2 and 3×1) guns; complement 1,000.

For submarines: ADAMANT

Except that her twin 4·5-inch D.P. and quadruple 2-pounder A.A. mountings have been removed, and a reduced number of 40mm. A.A. guns substituted, the ADAMANT has been little altered and only has limited support facilities for modern conventional submarines. She generally followed the lines of the TYNE but was slightly enlarged.

12,700/16,500 tons; 620(pp) 658(oa)×70½×20/21¼ feet; four Admiralty 3-drum boilers; two shafts; Parsons geared turbines, S.H.P. 8,000=17 knots; O.F. 2,600 tons; twelve 40mm. A.A. (2×4 and 2×2) guns; complement 750.

For submarines: AMBA

Scheduled for transfer to the Indian Navy 1968 from the U.S.S.R.

Left top: Destroyer depot ship *Tyne*.　**Left bottom:** Submarine depot ship *Adamant*.

Below: *Triumph*, former carrier converted to heavy repair ship.

FLEET TRAIN

For heavy repairs: **TRIUMPH**

This former light fleet aircraft carrier was converted to a heavy repair ship at H.M. Dockyard, Portsmouth, between 1958–65. All fixed wing aircraft capability was removed, the hangars were converted into workshops while additional workshops were added on the flight deck and store space provided below. Four cranes were stepped on the flight deck, a hangar to accommodate three helicopters for servicing added inboard of the island, and the bridge raised a deck in height. She can simultaneously maintain four modern escorts (two a side) and supply them with steam and electrical power, so that they can completely shut-down, from a harbour services plant situated between the forward and af.er machinery spaces which was formerly the aircraft fuel compartment. Limited accommodation is also available for the crews of escorts. The main and auxiliary machinery is remotely operated from a central control room and ABC defence measures incorporated.

13,350/17,000 tons; 630(pp) 699(oa) × 80¼ × 18¾/21¼ feet; four Admiralty 3-drum boilers (400 lb/in² at 700°F); two shafts; Parsons geared turbines, S.H.P. 40,000=24½ knots; O.F. 3,000 tons; four 40 mm.A.A. (4×1) guns; complement 1,639.

Pt. No.	Name	Builder	Laid down	Launched	Completed	Disposition
A.187	FORTH	Clydebank	30. 6.37	11. 8.38	14. 5.39	Far East
A.185	MAIDSTONE	Clydebank	17. 8.36	21.10.37	5. 5.38	Rosyth, for disposal
A.194	TYNE	Scotts	15. 7.33	28. 2.40	28. 2.41	Devonport reserve
A.164	ADAMANT	Harland & Wolff ...	18. 5.39	30.11.40	23. 2.42	Devonport reserve
A.108	TRIUMPH	Hawthorn Leslie ...	27. 1.43	2.10.44	9. 4.46	Singapore

Machinery contracts: All engined by builders.

The *Manxman* has had half her installed power and all her 4-inch A.A. guns removed, to serve as a minesweeper support ship

Pt. No.	Name	Builder	Laid down	Launched	Completed	Disposition
N.26	PLOVER	Denny...	7.10.36	8. 6.37	24. 9.37	Port Edgar, for disposal

Machinery contract: Engined by

Pt. No.	Name	Builder	Laid down	Launched	Completed	Disposition
N.70	MANXMAN	Stephen	24. 3.39	5. 9.40	20. 6.41	Singapore

Machinery contract: Engined by builder.

Pt. No.	Name	Builder	Laid down	Launched	Completed	Disposition
F.408	CULGOA	H.M.A. Dockyard (Williamstown)	15. 7.43	22. 9.45	17.12.46	Royal Australian Navy
DE 320	GRANBY (ex-*Victoriaville*)	G. T. Davie	26.11.43	23. 6.44	11.11.44	Royal Canadian Navy

Machinery contract: Culgoa engined by Thompson Eng. & Pipe Co., and *Granby* by Canadian Vickers.

Pt. No.	Name	Builder	Laid down	Launched	Completed	Disposition
K.07	LOFOTEN (ex-*LST(3).3027*)	Blyth Sbdg.	30. 5.44	25. 1.45	24.10.45	
L.3044	NARVIK (ex-*LST(3).3044*)	Vickers-Armstrongs (Barrow)	14.12.44	29. 7.45	4. 4.46	Faslane, for disposal
L.3515	STALKER (ex-*LST(3).3515*)	Canadian Yarrow ...	22. 4.44	16.12.44	5. 6.45	Londonderry
L.3522	TRACKER (ex-*LST(3).3522*)	Davie Sbdg.	....	9. 6.45	...10.45	Devonport

Machinery contracts: Stalker engined by Dominion Engineering Works, *Tracker* by Canadian Pacific Railways, and others by builders.

Pt. No.	Name	Builder	Laid down	Launched	Completed	Disposition
A.231	RECLAIM	Simons	9. 4.46	12. 3.46	00.10.48	Port Edgar

Machinery contract: Engined by Aitchison Blair.

For mine countermeasures: **PLOVER**

Completed as a coastal minelayer, the PLOVER performed sterling war service and laid over 15,000 mines: a figure only surpassed by five of the much larger auxiliary minelayers. She has been kept in continuous commission and employed for a variety of associated mining roles post-war, and is now classed as a mine countermeasures support vessel. She was slightly modified in 1955 when a deckhouse and pole mainmast were added aft.

805/1,020 tons: 180(pp) $195\frac{1}{4}$(oa)$\times37\frac{1}{2}\times$../10 feet; two .... boilers (... lb/in²); two shafts; reciprocating (VTE-cyl. .."$:..$"$:..$"$\times..$" stroke), I.H.P. 1,400$=14\frac{3}{4}$ knots; O.F. ... tons; complement 69.

For minesweepers: **MANXMAN**

This former minelayer was converted at H.M. Dockyard, Chatham, in 1962–63 to act as a parent ship for up to sixteen coastal minesweepers. The boiler power—and consequently engine power—was halved, and additional generator and evaporator capacity was installed in the forward boiler room, while the fore funnel was retained for ventilation and diesel exhaust trunking. The twin 4-inch A.A. mountings were removed, additional superstructure added aft, and two-thirds of the mining deck taken over for stores and offices. Of the other ships in this class three were war losses and two were scrapped.

3,000/4,000 tons; $400\frac{1}{2}$(pp) 418(oa)$\times39\times13/16$ feet; two Admiralty 3-drum boilers; two shafts; Parsons geared turbines, S.H.P. 36,000$=27$ knots; O.F. 750 tons; six 40mm. A.A. (1×2 and 4×1) guns; complement 238.

For minesweepers: **CULGOA**. For divers: **GRANBY**

Former "River" class frigates disarmed and used as an accommodation ship for minesweepers (CULGOA) and diving tender (GRANBY); the latter replaced a former "Bangor" class minesweeper of the same name. For other vessels of this class under surveying vessels (p. 159) and escort vessels (p. 86).

1,537/2,187 tons; 283(pp) $301\frac{1}{4}$(oa)$\times36\frac{3}{4}\times12\frac{3}{4}/14\frac{1}{2}$ feet; two Admiralty 3-drum boilers (225 lb/in²); two shafts; reciprocating (VTE—cyl. $18\frac{1}{2}$":31":$38\frac{1}{2}$"(2)$\times30$" stroke), I.H.P. 5,500$=20$ knots; O.F. 640 tons; complement 177.

Left and right: Bow and quarter views of helicopter support ship *Engadine*. **Bottom left:** *Abdiel*, support ship for MCM vessels. **Bottom right:** *Stalwart*, Australian support ship for escorts.

[All blocks
courtesy
Naval Record

FLEET TRAIN

For helicopters: **LOFOTEN.** *For submarines:* **NARVIK, STALKER.** *For nets and booms:* **TRACKER**

Former LST(3)'s converted for subsidiary duties. The LOFOTEN was modified at H.M. Dockyard, Devonport, in 1964 when the upper deck forward of the cargo hatch was made flush and strengthened to operate helicopters. The forward gun platform was fitted as a station for the flight deck control officer, and as a fuelling point connected to two 10,000-gal. tanks in the fore end of the tank deck. Abaft these a transverse bulkhead was worked-in separating them from the after end of the tank deck, and the bow doors welded-up. In the NARVIK and STALKER alterations were principally confined to utilising the tank deck space for accommodation and offices, and by providing heavy handling gear for booms and nets in the TRACKER.

2,140/4,820 except *Narvik* 4,980 tons; 330(pp) $345\frac{3}{4}$(oa) × 54 × $8\frac{1}{4}$ feet; two Admiralty 3-drum boilers (225 lb/in²); two shafts; reciprocating (VTE—cyl. $18\frac{1}{2}$″:31″$38\frac{1}{2}$″(2) × 30″ stroke), I.H.P. 5,500 = $12\frac{1}{2}$ knots; O.F. 1,400 tons; four except *Lofoten* two 40mm. A.A. (2/4 × 1) guns; six helicopters in *Lofoten* only; complement 110.

For mine countermeasures: **RECLAIM**

Laid down as an ocean salvage vessel of the "King Salvor" class, this vessel was altered while building to a deep diving and submarine rescue vessel and renamed RECLAIM. Except that the boat deck superstructure was extended to the ship's side, the modification was more one of equipment fitted than structual alteration.

1,200/1,800 tons; $200\frac{1}{4}$(pp) $217\frac{3}{4}$(oa) × $37\frac{3}{4}$ × $13\frac{1}{2}$/$15\frac{1}{2}$ feet; two S.E. cylindrical boilers (200 lb/in²); one shaft; reciprocating (VTE—cyl. 14″:23″:$38\frac{1}{2}$″ × 24″ stroke), I.H.P. 1,500 = 12 knots; O.F. 310 tons; complement 84.

For escorts: **STALWART**

Designed to maintain destroyers, frigates, and modern weapon systems including guided missiles. Mercantile type hull has fo'c'sle and long bridge deck extending nearly to the stern, and the machinery is arranged three-quarters aft. A landing pad for helicopters is provided at the stern.

14,500 tons; 470(pp) $515\frac{1}{2}$(oa) × $67\frac{1}{2}$ × 39d/$25\frac{1}{2}$ feet; two shafts; 6-cyl. Sulzer type RD.68 diesel engines, B.H.P. 14,400 = 17 knots; O.F. ... tons; four 40mm. A.A. (2 × 2) guns; complement 478.

For helicopters: ENGADINE

Designed to train helicopter crews in A/S warfare, it proved more cost effective to build and operate the ship on a commercial basis rather than have a naval-manned vessel constructed to warship standards. The permanent complement is made-up of both R.F.A. (for operating the ship) and R.N. (for maintenance duties) personnel; while helicopters, naval air crews and their associated training and support parties are only embarked for training and operational purposes. The helicopters are not permanently carried although provision is made to accommodate six of them.

8,000 tons (3,640 tons d.w.); 385(pp) 424½(oa) × 58 × 35¾d/22 feet; one shaft, 5-cyl. Sulzer type RD.68 turbocharged diesel engine B.H.P. 5,500 (at 135 r.p.m.) = 15 knots, O.F. ... tons; complement 63 R.F.A. + 122 R.N.

For mine countermeasures: ABDIEL

Multi-purpose vessel designed to act in support of mine countermeasures vessels, provide headquarters facilities for MCM operations, and lay and recover exercise minefield for minesweeper training. Design requirements fixed a speed and draught similar to that possessed by coastal minesweepers, so that they could closely co-operate, and the latter naturally limited overall dimensions. Despite her small size the ABDIEL possesses all the necessary qualities for her role and greatly extends the operational capability of her attached MCM squadron.

1,200 tons (1,460 tons full load); 245(pp) 264(oa) × 38½ × 9¼ feet; two shafts, 16-cyl. Davey Paxman type YJXM turbocharged diesel engines B.H.P. 2,670 (at 1,250 r.p.m.) = 16 knots; O.F. ... tons, complement 57 + 20 support party + 9 H.Q. staff.

Pt. No.	Name	Builder	Laid down	Launched	Completed	Disposition
A.215	STALWART	Cockatoo	... 3.64	7.10.66	8. 2.68	Building for Royal Australian Navy

Machinery contract: Engined by Scotts.

| K.08 | ENGADINE ... ... | Robb ... ... | 9. 8.65 | 16. 9.66 | 14.12.67 | Portland |

Machinery contract: Engined by Wallsend Slipway.

| N.21 | ABDIEL ... ... | Thornycroft ... ... | 23. 5.66 | 27. 1.67 | 17.10.67 | Port Edgar |

Machinery contract: Engined by Davey Paxman.

Pt. No.	Name	Builder	Laid down	Launched	Completed	Disposition
A.236	FORT CHARLOTTE (ex-*Buffalo Park*)	Pacific D.D.	....	....	6. 4.44	For disposal
A.237	FORT CONSTANTINE ...	Burrard	....	11. 5.44	25. 4.44	For disposal
A.160	FORT DUNVEGAN ...	Burrard	....	28. 2.44	14. 4.44	For disposal
A.230	FORT LANGLEY (ex-*Montebello Park*)	Victoria	....	....	18. 5.45	
A.186	FORT ROSALIE	United Shyds. ...	29. 8.44	18.11.44	7. 4.45	
A.316	FORT SANDUSKY ...	United Shyds. ...	11. 9.44	25.11.44	1. 8.45	Chatham

Machinery contracts: *Fort Charlotte* engined by John Inglis; *Fort Constantine*, *Fort Dunvegan*, and *Fort Langley* by Canadian Allis-Chalmers; and *Fort Rosalie* and *Fort Sandusky* by Dominion Engineering Works.

Pt. No.	Name	Builder	Laid down	Launched	Completed	Disposition
A.84	RELIANT (ex-mercantile *Somersby*)	Laing	....	9. 9.53	4. 3.55	Far East

Machinery contract: Engined by Hawthorn Leslie.

Pt. No.	Name	Builder	Laid down	Launched	Completed	Disposition
A.339	LYNESS	Swan Hunter	7. 4.65	7. 4.66	22.12.66	Far East
A.344	STROMNESS	Swan Hunter	5.10.65	16. 9.66	30. 3.67	
A.345	TARBATNESS	Swan Hunter	15. 4.66	27. 2.67	10. 8.67	

Machinery contracts: Engined by Wallsend Slipway.

For stores: **FORT CHARLOTTE, FORT CONSTANTINE, FORT DUNVEGAN.** *For armament stores:* **FORT LANGLEY, FORT ROSALIE, FORT SANDUSKY**

Standard war-built "Fort/Park" class cargo hulls acquired for naval use as store carriers while under construction. Helicopter landing pads are fitted aft in FORT CHARLOTTE and FORT DUNVEGAN. Of other ships in this class seven were sold-out commercially and three scrapped.

14,000 tons (10,300 tons d.w.); 416(pp) $441\frac{1}{2}$ except *Fort Duquesne* $439\frac{1}{4}$(oa) $\times 57 \times 27$ feet; two Babcock & Wilcox except *Fort Rosalie* and *Fort Sandusky* three S.E. cylindrical boilers (250 lb/in²); one shaft; reciprocating (VTE—cyl. $24\frac{1}{2}":37":70" \times 48"$ stroke), I.H.P. 2,500 = 11 knots; O.F. 1,600 tons; complement ....

For air stores: **RELIANT**

Former general cargo vessel purchases in 1956 and renamed on completion of conversion in 1958. Is fitted for replenishing aircraft carriers at sea with a wide range of air, naval, and victualling stores.

13,730 tons (9,290 tons d.w.); 440(pp) $468\frac{3}{4}$(oa) $\times 61\frac{1}{4} \times 26\frac{1}{4}$ feet; one shaft; 6-cyl. Doxford diesel engine, B.H.P. 8,250 = 18 knots; O.F. .,.... tons; complement 110.

For naval and air stores: **LYNESS** *For naval and victualling stores:* **STROMNESS, TARBATNESS**

Fitted for replenishing warships at sea with naval and victualling stores, these vessels incorporate modern cargo handling arrangements to effect a rapid transfer. The stores are palletised and are handled by fork lift trucks, pallet transporters, electric lifts, and powered roller conveyors, and are brought on to deck through side ports in the hatch trunkways. The helicopter landing deck aft is also served by a stores lift to provide a measure of vertical replenishment capability. Cranes and derricks are provided for loading purposes only.

15,500 tons (7,832 tons d.w.); 490(pp) $523\frac{1}{2}$(oa) $\times 72\frac{1}{4} \times 44\frac{3}{4}$d/$25\frac{1}{2}$ feet; one shaft; 8-cyl. Sulzer type RD.76 diesel engine, B.H.P. 11,520 = 20 knots; O.F. .,.... tons; two helicopters; complement 184.

Hartland Point, maintenance ship for escorts.

Pt. No.	Name	Builder			Laid down	Launched	Completed	Disposition
A.191	BERRY HEAD	Burrard			15. 6.44	21.10.44	7. 6.45	Devonport refitting
A.158	DUNCANSBY HEAD ...	Burrard			29. 7.44	17.11.44	9. 8.45	Rosyth reserve
A.262	HARTLAND POINT ...	Burrard			18. 7.44	4.11.44	12. 7.45	Portsmouth reserve
A.226	MULL OF KINTYRE ...	Pacific D.D.			21.12.44	5. 4.45	5.11.45	Singapore reserve
A.134	RAME HEAD	Pacific D.D.			12. 7.44	22.11.44	18. 8.45	Portsmouth reserve
ARE.100	CAPE BRETON (ex-*Flambrough Head*)	Burrard			5. 7.44	7.10.44	2. 5.45	Royal Canadian Navy (1951), Pacific reserve
ARE.101	CAPE SCOTT (ex-*Beachy Head*, ex-*R. Neth.N. Vulkaan*, ex-*Beachy Head*)	Burrard			8. 6.44	27. 9.44	27. 3.45	Royal Canadian Navy (1952), Atlantic reserve
A.387	GIRDLE NESS	Burrard			7.12.44	29. 3.45	6. 9.45	Rosyth

Machinery contracts: All engined Canadian Allis-Chalmers except *Mull of Kintyre* and *Girdle Ness* by Dominion Engineering Works.

For escorts: **BERRY HEAD, CAPE BRETON, CAPE SCOTT, HARTLAND POINT, RAME HEAD.** *For minesweepers:* **MULL OF KINTYRE.** *For accommodation:* **DUNCANSBY HEAD, GIRDLE NESS**

Standard war-built "Fort/Park" class hulls which were converted while building into maintenance vessels, a much larger degree of alteration being required than in the otherwise similar stores support ships.

Of the twenty-three vessels originally in this class five were cancelled and completed as mercantile vessels; one was transferred to the Royal Air Force—the ADASTRAL (ex-*Fife Ness*)—and was later sold-out commercially together with four others; two were transferred to the Royal Canadian Navy; and three were scrapped.

The GIRDLE NESS was converted into a guided weapons trials vessel by H.M. Dockyard, Devonport, in 1953–56, when considerable additions were made to the superstructure; two lattice masts replaced the pole masts; warning, tracking and guidance radar was added for the weapon system; and a triple launching ramp for Seaslug missiles was fitted on the foredeck. These duties were completed in 1962 when, jointly with the DUNCANSBY HEAD, she formed the COCHRANE establishment at Rosyth.

The remaining vessels in the Royal Navy were refitted between 1959–63 when cranes replaced the masts and derricks fore and aft, a lattice replaced the pole signalling mast abaft the bridge, addition were made to the superstructure, and fewer single 40mm. A.A. guns replaced the more numerous 20mm. A.A. guns previously carried. Space more than weight being at a premium, these alterations necessitated shipping over 2,000 tons of ballast to improve stability and keep them adequately immersed. Except that a landing pad for helicopters has been added aft the Royal Canadian Navy vessels have been little altered externally but completely re-equipped internally.

8,580 except *Heads* 9,000/11,270 except *Hartland Point* and *Mull of Kintyre* 10,200 tons, *Girdle Ness* 10,000/11,620 tons; 416(pp) 441½(oa) × 57 × 20/22½ except *Hartland Point* and *Mull of Kintyre* 21 feet; two Foster Wheeler boilers (200 lb/in²); one shaft; reciprocating (VTE—cyl. 24½″:37″:70″ × 48″ stroke), I.H.P. 2,500=11 knots; O.F. 1,600 tons except *Hartland Point* and *Mull of Kintyre* 1,000 tons; eleven 40mm. A.A. (11 × 1) guns except *Duncansby Head, Girdle Ness*, and *R.C.N. vessels* unarmed; complement 445 except *Cape Breton* 220 and *Cape Scott* 270.

Left: *Lofoten,* support ship for helicopters.

Below: *Lyness,* support ship for naval and air stores.

[Block courtesy *Naval Record*

Right: *Plover*, support ship for mine counter-measures.

Below: *Regent* replenishment vessel for ammunition and stores.

[Block courtesy *Naval Record*

Pt. No.	Name	Builder	Laid down	Launched	Completed	Disposition
A.280	RESURGENT (ex-mercantile *Chungchow*)	Scotts	7. 6.49	31. 7.50	51	
A.329	RETAINER (ex-mercantile *Chungking*)	Scotts	11.10.48	19. 1.50	50	

Machinery contracts: Both engined by builders.

AOR.508	PROVIDER...	Davie Sbdg.	1. 5.61	5. 7.62	28. 9.63	Royal Canadian Navy, Atlantic coast

Machinery contract: Engined by Canadian Westinghouse.

A.486	REGENT	Harland & Wolff ...	4. 9.64	9. 3.66	6. 6.67	
A.480	RESOURCE	Scotts	19. 6.64	11. 2.66	5. 6.67	

Machinery contracts: Both engined by A.E.I.

AOR.510	PRESERVER	St. Jonn Sbdg ...	67	....	15.11.69	Building for Royal Canadian Navy, Atlantic coast
AOR.509	PROTECTEUR	St. John Sbdg ...	67	2.11.68	16. 6.69	Building for Royal Canadian Navy, Pacific coast

Machinery contracts: Engined by Canadian-G.E.

Ex-mercantile conversions: **RESURGENT, RETAINER**

Former passenger/cargo liners purchased in 1952 and converted into replenishment ships for naval stores.

14,400 tons (7,500 tons d.w.); 450(pp) 477¼(oa)×62¾×29 feet; one shaft; 6-cyl. Doxford diesel engine, B.H.P. 6,600=15 knots; O.F. 925 tons; complement ....

R.C.N. type: **PROVIDER**

Generally similar but faster than contemporary vessels in the Royal Navy and provided with exceptionally complete cargo handling and replenishment at sea (R.A.S.) equipment. A large hangar for helicopters is arranged forward of the funnel with the landing deck abaft it, at the stern. She can stow 12,000 tons of oil fuel, 1,200 tons of diesel oil, 1,000 tons of avgas, and 250 tons of victualling stores together with limited quantities of naval stores and ammunition.

22,000 tons (14,700 tons d.w.); 523(pp) 555¼(oa)×76¼×31¾ feet; two Combustion Engineering boilers (650 lb/in² at 860°F), one shaft; Westinghouse geared turbines, S.H.P. 21,000=20 knots; O.F. 1,200 tons; six helicopters; complement 142.

Admiralty type: **REGENT, RESOURCE**

Designed to replenish the fleet at sea with ammunition and naval and victualling stores these vessels are extremely well equipped for this purpose, and generally follow the lines of the replenishment tankers but with the whole cargo deadweight devoted to dry stores.

19,000 tons (..,.... tons d.w.) 599¼(pp) 640(oa)×77¼×49½d/26¼ feet; two Foster Wheeler boilers (695 lb/in² at 850°F); one shaft; A.E.I. geared turbines, S.H.P. 20,000=19 knots; O.F. ..,.... tons; two 40mm. A.A. (2×1) guns, one helicopter; complement 182 (119 R.F.A.+63 R.N.).

R,C,N, type: **PRESERVER, PROTECTEUR**

Improved versions of the **PROVIDER** which, when completed, will greatly augment the Royal Canadian Navy's support at sea for its anti-submarine forces, and further reduce their dependency on shore facilities as each replenishment vessel can treble the number of escort vessels that can be kept on station in mid-ocean. They are also intended to double as military transports—should the need arise—and provide the sea-lift for vehicles, stores, helicopters, etc., and up to fifty army personnel. A close range A.A. G.W.S. is to be installed.

9,000/24,000 tons (13,250 tons d.w.); 519(pp) 564(oa)×76×40½d/30 feet; two Babcock & Wilcox boilers, one shaft, General Electric geared turbines S.H.P. 22,000=20 knots, O.F. ..,... tons, one Sea Sparrow G.W.S., one 3-inch D.P. gun, three helicopters; complement ....

Above: *Resurgent*, replenishment ship for air stores.

Left: *Supply*, Royal Australian Navy replenishment tanker.

Above: *Olna.* **Below:** *Tidepool.*

Pt. No.	Name	Builder	Laid down	Launched	Completed	Disposition
A.97	TIDEFLOW (ex-*Tiderace*)	Thompson	53	30. 8.54	25. 1.56	
A.96	TIDEREACH	Swan Hunter	53	2. 6.54	30. 8.55	
A.98	TIDESURGE (ex-*Tiderange*)	Laing	53	1. 7.54	30. 8.55	
AO.195	SUPPLY (ex-*Tide Austral*) ..	Harland & Wolff ...	53	1. 9.54	28. 5.55	Royal Australian Navy

Machinery contracts: Tideflow and Tidesurge engined by White; Tidereach by Wallsend Slipway; and Supply by builders.

| A.76 | TIDEPOOL... ... ... | Hawthorn Leslie ... | 4.12.61 | 11.12.62 | 28. 6.63 | |
| A.75 | TIDESPRING ... ... | Hawthorn Leslie ... | 24. 7.61 | 3. 5.62 | 18. 1.63 | |

Machinery contracts: Both engined by builders.

A.124	OLMEDA (ex-*Oleander*)	Swan Hunter	27. 8.63	19.11.64	18.10.65	
A.123	OLNA	Hawthorn Leslie ...	2. 7.64	28. 7.65	1. 4.66	
A.122	OLWEN (ex-*Olynthus*) ...	Hawthorn Leslie ...	11. 7.63	10. 7.64	21. 6.65	

Machinery contracts: Olmeda engined by Wallsend Slipway, and others by builders.

These vessels differed from earlier Admiralty tankers in that a portion of the deadweight was devoted to dry cargo (ammunition, victualling and naval stores, etc.) which, together with oil and aircraft fuel, could all be transferred while undeṣway at sea to the combatant vessels. Unlike contemporary mercantile tankers the bridge has been retained amidships, and a full width flying deck connects the fo'c'sle and poop on which is stepped the samson posts and derricks for replenishment at sea. The last five differ from the earlier units in that the fo'c'sle side plating is extended to the bridge, and a helicopter hangar is provided forward of the funnel with a landing deck abaft it. The TIDE AUSTRAL was operated by the Royal Navy until 1962 when she was retroceded to the Royal Australian Navy and renamed SUPPLY. During 1967 the OLEANDER and OLYNTHUS were renamed because of the liability of phonetic error with the frigate LEANDER and the submarine OLYMPUS.

Admiralty type: **SUPPLY, TIDEFLOW, TIDEREACH, TIDESURGE**

26,000 tons (16,800 except *Supply* 17,700 tons d.w.); 550(pp) $583\frac{1}{4}$(oa)$\times 71\frac{1}{4}\times 32$ feet; three Babcock & Wilcox boilers (625 lb/in² at 800°F), one shaft, Pametrada geared turbines, S.H.P. 15,000=17 knots; O.F. .,... tons; six 40mm. A.A. (3×2) guns in *Supply* only; complement 90 except *Supply* 133.

Admiralty type: **TIDEPOOL, TIDESPRING**

25,930 tons (17,400 tons d.w.); 550(pp) $583\frac{3}{4}$(oa)$\times 71\frac{1}{4}\times 32$ feet; two Babcock & Wilcox boilers (680 lb/in² at 850°F); one shaft; Pametrada geared turbines, S.H.P. 15,000=17 knots; O.F. .,... tons; eight Seacat (2×4) G.W.S., two helicopters; complement 110.

Admiralty type: **OLMEDA, OLNA, OLWEN**

32,200 tons (22,300 tons d.w.); 610(pp) 648(oa)$\times 84\frac{1}{4}\times 34$ feet; two Babcock & Wilcox boilers (750 lb/in² at 950°F); one shaft; Pametrada geared turbines, S.H.P. 26,500 =19 knots; O.F. .,... tons; two 40mm. A.A. (2×1) guns, two helicopters; complement 87.

Owing to the closure of the Suez Canal following the Arab-Israeli war, and the continuing need to support fleet units in the Indian Ocean and Far East, three large commercial tankers were chartered in 1967. They were all given limited modifications enabling them to replenish fleet units at sea, the conversion work being undertaken by Cammell Laird (DEWDALE), Palmers (ENNERDALE), and Swan Hunter (DERWENTDALE). Unlike their naval-built counterparts they all have their bridge and machinery positioned aft.

Mercantile type: **ENNERDALE**

30,112 tons gross (47,270 tons d.w.); $680\frac{3}{4}$(pp) 710(oa) $\times 98\frac{1}{2} \times 51\frac{3}{4}$d/$37\frac{1}{2}$ feet; one shaft, 8-cyl. B. & W. type 84.VT2BF.180 diesel engine B.H.P. 16,800 = $15\frac{1}{2}$ knots, O.F. 2,766 tons; complement 58.

Mercantile type: **DERWENTDALE**

..,.... tons gross (67,729 tons d.w.); $761\frac{1}{4}$(pp) 799(oa) $\times 117\frac{1}{2} \times 55\frac{1}{4}$d/40 feet; one shaft, 9-cyl. B. & W. type 84.VT2BF.180 diesel engine B.H.P. 20,700 = $15\frac{1}{2}$ knots, O.F. 3,072 tons; complement ....

Mercantile type: **DEWDALE**

38,805 tons gross (60,600 tons d.w.); 747(pp) $774\frac{1}{2}$(oa) $\times 107\frac{1}{2} \times 55$d/40 feet; one shaft, 9-cyl. B. & W. type 84.VT2BF.180 diesel engine B.H.P. 18,000 = 16 knots, O.F. ..,... tons; complement ....

Pt. No.	Name	Builder	Laid down	Launched	Completed	Remarks
A.213	ENNERDALE (ex-mercantile *Naess Scotsman*)	Kieler Howaldtswerke	....	... 8.63	...12.63	Acquired 1967
A.221	DERWENTDALE (ex-mercantile *Halcyon Breeze*)	Hitachi (Innoshima) ...	10.10.63	8. 1.64	30. 4.64	Acquired 1967
A.219	DEWDALE (ex-mercantile *Edenfield*)	Harland & Wolff ...	....	5. 3.65	... 7.65	Acquired 1967

Machinery contracts: Ennerdale engined by Fried. Krupps (Essen), *Derwentdale* by Hitachi (Osaka) and *Dewdale* by builders.

Admiralty type: **BLUE ROVER, GREEN ROVER, GREY ROVER**

To rapidly replenish detached units and escorts at sea under all conditions, and be capable of providing aviation and ground fuels for forces ashore in operational areas, a smaller class of replenishment tanker was put in hand. Limited provision was also made to supply fresh water, and dry and refrigerated stores to ships or ground forces, and a helicopter landing deck provided for vertical replenishment. An innovation was the adoption of a twin diesel installation geared to a single shaft.

..,... tons (7,060 tons d.w.); 430(pp) 461(oa)×63×39½d/24 feet; one shaft, 16-cyl. Ruston & Hornsby type AO diesel engines (two/shaft) B.H.P. 16,000=19 knots, O.F. .,... tons; complement 43.

Pt. No.	Name	Builder	Laid down	Launched	Completed	Disposition
	BLUE ROVER	Swan Hunter & Tyne (Hebburn)	... 1.69	....	....	Building
A.	GREEN ROVER	Swan Hunter & Tyne (Hebburn)	28. 2.68	19.12.68	... 8.69	
A.269	GREY ROVER	Swan Hunter & Tyne (Hebburn)	28. 2.68	17.. 4.69	....	Building

Machinery contracts: Engined by Ruston & Hornsby.

Admiralty type: **ONE** unnamed vessel

A sea-going experimental and trials vessel for weapons and equipment to replace the SARPETA (a 465-ton former mercantile vessel completed in 1920), which will be manned by the R.F.A. A passive stabilising tank and active rudders will be fitted, with electric power supplied by four 350kW alternators.

2,900 tons; ...(pp) 320(oa)×48×... feet; two shafts, 12-cyl. Davey Paxman type YLCM diesel engines, B.H.P. 3,400 (at 900 r.p.m.) =15½ knots, O.F. ... tons; complement 42+21 scientific staff.

	Unnamed	Scotts	69	70	71	Building

Machinery contract: Engined by Davey Paxman.

MISCELLANEOUS VESSELS

Before the Second World War fleet tugs ("Nimble" class) were principally used for berthing duties and target towing, but following the outbreak of war they were soon pressed into the more urgent task of towing damaged ships back to port. Re-designated rescue tugs, a considerable war programme was put in hand and design and construction entrusted to Cochrane ("Assurance" and "Envoy" classes) and Robb ("Bustler" class): commercial builders with an established reputation in this field. The former adhered to reciprocating machinery while the latter adopted diesel propulsion. Under the terms of Lend/Lease two further classes of single-screw tugs were built for the Royal Navy in the United States. The "ATR.1" type were wood-hulled and reciprocating-engined while the "ATR.41" type were steel-hulled with diesel-electric drive. The Royal Canadian Navy also built a small series of rescue tugs ("Clifton" class) with direct diesel drive.

Post-war, the "Samson" class were practically repeat editions of the earlier "Nimble" class, but the succeeding "Confiance" and "Adept" classes had twin-input/single-output diesel engines on each shaft with controllable pitch propellers, while the Royal Canadian Navy "Saint" class had a straight diesel installation. A feature of the Admiralty designed tugs—which distinguished them from the commercial and American designs—was their marked tumblehome, in addition to stout belting, so that the upper deck would ride cleat of any projections on the sides of warships. For handling larger vessels in the restricted confines of dockyards, side paddle propulsion with diesel-electric chain drive was selected for the "Director" class, as for this particular duty paddle tugs were still considered superior to their screw counterparts. To allow for the considerable overhang in aircraft carriers the bow was raked back, the foremast hinged, and the funnels kept low. The diesel-engined TYPHOON, intended for ocean towing and consequently single screw, was fitted with a controllable pitch propeller and was also equipped as a salvage vessel. In 1959 the United States Navy transferred a tug of the "AT.64" type to the Pakistani Navy under MDAP.

The fleet tugs are disposed as follows, those marked * being earmarked for disposal: *Chatham:* *JAUNTY. *Devonport:* ADVICE, BUSTLER, CAREFUL, DIRECTOR, FAITHFUL, FAVOURITE, SEAGIANT, SUPERMAN. *Mediterranean:* CONFIANCE, DEXTEROUS. *Portland:* ANTIC. *Portsmouth:* AGILE, CAPABLE, CONFIDENT, CYCLONE, FORCEFUL, GRINDER, REWARD, SAMSON, SAMSONIA, TYPHOON, WARDEN. *Rosyth:* ACCORD, GRIPER. *Singapore:* ENCORE, NIMBLE. *Disposition unknown:* PROSPEROUS. *Royal Australian Navy:* SPRIGHTLY. *Royal Canadian Navy:* CLIFTON, HEATHERTON, ST. ANTHONY, ST. CHARLES, ST. JOHN, RIVERTON. *Pakistani Navy:* MADADGAR.

MISCELLANEOUS VESSELS

Pt. No.	Name	Builder	Launched
A.508	CAPABLE	Hall Russell ...	22.11.45
A.293	CAREFUL	Alex. Hall	23.10.45
A.223	NIMBLE	Fleming & Ferguson	4.12.41

Machinery contracts: All engined by builders.

Pt. No.	Name	Builder	Launched
A.141	ANTIC	Cochrane	24. 3.43
A.140	JAUNTY	Cochrane	11. 6.41

Machinery contracts: All engined by Holmes.

Pt. No.	Name	Builder	Launched
A.240	BUSTLER	Robb	4.12.41
A.111	CYCLONE (ex-*Growler*)	Robb	10. 9.42
A.264	REWARD	Robb	13.10.44
A.218	SAMSONIA ...	Robb	1. 4.42
A.309	WARDEN	Robb	28. 6.45

Machinery contracts: All engined by British Polar.

Pt. No.	Name	Builder	Launched
A.42	MADADGAR (ex-*U.S.N. Yuma*)	Commercial I.W. ...	17. 7.43

Machinery contracts: Engined by General Motors.

Pt. No.	Name	Builder	Launched
A.203	SPRIGHTLY (ex-*U.S.N. BAT.12*)	Levingston	7. 8.42

Machinery contracts: Engined by General Motors.

Pt. No.	Name	Builder	Launched
A.379	ENCORE	Cochrane	2.12.44

Machinery contracts: Engined by Holmes.

Pt. No.	Name	Builder	Launched
ATA.529	CLIFTON	Canadian Bridge ...	31. 7.44
ATA.527	HEATHERTON ...	Canadian Bridge ...	29. 6.43
ATA.528	RIVERTON ...	Montreal D.D. ...	15. 1.44

Machinery contracts: All engined by Dominion Engineering.

Pt. No.	Name	Builder	Launched
A.390	SAMSON	Alex. Hall	14. 5.53
A.298	SEA GIANT ...	Alex. Hall	2. 6.54
A.	SUPERMAN ...	Alex. Hall	23.11.55

Machinery contracts: All engined by builders.

Pt. No.	Name	Builder	Launched
A.289	CONFIANCE ...	Inglis	15.11.55
A.290	CONFIDENT ...	Inglis	17. 1.56

Machinery contracts: Both engined by Davey Paxman.

Admiralty type: **CAPABLE, CAREFUL, NIMBLE**

Of the original four units comprising this class, one—the EXPERT—was sold-out commercially.

890/1,190 tons; 165(pp) 175(oa) $\times$ 35$\frac{3}{4}$ $\times$ 11f13$\frac{3}{4}$ feet; two Admiralty 3-drum boilers (... lb/in²); two shafts; reciprocating (VTE—cyl. ..":..":.." $\times$ .." stroke), I.H.P. 3,500 = 16 knots; O.F. 300 tons; complement 42.

"Assurance" class: **ANTIC, JAUNTY**

Of the original twenty-one units comprising this class six were war losses and thirteen were sold-out commercially.

700/1,055 tons; 142$\frac{1}{2}$(pp) 156$\frac{3}{4}$(oa) $\times$ 33$\frac{1}{4}$ $\times$ 10$\frac{1}{2}$/14$\frac{3}{4}$ feet; one S.E. cylindrical boiler (200 lb/in²); one shaft; reciprocating (VTE—cyl. 17":28":46" $\times$ 33" stroke), I.H.P. 1,350 = 12 knots; O.F. 262 tons; complement 31.

"Bustler" class: **BUSTLER, CYCLONE, REWARD, SAMSONIA, WARDEN**

Of the original eight units comprising this class one was a war loss and two were sold-out commercially, while most of the remainder have been loaned for commercial charters as the circumstances have arisen.

1,120/1,630 tons; 190(pp) 205(oa) $\times$ 38$\frac{1}{2}$ $\times$ 12$\frac{1}{2}$/16$\frac{3}{4}$ feet; one shaft; 8-cyl. Polar diesel engines (two/shaft), B.H.P. 4,000 = 16 knots; O.F. 405 tons; complement 42.

"AT.64" class: **MADADGAR**

Former United States Navy ocean towing tug transferred to the Pakistani Navy in 1959 under MDAP, and also equipped for salvage work.

1,235/1,675 tons; 195(wl) 205(oa) $\times$ 38$\frac{1}{2}$ $\times$ ../15$\frac{1}{4}$ feet; one shaft; 12-cyl. G.M. diesel engines (four/shaft) and electric motors, B.H.P./S.H.P. 3,750/3,000 = 16 knots; O.F. ... tons; two 40mm. A.A. (2 $\times$ 1) guns; complement 85.

239

Pt. No.	Name	Builder	Launched
ATA.531	ST. ANTHONY ...	St. John D.D. ...	2.11.55
ATA.533	ST. CHARLES ...	St. John D.D. ...	10. 7.56
ATA.535	ST. JOHN	St. John D.D. ...	14. 5.56

Machinery contracts: All engined by Canadian Locomotive.

A.93	DEXTEROUS ...	Yarrow	21. 8.56
A.94	DIRECTOR ...	Yarrow	11. 6.56
A.85	FAITHFUL	Yarrow	14. 6.57
A.87	FAVOURITE ...	Ferguson Bros. ...	1. 7.58
A.86	FORCEFUL ...	Yarrow	20. 5.57
A.92	GRINDER	Simons	6. 5.58
A.91	GRIPER	Simons	6. 3.58

Machinery contracts: Engined by Davey Paxman (diesel engines) and British Thompson Houston (electric motors).

A.90	ACCORD	Inglis	17. 9.57
A.89	ADVICE	Inglis	16.10.58
A.88	AGILE	Goole Sbdg. ...	2. 7.58

Machinery contracts: All engined by Davey Paxman.

Pt. No.	Name	Builder	Launched
A.95	TYPHOON ...	Robb	14.10.58

Machinery contract: Engined by Vickers-Armstrongs (Barrow).

A.	A	Holmes	....
A.	B	Holmes	....

Machinery contracts: Engined by Mirrless

"ATR.41" class: SPRIGHTLY

This class of ocean towing tugs was built in the United States for the Royal Navy under Lend/Lease, and were reduced editions of the "AT.64" class with half the propulsive power. Of the twenty-four units originally comprising this class one was retained by the United States Navy (since sold-out commercially), one was a war loss, three were transferred to the Royal Australian Navy (one since scrapped and another sold-out commercially), and the remaining nineteen were returned to the United States Navy after the Second World War, leaving the R.A.N. SPRIGHTLY as the only surviving unit.

534/783 tons; $134\frac{1}{2}$(wl) 143(oa) $\times 33\frac{1}{4} \times 12\frac{3}{4}/13\frac{1}{2}$ feet; one shaft; 12-cyl. G.M. diesel engines (two/shaft) and electric motor, B.H.P./S.H.P. 1,875/1,500 = 13 knots; O.F. 186 tons; three 40mm. A.A. (3 $\times$ 1) guns; complement 43.

"*Envoy* ' *class:* **ENCORE**

Of the original six units comprising this class one was lost post-war, three were sold-out commercially, and one was scrapped.

868/1,332 tons; 160(pp) $174\frac{1}{4}$(oa) $\times 34\frac{1}{4} \times 11\frac{1}{4}/15\frac{3}{4}$ feet; two S.E. cylindrical boilers (220 lb/in²); one shaft; reciprocating (VTE—cyl. 18″:$29\frac{1}{2}$″:49″ $\times$ 34″ stroke), I.H.P. 1,700 = 13 knots; O.F. 398 tons; complement 33.

Modified "*Norton*" *class:* **CLIFTON, HEATHERTON, RIVERTON**

Of the five units originally comprising this class one was lost post-war and another sold-out commercially.

462/... tons; 104(pp) $111\frac{3}{4}$(oa) $\times 28 \times 11$ feet; one shaft; 9-cyl. Sulzer diesel engine, B.H.P. 1,000 = 11 knots; O.F. ... tons; complement 17.

"*Samson*" *class:* **SAMSON, SEAGIANT, SUPERMAN**

850 tons *gross*; 165(pp) 177(oa) $\times 37 \times 11\frac{1}{2}/15\frac{3}{4}$ feet; two S.E. cylindrical boilers (.. lb/in²); two shafts; reciprocating (VTE—cyl. 18″:30″:47″ $\times$ 28″ stroke), I.H.P. 3,000 = 16 knots; O.F. ... tons; one 40mm. A.A. gun; complement ....

"*Confiance*" *class:* **CONFIANCE, CONFIDENT**

.../760 tons; 140(pp) $154\frac{3}{4}$(oa) $\times 35 \times 16$d/11 feet; two shafts (KaMeWa c.p. propellers); 12-cyl. Davey Paxman type YHAXM diesel engines (two/shaft), B.H.P. 1,600 = 13 knots; O.F. ... tons; one 40mm. gun; complement 29 + 13 salvage party.

"*Saint*" *class:* **ST. ANTHONY, ST. CHARLES, ST. JOHN**

.../840 tons; ...(pp) $151\frac{1}{2}$(oa) $\times 34\frac{1}{4} \times 14/17$ feet; 12-cyl. Fairbanks-Morse diesel engine, B.H.P. 1,920 = 14 knots; O.F. ... tons; two 40mm. A.A. (2×1) guns; complement ....

MISCELLANEOUS VESSELS

"Director" class: **DEXTEROUS, DIRECTOR, FAITHFUL, FAVOURITE, FORCEFUL, GRINDER, GRIPER**

.../710 tons; 145(pp) 157¼(oa) × 30 (60 across PB) × 10 feet; side paddle wheels; 12-cyl. Davey Paxman diesel engines (two/shaft) and B.T.H. electric motors, B.H.P./S.H.P. 2,000/1,600 = 13 knots; O.F. ... tons; complement 21.

"Accord" class: **ACCORD, ADVICE, AGILE**

640 tons *gross*; 140(pp) 151½ except *Agile* 151¼(oa) × 35 × 13 feet; two shafts; 12-cyl. Davey Paxman diesel engines (two/shaft), B.H.P. 1,600 = 13 knots; O.F. ... tons; one 40mm. A.A. gun; complement ....

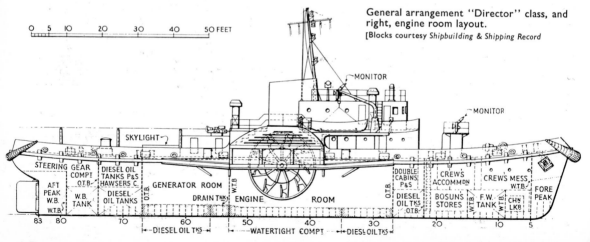

General arrangement "Director" class, and right, engine room layout.
[Blocks courtesy *Shipbuilding & Shipping Record*

Admiralty type: **TYPHOON**

.,../1,380 tons; 188(pp) 199¾(oa) × 38½ × 13/14½ feet; one shaft; 12-cyl. **ASR.1** diesel engines (two/shaft), B.H.P. 2,750 = 16 knots; O.F. ... tons; complement ....

Admiralty type: **TWO** unnamed vessels

Advance orders have been placed for diesel engines and c.p. propellers for the two twin-screw tugs. The diesel engines are 6-cyl. Mirrlees units, each developing 2,250 B.H.P. at 500 r.p.m. and driving through reduction gearing.

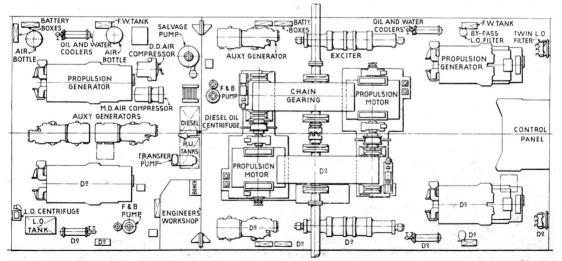

Screw tug *Confiance*

Paddle tug *Director*

The "Bar" class was the outcome of experience secured with earlier mooring and dumb gate vessels during, and after the First World War, and combined their roles in a dual-purpose vessel capable of world-wide employment. They were provided with reciprocating machinery with which trawler reserve personnel—who manned them in wartime—would be familiar.

During the Second World War reversion was made to a small programme of mooring vessels ("Moor" class) for handling heavier gear than that associated with booms, and which more followed mercantile lines than the naval "Bar" class. They were rigged with a short heavy derrick stepped from a tripod mast forward of the bridge. The freeboard was kept low forward to facilitate handling bulky and awkward gear on, and off, the upper deck, and they were also equipped as salvage vessels.

The high rate of mercantile losses during the Second World War necessitated sunken vessels being salved, wherever possible, in addition to which wrecks in the fairways hindered the free flow of vessels entering, or leaving, harbours. To ease the situation a modest programme of salvage vessels of two types were put in hand: the larger ("King Salvor" class) were capable of proceeding overseas, while the smaller type ("Kin" class) were intended for coastal work. Both types were similarly equipped except that the latter were also provided with heavy lift equipment in the bows as the bulk of their work was undertaken in shallow waters where it could be utilised.

In 1950 the Royal Canadian Navy embarked on a series of gate vessels which lacked the heavy lift capability of the Royal Navy vessels, while the Royal Australian Navy adhered to the "Bar" design for a single unit built three years later.

The close affinity between boom defence and mooring vessels, which only needed the provision of salvage equipment to adapt them for this role as well, resulted in all these duties being merged in the Royal Navy's multi-purpose "Lay" class, which can lift 200 tons over the bow apron and were dimensionally enlarged to stow a full range of salvage gear. The "Wild Duck" class that followed were generally similar except that they adopted twin-input/single-output diesel propulsion with controllable pitch propellers. Although provision is made to ship armament none of these vessels mount their guns in peacetime.

These vessels are disposed as follows, those marked thus * being earmarked for disposal: 1st *Boom Defence Squadron:* BARNSTONE, LAYMOOR. 2nd *Boom Defence Squadron:* BARNARD, BARRAGE, BARRINGTON. *Royal Australian Navy:* KANGAROO, KIMBLA (trials vessel), KOALA. *Royal Canadian Navy:* PORTE DE LA REINE, PORTE QUEBEC, PORTE ST. JEAN, PORTE ST. LOUIS. *Chatham:* KINBRACE. *Clyde:* BARHILL, MANDARIN, MOORSMAN, SUCCOUR. *Devonport:* BARBASTEL, MOORPOUT, PINTAIL, SALVICTOR. *Greenock:* KINGART, SUCCOUR. *Mediterranean:* LAYBURN, MOORLAND, MOORHEN, SEA SALVOR. *Portland:* BARCLIFF, GARGANEY. *Portsmouth:* BARFOSS (D/G vessel), BARNDALE, KINLOSS. *Rosyth:* BARCAROLE, BARFIELD, BARFOOT. *Singapore:* *BARFORD, BARFOIL, BARMOND. *Disposition unkown:* BARBAIN, BARBECUE, BARFOAM, BARGLOW, BARTIZAN, GOLDENEYE, *LIFELINE, *MOORBURN, *MOORESS, *MOORFIELD, *MOOR MYRTLE, SALVALOUR, SALVEDA, SALVESTOR, SWIN, UPLIFTER.

MISCELLANEOUS VESSELS

Pt. No.	Name	Builder	Launched
P.201	BARBAIN	Blyth D.D.	8. 1.40
P.279	BARBASTEL ...	Philip	26. 7.45
P.214	BARBECUE ...	Ardrossan D.D. ...	19.12.44
P.287	BARCAROLE ...	Ardrossan D.Y. ...	14. 3.45
P.244	BARFIELD	Lewis	28. 7.38
P.282	BARFOAM... ...	Simons	8. 9.41
P.294	BARFOIL	Philip	18. 7.42
P.202	BARFOOT	Lewis	25. 9.42
P.	BARFORD	Simons	21.10.41
P.200	BARFOSS	Simons	17. 2.42
P.205	BARGLOW ...	Lewis	10.11.42
P.225	BARHILL	Ferguson	26.11.42
P.232	BARMOND ...	Simons	24.12.42
P.241	BARNARD... ...	Lewis	1. 7.42
P.215	BARNDALE ...	Lobnitz	30.11.39
P.297	BARNSTONE ...	Blyth D.D.	25.11.39
P.254	BARRAGE	Hall Russell ...	2.12.37
P.259	BARRINGTON ...	Simons	15.11.40

Pt. No.	Name	Builder	Launched
P.261	BARTIZAN ...	Ardrossan D.Y. ...	20. 5.43
P.80	KANGAROO ...	Cockatoo	4. 5.40
P.69	KOALA	Cockatoo	4.11.39
P.	KIMBLA	Walkers	23. 3.55

Machinery contracts: Barbain and *Barnstone* engined by North-Eastern Marine; *Barbastel* by C. D. Holmes; *Barbecue,* *Bacarole* and *Bartizan* by Lonbitz; *Barfoil* by Plenty; *Somerset* by Swan Hunter; and others by builders.

A.267	MOORBURN ...	Goole Sbdg. ...	16. 4.42
A.271	MOORESS	Goole Sbdg. ...	16. 9.43
A.483	MOORHEN ...	Goole Sbdg. ...	30. 9.43
A.268	MOOR MYRTLE ...	Goole Sbdg. ...	15. 3.45
A.223	MOORPOUT ...	H.M. Dockyard ... (Chatham)	24. 7.4†
A.284	MOORSMAN ...	H.M. Dockyard ... (Chatham)	24. 7.4†

Machinery contracts: All engined by builders except *Moorpout* and *Moorsman* by Fleming & Ferguson.

"Bar" class: **BARBAIN, BARBASTEL, BARBECUE, BARCAROLE, BARFIELD, BARFOAM, BARFOIL, BARFOOT, BARFORD, BARFOSS, BARGLOW, BARHILL, BARMOND, BARNARD, BARNDALE, BARNSTONE, BARRAGE, BARRINGTON, BARTIZAN, KANGAROO, KIMBLA, KOALA**

Of the seventy-eight vessels originally comprising this class, two were cancelled; two were war losses; four (one since scrapped) were built for the Royal Australian Navy, three were transferred to the Turkish Navy, and two to the South African Navy (one since scrapped), and five were sold-out commercially; and forty-one were scrapped.

790/975 tons; 150(pp) $173\frac{3}{4}$(oa)$\times 32\frac{1}{4}\times 11\frac{1}{2}$ feet; two S.E. cylindrical boilers (200 lb/in²); one shaft; reciprocating (VTE—cyl. $14\frac{3}{4}$″:$23\frac{1}{2}$″:39″$\times 24$″ stroke), I.H.P. $850 = 11\frac{3}{4}/9$ knots; coal 124 tons except *R.A.N. vessels* O.F. 150 tons; one 40mm. A.A. gun; complement 32.

Mercantile type: **MOORLAND**

720/000 tons; 135(pp) 145(oa)$\times 31\times 12$ feet; two S.E. cylindrical boilers (200 lb/in²); one shaft; reciprocating (VTE—cyl. 12″:20″:30″$\times 24$″ stroke), I.H.P. $500 = 10$ knots; coal ... tons; complement ....

Admiralty type: **MOORBURN, MOORESS, MOORHEN, MOOR MYRTLE, MOORPOUT, MOORSMAN**

Of the thirteen units originally comprising this class, two were lost incomplete while building in the Far East during the Second World War, two were sold-out commercially, and five were scrapped.

1,000 tons; 149(pp) $163\frac{1}{2}$(oa)$\times 37\times 12\frac{1}{4}$ feet; two S.E. cylindrical boilers (200 lb/in²); one shaft; reciprocating (VTE—cyl. 12″:30″:30″$\times 24$″ stroke), I.H.P. $500 = 9$ knots; coal ... tons; one 40mm. A.A. gun; complement ....

"King Salvor" class: **SALVALOUR, SALVESTOR, SALVICTOR, SEA SALVOR**

Of the thirteen vessels originally comprising this class one was a war loss; one was modified while under construction to a submarine rescue vessel and is listed with the fleet train; one each were sold to the Argentinian and Royal Hellenic navies together with five sold-out commercially (one since lost).

1,440/1,700 tons; $200\frac{1}{4}$(pp) 217(oa)$\times 38\times ../13$ feet; two S.E. cylindrical boilers (200 lb/in²); two shafts; reciprocating (VTE—cyl. 14″:23″:$38\frac{1}{2}$″$\times 24$″ stroke), I.H.P. $1,500\times 12$ knots; O.F. 310 tons; complement 72.

MISCELLANEOUS VESSELS

Australian tug *Sprightly*

Australian boom defence vessel *Kimbla* is now employed as a research vessel.

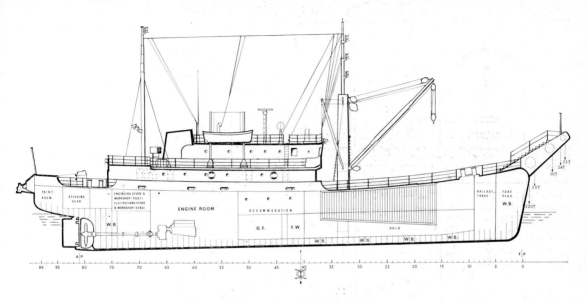

Profile of boom defence/mooring/salvage vessels *Garganey* and *Goldeneye*.

[Block courtesy *Naval Record*

Pt. No.	Name	Builder	Launched
A.431	MOORLAND ...	Simons	22.11.38

Machinery contract: Engined by builder.

Pt. No.	Name	Builder	Launched
A.494	SALVALOUR ...	Goole Sbdg. ...	2.11.44
A.499	SALVESTOR ...	Simons	28. 8.42
A.500	SALVICTOR ...	Simons	11. 3.44
A.503	SEA SALVOR ...	Goole Sbdg. ...	22. 4.43

Machinery contracts: Salvalour engined by Blair, *Sea Salvor* by White's Marine Engineering, and others by builders.

A.497	SALVEDA	Cammell Laird ...	9. 2.43

Machinery contract: Engined by builder.

A.281	KINBRACE ...	Alex. Hall	17. 1.45
A.	KINGARTH (ex-*Sledway*)	Alex. Hall ...	22. 5.44
A.482	KINLOSS ...	Alex. Hall ...	14. 4.45
A.	LIFELINE	Smiths Dock	17. 8.43
A.505	SUCCOUR...	Smiths Dock	18. 8.43
A.506	SWIN (ex-*Shipway*)	Alex. Hall	25. 3.44

Pt. No.	Name	Builder	Launched
A.507	UPLIFTER	Smiths Dock ...	29.11.43

Machinery contracts: All engined by builders.

YMG.184	PORTE DE LA REINE	Victoria M.D. ...	28.12.51
YMG.185	PORTE QUEBEC ...	Burrard	28. .851
YMG.180	PORTE ST. JEAN...	G. T. Davie ...	21.11.50
YMG.183	PORTE ST. LOUIS	G. T. Davie ...	22. 7.52

Machinery contracts: All engined by Dominion Engineering.

P.191	LAYBURN... ...	Simons	14. 4.60
P.190	LAYMOOR ...	Simons	6. 8.59

Machinery contracts: Both engined by builder.

P.192	MANDARIN ...	Cammell Laird ...	17. 9.63
P.193	PINTAIL	Cammell Laird ...	3.12.63
P.194	GARGANEY ...	Brooke Marine ...	13.12.65
P.195	GOLDENEYE ...	Brooke Marine ...	31. 3.66

Machinery contracts: All engined by Davey Paxman.

Admiralty type: **SALVEDA**

1,250/1,360 tons; 185(pp) 195(oa) $\times$ 34$\frac{3}{4}$ $\times$ 11$\frac{1}{4}$/13 feet; two S.E. cylindrical boilers (200 lb/in^2); one shaft; reciprocating (VTE—cyl. 17$''$:28$''$:47$''$ $\times$ 28$''$ stroke), I.H.P. 1,200=12 knots; O.F. 150 tons; complement 62.

"Kin" class: **KINBRACE, KINGARTH, KINLOSS, LIFELINE, SUCCOUR, SWIN, UPLIFTER**

Of the eleven vessels originally comprising this class two were cancelled and two were sold-out commercially. The KINGARTH and UPLIFTER were re-engined by St. Andrews Engineering (Hull), and the KINBRACE by Jas. Lamont (Greenock), with diesel engines.

950/1,050 tons; 150(pp) 179$\frac{1}{2}$(oa) $\times$ 35$\frac{3}{4}$ $\times$ 9$\frac{1}{2}$/12 feet; one S.E. cylindrical boiler (225 lb/in^2); one shaft; reciprocating (VTE—cyl. 11$\frac{3}{4}''$:19$\frac{3}{4}''$:34$''$ $\times$ 24$''$ stroke), I.H.P. 600=9 knots; O.F. 125 tons; complement 34.

"Porte" class: **PORTE DE LA REINE, PORTE QUEBEC, PORTE ST. JEAN, PORTE ST. LOUIS**

One unit of this class, the PORTE DAUPHINE, was transferred to the Canadian Coast Guard in 1963.

.../429 tons; 125$\frac{1}{2}$(pp) ...(oa) $\times$ 26$\frac{1}{4}$ $\times$ .../13 feet; one shaft; 6-cyl. Fairbanks-Morse diesel engine, B.H.P. 600=11 knots; O.F. ... tons; one 40mm. A.A. gun; complement 23.

"Lay" class: **LAYBURN, LAYMOOR**

800/1,050 tons; 160(pp) 192$\frac{1}{4}$(oa) $\times$ 34$\frac{1}{4}$ $\times$ 11$\frac{1}{2}$ feet; two Foster Wheeler boilers (200 lb/in^2); two shafts; reciprocating (VTE—cyl. 14$\frac{3}{4}''$:25$''$:44$''$ $\times$ 24$''$ stroke), I.H.P. 1,300=14 knots; O.F. ... tons; two 40mm. A.A. (2$\times$1) guns; complement 31/36.

"Wild Duck" class: *First group* — **MANDARIN, PINTAIL.** *Second group* — **GARGANEY, GOLDENEYE**

950/.,... tons; *first group* 150$\frac{1}{4}$(pp) 181$\frac{3}{4}$(oa) $\times$ 36$\frac{1}{2}$ $\times$ 17$\frac{1}{2}$d/10$\frac{1}{2}$ feet, *second group* 155(pp) 189$\frac{3}{4}$(oa) $\times$ 36$\frac{1}{2}$ $\times$ 18d/10$\frac{1}{2}$ feet; one shaft (Slack & Parr c.p propeller), 16-cyl. Davey Paxman type RPHM diesel engine B.H.P. 600 (at 1,140 r.p.m.)= 10 knots, O.F. ... tons (3,000m. at 10k.); complement 24 (*first group*), 25 (*second group*).

MISCELLANEOUS VESSELS

Layburn, multi-purpose boom defence, mooring, and salvage vessel.

Garganey was developed from *Layburn* above and had diesel main propulsion and a c.p. propeller.

[Block courtesy *Naval Record*

Above: *Britannia*

Right: *Valiant*

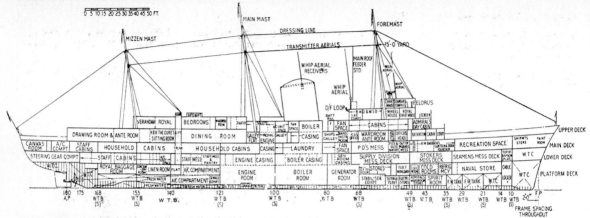

Profile of *Britannia* as Royal yacht (above) and hospital ship (below).

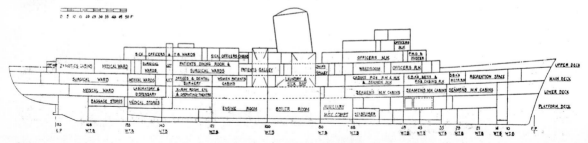

Camper & Nicholsons type: **ACHIMOTA**

Served in the Royal Navy as the armed yacht RADIANT (ex-*Saracen*, ex-*Crusader*) 1939–46, and was then sold-out commercially. Purchased by Ghanaian Government in 1958 as a state yacht, and transferred to the Ghanaian Navy in 1963 and classed as a training/depot ship.

600/... tons; 160(pp) 173½(oa)×27½×12/14 feet; two shafts; 6-cyl. Crossley diesel engines, B.H.P. 880=13 knots; O.F. 60 tons; complement 35+30 official passengers.

Admiralty type: **BRITANNIA**

Designed as combined Royal yacht and hospital ship, the BRITANNIA is naval-manned in the former role, and mercantile manned in the latter but with a Naval medical staff. Conversion can be undertaken with little structural alteration and features common to both roles included full air-conditioning of the Royal accommodation aft, which would be adapted as hospital wards, operating theatres, etc.; fin stabilisation to reduce rolling; and elimination of machinery vibration and noise. In addition, the after sun deck was stiffened for use as a helicopter landing deck, if required. Yacht features included the shell plating worked flush above the light waterline, and a three-masted rig for wearing the required standards and flags. As a hospital ship she will accommodate about 200 patients and have a medical staff of 60.

3,990/4,715 tons; 360(pp) 412¼(oa)×55×.../15¾ feet; two Admiralty 3-drum boilers (300 lb/in² at 660°F); two shafts; Pametrada geared turbines, S.H.P. 12,000=21 knots; O.F. 330 tons (440 tons max.); two 3-pounder saluting (2×1) guns; complement 271+52 Royal household.

Yarrow type: **VALIANT**

Designed as a shallow draught river and esturial vessel for the then Governor-General (now President) of Nigeria with screws working in tunnels. The President's suite is at the for end of the upper deck, with a saloon and six single cabins for the staff at the after end. The remainder of the crew are berthed on the main deck; the officers and servants forward and the ratings aft, with the boiler and engine room casing intervening.

325/381 tons; 130(pp) 135¼(oa)×29×4¼ feet; one S.E. cylindrical boiler (... lb/in²); two shafts; reciprocating (VTE—cyl. 6¼":11":17½"×17½" stroke), I.H.P. 450=9 knots; O.F. 35 tons; two 3-pounder saluting (2×1) guns; complement 37+8 official passengers.

MISCELLANEOUS VESSELS

Antartic patrol ship: **PROTECTOR**

Former netlayer converted to present role in 1955 when the bridge was enclosed and re-modelled, a hangar and landing deck for helicopters were added aft which supplanted the twin 4-inch A.A. mounting which was resited forward, and the hull strengthened for navigation in ice. A tripod mainmast and crane were subsequently added. A near sister ship, the GUARDIAN, was scrapped in 1962.

3,450/4,250 tons; 310(pp) 338(oa)×53×15¼/... feet; two Admiralty 3-drum boilers; two shafts; B.T.H. geared turbines, S.H.P. 9,000=20 knots; O.F. 690 tons; two 4-inch A.A. (1×2), four 3-pounder saluting (4×1), four 20mm. A.A. (2×2) guns; two helicopters; complement 238.

Antartic support ship: **ENDEAVOUR**

Former United States Navy petrol carrier of the "Patapsco" class, strengthened for navigation in ice, and transferred to the Royal New Zealand Navy in 1962 under MDAP.

1,850 tons; 292(wl) 310¾(oa)×48½×15¾ feet; two shafts; ..-cyl. G.M. diesel engines and electric motors, B.H.P. 3,300=14 knots; O.F. ... tons; complement 70.

Antarctic patrol ship: **ENDURANCE**

To replace the ageing PROTECTOR—following the cancellation of the proposed icebreaker TERRA NOVE (A.347) in 1966—a cargo vessel with a hull specially strengthened for navigation in ice was purchased from J. Lauritzen Lines, Copenhagen, in 1967. She was modified by Harland & Wolff to incorporate extra accommodation, increased naval communications equipment, and provided with hangar space and a loading deck for two helicopters. Her hull is painted a distinctive red.

3,600 tons; 273½(pp) 305(oa)×46×25¾d/16½ feet; one shaft, 5-cylinder B. & W. type 50.VT2BF.110 diesel engine B.H.P. 2,900=14 knots, O.F. 545 tons (12,000m. at 14k.); two 20mm. A.A. (2×1) guns, two helicopters; complement 119+11 spare.

"*Bangor*" *class:* **KONKAN**

Former minesweeper ("Bangor" class) which received either diesel (built in U.K. and Canadian yards), reciprocating (built in U.K., Canadian, Hong Kong and Indian yards), or turbine (built in U.K. yards only) machinery. Of the original one hundred and thirteen units comprising this class (fifty-two Royal Navy, forty-eight Royal Canadian Navy and thirteen Royal Indian Navy), ten were war losses; two were transferred to the marine divisions of the Royal Air Force (both since scrapped) and six to the Royal Canadian Mounted Police (four since scrapped and two sold-out commercially) post-war; seventeen—three Egyptian Navy (one since lost), two Royal Norwegian Navy (both since scrapped), two Portuguese Navy, and ten Turkish Navy (one since scrapped)—were sold, together with nine others (two doubtful) sold-out commercially; four were captured incomplete by the Imperial Japanese Navy at Hong Kong in 1941 (two were war losses, one scrapped, and one sold-out commercially); and sixty-four were scrapped. The sole Commonwealth survivor—Indian Navy KONKAN—is now used for training purposes.

672/825 tons; 171½(pp) 180(oa) × 28½ × 8¼/9½ feet; two Admiralty 3-drum boilers, two shafts, reciprocating (VTE) I.H.P. 2,400 × 16 knots, O.F. 160 tons; one 12 pdr. A.A., one 40mm. A.A. guns; complement 87.

"*Bathurst*" *class:* **CASTLEMAINE**

Former minesweeper used as a sea-going training ship for ERA's by the Royal Australian Navy.

815/1,025 tons; 162(pp) 186(oa) × 31 × 8¼/9½ feet; two Admiralty 3-drum boilers; two shafts; reciprocating (VTE—cyl. 13″:21″:34″ × 21″ stroke), I.H.P. 1,800 = 15½ knots; O.F. 170 tons; complement 85.

"*River*" *class:* **GAJABAHU, TIR**

Former frigates used for training purposes by the Indian Navy (TIR) and Singhalese Navy (GAJABAHU). The TIR was converted by Bombay D.Y. in 1948 when additions were made to the bridge, the fo'c'sle side plating extended further aft to provide additional accommodation, and the after guns and all A/S weapons removed. The GAJABAHU, together with a sister vessel—the MAHASENA (now scrapped)—were purchased from the Israeli Navy in 1950 who had removed all A/S weapons and had shipped an additional 4-inch gun on the fo'c'sle.

Gajabahu 1,445/2,360 tons, *Tir* 1,465/1,935 tons; 283(pp) 301¼(oa) × 36¾ × 12/13¾ feet; two Admiralty 3-drum boilers (225 lb/in²); two shafts; reciprocating (VTE—cyl. 18½″:31″:38½″(2) × 30″ stroke), I.H.P. 5,500 = 20/18 knots; O.F. 585 except *Tir* 385 tons; one 4-inch, *Tir* one/*Gajabahu* three 40mm. A.A. (1/3 × 1), two 20mm. A.A. (2 × 1-*Tir only*) guns; complement *Tir* 135, *Gajabahu* 160.

MISCELLANEOUS VESSELS

"Balao/Tench" class: GHAZI, GRILSE, RAINBOW

These submarines were transferred for anti-submarine training duties to the Royal Canadian Navy (GRILSE and RAINBOW) in 1961 and 1968, and Pakistani Navy (GHAZI) in 1964.

1,570/2,415 tons except *Grilse* 1,525/2,390 tons; ... (wl) 311¾ except *Grilse* 311½(oa)×27¼×15¼/17 feet; two shafts; Fairbanks-Morse diesel engines (two/shaft) and Elliott electric motors, B.H.P./S.H.P. 5,400/2,740 = 20/8¾ knots; O.F. 300 tons; ten except *Grilse* six 21-inch (six forward and four aft—not in *Grilse*) T.T.; complement 85 except *Grilse* 79+11 for training.

Pt. No.	Name	Builder	Launched
A.15	ACHIMOTA (ex-mercantile *Kantamento*, ex-*Radiant*)	Camper & Nicholson	00.00.26

Machinery contract: Re-engined by Crossley (1951).

Pt. No.	Name	Builder	Launched
A.00	BRITANNIA	Clydebank ...	16. 4.53

Machinery contract: Engined by builder.

Pt. No.	Name	Builder	Launched
	VALIANT ...	Yarrow ...	14. 2.57

Machinery contract: Engined by Lobnitz.

Pt. No.	Name	Builder	Launched
A.146	PROTECTOR ...	Yarrow ...	20. 8.36

Machinery contract: Re-engined by British Thomson-Houston (1945).

Pt. No.	Name	Builder	Launched
A.184	ENDEAVOUR (ex-U.S.N. *Namakagon*)	Cargill ...	4.11.44

Machinery contract: Engined by General Motors.

Pt. No.	Name	Builder	Launched
A.171	ENDURANCE (ex-mercantile *Anita Dan*)	Krögerwerft ...	26. 5.56

Machinery contract: Engined by Burmeister & Wain.

Pt. No.	Name	Builder	Launched
M.228	KONKAN (ex-*Tilbury*)	Lobnitz ...	18. 2.42

Machinery contract: Engined by builder.

Pt. No.	Name	Builder	Launched
M.244	CASTLEMAINE (ex-*Castle Harbour*)	H.M.A. Dockyard (Williamstown)	7. 8.41

Machinery contract: Engined by Thompsons Eng. & Pipe Co.

Pt. No.	Name	Builder	Launched
F.232	GAJABAHU (ex-*Misnak*, ex-*Hallowell*)	Canadian Vickers ...	8. 8.44
F.256	TIR (ex-*Bann*) ...	Hill ...	29.12.42

Machinery contracts: Tir engined by Bellis & Morcom, and *Gajabahu* by builders.

Pt. No.	Name	Builder	Launched
	GHAZI (ex-U.S.N. *Diablo*)	Portsmouth N.Y. ...	30.11.44
S.71	GRILSE (ex-U.S.N. *Burrfish*, ex-*Arnillo*)	Electric Boat ...	18. 6.43
S.75	RAINBOW (ex-U.S.N. *Argonaut*)	Portsmouth N.Y. ...	1.10.44

Machinery contracts: All engined by Fairbanks-Morse (diesel engines) and Elliott Motors (electric motors).

Protector, former netlayer adapted for Antarctic patrol work.

Endurance, converted from former ice-strengthened mercantile vessel for Antarctic patrol work to replace the *Protector* above.
[Block courtesy
   Shipbuilding & Shipping Record

MISCELLANEOUS VESSELS

"Ranger" class: First group **BLACK RANGER, BLUE RANGER, BROWN RANGER.** *Second group* **GOLD RANGER' GREEN RANGER**

One unit of this class, the GRAY RANGER, was a war loss. Bridge and machinery arranged aft with the funnel offset to port.

First group: 3,500 tons *gross* (3,435/3,631 tons d.w.); 349½(pp) 365¾(oa) × 47 × 20¼ feet; one shaft; 6-cyl. B. & W. diesel engine, B.H.P. 2,750=12 knots; O.F. .,... tons; complement .... *Second group:* 3,300 tons *gross* (3,788 tons d.w.); 339½(pp) 355¼(oa) × 48¼ × 20¼ feet; one shaft; 4-cyl. Doxford diesel engine, B.H.P. 2,750=12 knots; O.F. .,... tons; complement ....

T2.SE.A1 type: **DACCA**

Former United States Navy tanker of standard war design transferred to the Pakistani Navy in 1963 under MDAP.

22,380 tons (16,350 tons d.w.); 503(wl) 523½(oa) × 68 × 30¾ feet; two Babcock & Wilcox boilers (... lb/in²); one shaft; G.E. turbines and electric motor, S.H.P. 6,000=15 knots; O.F. 1,460 tons; complement 160.

Pt. No.	Name	Builder	Launched
A.163	BLACK RANGER...	Harland & Wolff (Govan)	22. 8.40
A.157	BLUE RANGER ...	Harland & Wolff (Govan)	29. 1.41
A.169	BROWN RANGER	Harland & Wolff (Govan)	12.12.40
A.130	GOLD RANGER ...	Caledon ...	12. 3.41

Pt. No.	Name	Builder	Launched
A.152	GREEN RANGER...	Caledon	21. 8.41

Machinery contracts: Gold Ranger and Green Ranger engined by Doxford' others by builders.

Pt. No.	Name	Builder	Launched
A.41	DACCA (ex-U.S.N. *Mission Santa Clara*)	Marinship	8. 9.43

Machinery contract: Engined by G.E.C.

"Wave" class: ‡WAVE BARON, *WAVE CHIEF, *WAVE DUKE, *WAVE LAIRD, WAVE PRINCE, ‡WAVE RULER

Fast standard war-built tankers all acquired by the Royal Navy while under construction. Of the twenty units originally comprising this class one—the WAVE VICTOR—was transferred to the Royal Air Force and hulked in the Maldive Islands, one was sold-out commercially, and twelve were scrapped.

16,480 tons (11,226/11,950 tons d.w.); 465¼(pp) 493¾ except ‡ 491(oa) × 64 except ‡ 64¼ × 28½ feet; two Admiralty 3-drum boilers (490lb/in²); one shaft; Parsons except * Metrovick geared turbines S.H.P. 6,800 = 15 knots; O.F. .,.... tons; complement ....

"Surf" class: SURF PATROL, SURF PIONEER

15,800 tons (11,500 tons d.w.); 445(pp) 469½(oa) × 60½ × 27½ feet; one shaft; 4-cyl. Doxford diesel engine, B.H.P. 4,250 = 13¾ knots; O.F. .,... tons; complement ....

Pt. No.	Name	Builder	Launched
A.242	WAVE BARON (ex-mercantile *Empire Flodden*)	Furness Sbdg. ...	19. 2.46
A.265	WAVE CHIEF (ex-mercantile *Empire Edgehill*)	Harland & Wolff (Govan)	4. 4.46
A.246	WAVE DUKE (ex-mercantile *Empire Mars*)	Laing	16.11.44
A.119	WAVE LAIRD (ex-mercantile *Empire Dunbar*)	Laing	3. 4.46
A.207	WAVE PRINCE (ex-mercantile *Empire Herald*)	Laing	27. 7.45

Pt. No.	Name	Builder	Launched
A.212	WAVE RULER (ex-mercantile *Empire Evesham*)	Furness Sbdg. ...	17. 1.46

Machinery contracts: Wave Baron and *Wave Ruler* engined by Richardson Westgarth; *Wave Chief* and *Wave Duke* by Metropolitan Vickers; and *Wave Prince* by Barclay Curle.

Pt. No.	Name	Builder	Launched
A.357	SURF PATROL (ex-mercantile *Tatry*)	Bartram	7. 2.51
A.365	SURF PIONEER (ex-mercantile *Beskidy*)	Bartram	23. 4.51

Machinery contracts: Surf Patrol engined by Richardson Westgarth, and *Surf Pioneer* by North-Eastern Marine.

The *Orangeleaf* is typical of the mercantile conversions to freighting tankers, and is fitted for replenishment at sea.

Pt. No.	Name	Builder	Launched
A.83	APPLELEAF (ex-mercantile *George Lyras*)	Bartram	22. 4.55
A.79	BAYLEAF (ex-mercantile *London Integrity*)	Furness Sbdg.	28.10.54
A.81	BRAMBLELEAF (ex-mercantile *London Loyalty*)	Furness Sbdg.	16. 4.53

Pt. No.	Name	Builder	Launched
A.80	ORANGELEAF (ex-mercantile *Southern Satellite*)	Furness Sbdg. ...	8. 2.55
A.77	PEARLEAF (ex-mercantile)	Blythswood ...	15.10.59
A.78	PLUMLEAF (ex-mercantile)	Blyth Sbdg. ...	29. 3.60

Machinery contracts: All were engined by North-Eastern Marine except *Pearleaf* by Rowan.

All the following mercantile tankers were chartered by the Royal Navy in 1959 for the world-wide carriage of oil fuel to bases and fuelling stations, and a further vessel—the CHERRYLEAF (A.82—ex-mercantile *Laurelwood*)—was returned to commercial ownership in 1966.

Mercantile type: **APPLELEAF**
22,980 tons (16,850 tons d.w.); 525¾(pp) 557½(oa) × 67¾ × 38d/29¾ feet; one shaft; 6-cyl. Doxford diesel engine, B.H.P. 6,800 = 14 knots; O.F. 1,480 tons; complement 67.

Mercantile type: **BAYLEAF, BRAMBLELEAF**
23,460 tons, (17,930 and 17,960 tons d.w. respectively), 525(pp) 556½(oa) × 71 × 39¼d/30½ feet; one shaft; 6-cyl. Doxford diesel engine, B.H.P. 6,800 = 15 knots; O.F. 1,470 tons; complement ....

Mercantile type: **ORANGELEAF**
22,975 tons (17,475 tons d.w.); 525(pp) 556½(oa) × 71 × 39d/30½ feet; one shaft; 6-cyl. Doxford diesel engine, B.H.P. 6,800 = 15 knots; O.F. 1,610 tons; complement ...

Mercantile type: **PEARLEAF**
23,900 tons (18,150 tons d.w.); 535 (pp)568(oa) × 71¼ × 39d/30 feet; one shaft; 6-cyl. Doxford diesel engine B.H.P. 8,800 = 15¼ knots; O.F. .,... tons; complement ...

Mercantile type: **PLUMLEAF**
24,920 tons (18,900 tons d.w.); 534(pp) 568(oa) × 71¼ × 39d/30 feet; one shaft; 6-cyl. Doxford diesel engine, B.H.P. 9,350 = 15¼ knots; O.F. .,... tons; complement ...

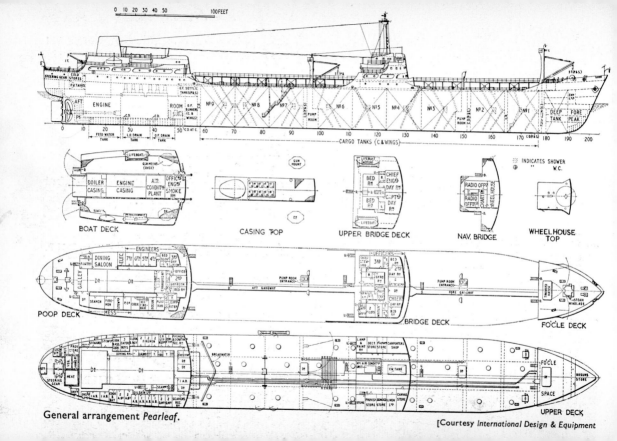

General arrangement *Pearleaf*.

[Courtesy *International Design & Equipment*

Right: Coastal tanker
Eddyfirth.

Below: Store carrier
Bacchus.

MISCELLANEOUS VESSELS

Pt. No.	Name	Builder	Launched
A.204	ROBERT DUNDAS	Grangemouth D.Y.	28. 7.38
A.241	ROBERT MIDDLETON	Grangemouth D.Y.	29. 6.38

Machinery contracts: Both engined by British Auxiliaries.

Pt. No.	Name	Builder	Launched
A.192	SPA	Philip	11.10.41
A.224	SPABROOK ...	Philip	24. 8.44
A.257	SPABURN	Philip	5. 1.46
A.260	SPALAKE	Hill	10. 8.46
A.222	SPAPOOL	Hill	28. 2.46

Machinery contracts: *Spalake* and *Spapool* engined by Holmes, and others by builders.

Pt. No.	Name	Builder	Launched
A.378	KINTERBURY ...	Philip	14.11.42
A.	THROSK	Philip	28. 9.43

Machinery contracts: Both engined by Lobnitz.

Pt. No.	Name	Builder	Launched
A.127	BIRCHOL	Lobnitz	19. 2.46

Pt. No.	Name	Builder	Launched
A.300	OAKOL	Lobnitz	28. 8.46
A.284	ROWANOL (ex-*Rowanol*, ex-*Ebonol*)	Lobnitz	15. 5.46
A.167	TEAKOL	Lobnitz	14.11.46

Machinery contracts: All engined by builders.

Pt. No.	Name	Builder	Launched
A.26	EDDYFIRTH ...	Lobnitz	10. 2.54
A.295	EDDYNESS ...	Blyth D.D. ...	11.10.54

Machinery contracts: All engined by Lobnitz.

Pt. No.	Name	Builder	Launched
A.404	BACCHUS	Robb	4. 6.62
A.406	HEBE	Robb	7. 3.62

Machinery contracts: Both engined by Swan Hunter.

Pt. No.	Name	Builder	Launched
Y.17	WATERFALL ...	Drypool	30. 3.66
Y.18	WATERSHED ...	Drypool	2. 8.66
Y.19	WATERSPOUT ...	J. R. Hepworth ...	28.12.66
Y.20	WATERSIDE ...	Drypool	4. 6.67

Machinery contracts: All engined by Lister Blackstone.

Coastal store carriers: **ROBERT DUNDAS, ROBERT MIDDLETON**

1,900 tons (1,000 tons d.w.); 210(pp) 220 except *Robert Dundas* 222½(oa) · 35¼ × 13½ feet; one shaft; 6-cyl. Polar diesel engine, B.H.P. 960=10½ knots; O.F. 60 tons; complement 17.

Coastal water carriers: **SPA, SPABROOK, SPABURN, SPALAKE, SPAPOOL**

1,220 tons (500 tons d.w.); 160(pp) 172(oa) × 30 × 12 feet; one S.E. cylindrical boiler (180 lb/in²); one shaft; reciprocating (VTE—cyl. 13½″:23″:38″ × 27″ stroke), I.H.P. 675=9 knots; O.F. 90 tons; complement …

Coastal armament carriers: **KINTERBURY, THROSK**

1,770 tons (769 tons d.w.); 185(pp) 199¾(oa) × 34¼ × 13 feet; one S.E. cylindrical boiler (… lb/in²); one shaft; reciprocating (VTE—cyl. …″:…″:…″ × …″ stroke), I.H.P. 900=11 knots; coal 154 tons; complement …

Coastal tankers: **BIRCHOL, OAKOL, ROWANOL, TEAKOL**

2,670 tons (1,638 tons d.w.); 218(pp) 231¼(oa) × 38¼ × 15¾ feet; two S.E. cylindrical boilers (250 lb/in²); one shaft; reciprocating (VTE—cyl. 13½″:23″:36″ × 18″ stroke), I.H.P. 1,140=11 knots; O.F. … tons; complement 26.

Coastal tankers: **EDDYFIRTH, EDDYNESS.**

Of the eight units originally comprising this class three were sold-out commercially and the remaining three were scrapped.
4,160 tons (2,200 tons d.w.); 270(pp) 287½(oa) × 46¼ × 17¼ feet; two S.E. cylindrical boilers (250 lb/in²); one shaft; reciprocating (VTE—cyl. 16″:27½″:43½″ × 21″ stroke), I.H.P. 1,750=12 knots; O.F. … tons; complement …

Mercantile type: **BACCHUS, HEBE**

Both these vessels were hired by the Royal Navy on long-term charter for the carriage of a wide variety of naval stores, and their holds were specially fitted out for this purpose.

7,960 tons (5,128 tons d.w.); 350(pp) 379¼(oa) × 55¼ × 22 feet; 5-cyl. Sulzer diesel engine, B.H.P. 5,500=15 knots; O.F. 720 tons; complement 57.

Water carriers: **WATERFALL, WATERSHED, WATERSIDE, WATERSPOUT**

285 tons **gross**; 123(pp) 131½(oa) × 24¾ × 11½d/8 feet; one shaft, 8-cyl. Lister Blackstone type ERS8 diesel engine B.H.P. 600=11 knots; O.F. 23 tons; complement 11.

MISCELLANEOUS VESSELS

Pt. No.	Name	Builder	Launched
	COLAC	Morts Dock ...	13. 8.41

Machinery contract: Engined by

Pt. No.	Name	Builder	Launched
P.40	BERN	Cook, Welton & Gemmell	2. 5.42
A.332	CALDY	Lewis	31. 8.43
A.333	COLL	Ardrossan D.Y. ...	7. 4.42
A.342	FOULNESS ...	Lewis	23. 3.42
A.340	GRAEMSAY ...	Ardrossan D.Y. ...	3. 8.42
A.366	LUNDY	Cook, Welton & Gemmell	29. 8.42
A.338	SKOMA	Lewis	17. 6.43
A.346	SWITHA	Inglis	3. 4.42

Machinery contracts: Bern and Lundy engined by Holmes; Coll and Graemsay by Plenty; Switha by Aitchison Blair; and others by builders.

	Name	Builder	Launched
A.	BRITANNIC (ex-*Miner V*, ex-*M.5*)	Philip	2.11.40
N.12	GOSSAMER (ex-*Miner II*, ex-*M.2*)	Philip	18. 8.39

Pt. No.	Name	Builder	Launched
N.13	MINER III (ex-*M.3*)	Philip	16.11.39
N.16	MINER VI (ex-*M.6*)	Philip	7. 2.42
N.11	MINSTREL (ex-*Miner I*, ex-*M.I*)	Philip	6. 7.39
N.17	STEADY (ex-*ETV.7*, ex-*Miner VII*, ex-*M.7*)	Philip	29. 1.44

Machinery contracts: All engined by Ruston & Hornsby.

	Name	Builder	Launched
Y....	OILBIRD	Appledore	21.11.68
Y....	OILFIELD	Appledore	5. 9.68
Y....	OILMAN	Appledore	18. 2.69
Y....	OILPRESS	Appledore	10. 6.68
Y....	OILSTONE	Appledore	11. 7.68
Y....	OILWELL	Appledore	20. 1.69

Machinery contracts: All engined by Lister Blackstone.

	Name	Builder	Launched
	DACHET	Vosper Thornycroft Uniteers (Singapore)	68

Machinery contract: Engined by Gray.

Coastal tankers: **OILBIRD, OILFIELD, OILMAN, OILPRESS, OILSTONE, OILWELL**

250 tons d.w.; 130(pp) 138(oa) × 24½ × 11¾d/8½ feet; one shaft, 6-cyl. Lister Blackstone type ERS diesel engine B.H.P. 405 = 10 knots; complement 11.

"Bathurst" class: **COLAC**

Former minesweeper converted into a tank cleaning vessel by the Royal Australian Navy.

815/1,025 tons; 162(pp) 186(oa) × 31 × 8½/9¼ feet; two Admiralty 3-drum boilers; two shafts; reciprocating (VTE—cyl. 13":21":34" × 21" stroke), I.H.P. 1,800 = 15½ knots; O.F. 170 tons; complement 55.

"Isles" class: **BERN, CALDY, COLL, FOULNESS, GRAEMSAY, LUNDY, SKOMA, SWITHA**

Former general purpose naval trawlers converted to tank cleaning vessels 1950–53. Of the one hundred and forty-five vessels originally comprising this class, fourteen were war losses; two were transferred to the West German Navy, eleven to the Italian Navy (all since scrapped), four to the Royal New Zealand Navy (all since scrapped), five to the Royal Norwegian Navy (all since sold-out commercially), and six to the Portuguese Navy (one since lost, one sold-out commercially, and three scrapped), together with fifty sold-out commercially; and forty-six were scrapped.

560/770 tons; 150(pp) 164(oa) × 27½ × 10½/14 feet; one S.E. cylindrical boiler (250 lb/in²); one shaft; reciprocating (VTE—cyl. 13½":23":38" × 27" stroke), I.H.P. 800 = 12 knots; coal 183 tons; complement . . .

Admiralty type: **BRITANNIC, GOSSAMER, MINER III, MINER VI, MINSTREL, STEADY**

Former controlled minelayers converted to various duties as tenders; BRITTANIC as a DG cable layer, GOSSAMER and MINER VI for torpedo trials, MINER III for clearance divers, MINSTREL for submarines, and STEADY for stabilisation trials. Of the nine vessels originally comprising this class the original *M.7* was lost incomplete at Singapore during the Second World War, and two were scrapped.

300/350 tons; 110¼(pp) 122½(oa) × 26½ × 8 feet; two shafts; 6-cyl. Ruston & Hornsby diesel engines, B.H.P. 360 = 10 knots; O.F. . . . tons; complement . . .

Diving tender: **DACHET**

Hull of steel construction with wood superstructure, and fitted with a compression chamber on deck handled by a derrick.

70 tons; . . . (pp) 75(ca) × 19 × 4 feet; two shafts, Gray diesel engines B.H.P. 500 = 12 knots; complement 5.

Above: Coastal water tanker *Waterfall*
[C. Taylor & S. Waters

Left: Diving tender *Dachet*

Admiralty type: **ABERDOVEY, ABINGER, ALNESS, ALNMOUTH, APPLEBY, ASHCOTT, BEAULIEU, BEDDGELERT, BEMBRIDGE, BIBURY, BLAKE-NEY, BRODICK**

Multi-purpose vessels intended to replace the large variety of craft employed as tenders by a standardised design able to meet most requirements. Height was restricted to 23 feet so that they can position themselves under the over-hangs of aircraft carriers. The all-welded steel hull is made up from twelve pre-fabricated sections, and they can carry either 25 tons d.w. or 3,000ft^3 of stores, or 200 standing passengers and two $1\frac{3}{4}$-ton torpedoes stowed in chocks abreast the main hatch, to port and starboard. The original provision was to build sixty of these vessels over a 10-year period.

Steel tender *Beaulieu*

$117\frac{1}{2}$ tons (full load—25 tons d.w.); 75(pp) $79\frac{3}{4}$(oa) $\times$ 18 $\times$ $8\frac{1}{4}$d/$5\frac{1}{2}$ feet; one shaft; 4-cyl. Lister Blackstone diesel engine, B.H.P. 225 (at 750 r.p.m.) = $10\frac{1}{2}$ knots; O.F. $3\frac{3}{4}$ tons; complement 6.

Pt. No.	Name		Builder		Launched
Y.10	ABERDOVEY	..	Pimblott	..	11.12.63
Y.11	ABINGER ..	..	Pimblott	..	25. 3.64
Y.12	ALNESS ..	..	Pimblott	..	18. 6.64
Y.13	ALNMOUTH	..	Pimblott	..	5.10.64
Y.14	APPLEBY ..	..	Pimblott	..	3. 2.65
Y.16	ASHCOTT ..	..	Pimblott	..	29. 5.65
Y.	BEAULIEU ..	..	Doig	..	20. 9.63
Y.	BEDDGELERT	..	Doig	..	13.11.63
Y.	BEMBRIDGE	..	Doig	..	15. 1.64
Y.	BIBURY ..	..	Doig	..	19. 2.64
Y.	BLAKENEY	..	Doig	..	12. 5.64
Y.	BRODICK ..	..	Doig	..	10. 7.64

Machinery contracts: All engined by Lister Blackstone.

Admiralty type: **CARTMEL, CAWSAND, DENMEAD, DUNSTER, ELKSTONE, ELSING, EPWORTH, ETTRICK, FOTHERBY, FULLBECK,** and **TWELVE** more unnamed

The second group of tenders were given a round bilge as opposed to double chine hull form as in the first group, greater beam, and had the diesel engine uprated to maintain speed. They comprise three variants, all with the same basic hull particulars and machinery: *type A* which is only fitted for the carriage of cargo, *type B* which is fitted to carry either cargo or passengers, and *type C* which is fitted to accommodate 12 R.F.A. personnel for training purposes. Of the twenty units building eight are of type A, ten of type B, and two of type C.

143 tons (full load—25 tons d.w.); 75(pp) 80(oa)×21× 10d/6½ feet; one shaft, 4-cyl. Lister Blackstone diesel engine B.H.P. 320 (at 750 r.p.m.)=10½ knots, O.F. 4¼ tons; complement 6.

Pt. No.	Name	Launched	Launched
Y.	CARTMEL	Pimblott	68
Y.	CAWSAND ...	Pimblott	68
Y.	C	Pimblott	69
Y.	C	Pimblott	69
Y.	C	Pimblott	....
Y	C	Pimblott	....
Y.	DUNSTER	Dunston (Thorne)	16. 7.69
Y.	FOTHERBY ...	Dunston (Thorne)	27. 8.69
Y.	D	Dunston (Thorne)	69
Y.	D ...	Dunston (Thorne)	....
Y.	ELKSTONE ...	Cook	69
Y.	ELSING	Cook	69
Y.	EPWORTH ...	Cook	....
Y.	ETTRICK	Cook	....
Y.	DENMEAD ...	Holmes (Beverley)	I. 8.69
Y.	FULLBECK ...	Holmes (Beverley)	27. 6.69
Y.	F	Holmes (Beverley)	....
Y.	F	Holmes (Beverley)	....
Y.	G	Lewis	70
Y.	G	Lewis	70
Y.	G ...	Lewis	70
Y.	G	Lewis	70

Machinery contracts: All engined by Lister Blackstone.

Admiralty type: **BEE, CICALA, CRICKET, GNAT, LADYBIRD, SCARAB**

The third group of tenders were enlarged all round to undertake coastal voyages. Similarly, there are three variants, all with the same basic hull particulars and machinery: *type 1* which is fitted to carry cargo and is rigged with two cranes, *type 2* which is fitted to carry cargo or armament stores and is rigged with a 2-ton crane, and *type 3* which is fitted to lift 10 tons over the bow as a mooring vessel and is rigged with a 3-ton crane.

450 tons (full load—200 tons d.w.); 100(pp) 111¾(oa)× 28×13½d/11 feet; one shaft, 8-cyl. Lister Blackstone diesel engine B.H.P. 660 (at 750 r.p.m.)=10½ knots, O.F. 24½ tons; complement 10.

Pt. No.	Name	Builder	Launched
	BEE	Holmes	5. 6.69
	CICALA	Holmes	....
	CRICKET	Holmes	30. 8.69
	GNAT	Holmes	....
	LADYBIRD ...	Holmes	....
	SCARAB	Holmes	....

Machinery contracts: All engined by Lister Blackstone.

A

B

C

D

E

F

G

H

I

J

K

L

M

P

Q

R

T

U

V

W

Y

Z

RAF	= Royal Air Force	KN	= Kenyan Navy	RNZN	= Royal New Zealand Navy
RAN	= Royal Australian Navy	IN	= Indian Navy		
RCN	= Royal Canadian Navy	JCG	= Jamaican Coast Guard	PN	= Pakistani Navy
CCG	= Canadian Coast Guard	RMN	= Royal Malaysian Navy	SN	= Singhalese Navy
RCT	= Royal Corp of Transport	MOT	= Ministry of Transport	T&TCG	= Trinidad & Tobago Coast Guard
GN	= Ghanaian Navy	NN	= Nigerian Navy		